PRAISE FOR NICHOLAS T. PARSONS

On *The Shortest History of Austria*

'Erudite, insightful, lucid and entertaining. A wonderful introduction to the mysteries of Austrian history and the rituals of Austrian culture' LONNIE R. JOHNSON, author of *Central Europe: Enemies, Neighbours, Friends*

'A great deal of world history starts in Austria. Some ends there too. But Austria and Vienna have shown themselves capable of endless reinvention in all the arts of civilisation including the making of history. That makes them ideal topics for Nicholas Parsons' wittily ironic pen and capacious imagination' JOHN O'SULLIVAN, The Danube Institute

On *Worth the Detour*

'What is a guidebook for? Tutor, art critic, counsellor, companion – Parsons traces in scholarly detail the mutation of the genre over time... He is rigorous, sophisticated, sharp and humorous. And he writes very well' CHRISTIAN TYLER, *Financial Times*

* * *

NICHOLAS T. PARSONS is the author of *Blue Guide Austria* and *Vienna: A Cultural and Literary History*, as well as *Worth the Detour*, a history of the guidebook as a literary genre, and *The Joy of Bad Verse*, a celebration of successfully bad poets. His most recent books are *Civilisation and its Malcontents* (2019) and *Democracy: A Narrative from Aristotle to Trump* (2023). For thirty years, he has been writing about Central Europe, and in particular Austria, which he regards as a second home.

ALSO BY NICHOLAS T. PARSONS

Vienna: A Cultural and Literary History
Blue Guide Vienna
Worth the Detour: A History of the Guidebook
The Joy of Bad Verse
Civilisation and Its Malcontents
Democracy: A Narrative from Aristotle to Trump

THE SHORTEST HISTORY
of
AUSTRIA

Nicholas T. Parsons

Published in Great Britain in 2025 by
Old Street Publishing Ltd
Notaries House, Exeter EX1 1AJ

www.oldstreetpublishing.co.uk

ISBN 978-1-91308-353-3
Ebook ISBN 978-1-91308-354-0

The right of Nicholas T. Parsons to be identified as the author of this work has been asserted by him in accordance with the Copyright, Designs and Patents Act 1988.

Copyright © 2025 by Nicholas T. Parsons

Illustrations and maps © 2025 by James Nunn

Every effort has been made to secure permissions for all images reproduced in this volume. Please contact the publisher directly for further information.

All rights reserved. No part of this publication may be reproduced, stored in or introduced into a retrieval system, or transmitted, in any form, or by any means (electronic, mechanical, photocopying, recording or otherwise) without the prior written permission of the publisher.

10 9 8 7 6 5 4 3 2 1

A CIP catalogue record for this title is available from the British Library.

Printed and bound in Great Britain.

For Ilona

CONTENTS

Timeline	viii
Habsburg Family Tree	xii
Prelude	1
1. Austrians and Pre-Austrians	5
2. Babenbergs and Early Habsburgs	17
3. The Habsburgs as Holy Roman Emperors	33
4. Protestants and the Empire	49
5. Internal and External Enemies	69
6. Baroque Culture	81
7. Enlightened Absolutism	91
8. Napoleonic Wars and the Biedermeier Age	103
9. From Austrian Empire to Dual Monarchy	123
10. *Fin de siècle* to *Finis Austriae*: 1873–1918	137
11. The Road to War and Disaster	153
12. The First Republic	161
13. The Second Republic	189
14. Post-Millennium Austria in the EU	217
Further Reading	232
Endnotes	233
Acknowledgements	235
Image Credits	236

A Timeline of Austrian History

750–400 BC. Hallstatt Civilisation (early Iron Age)

150 BC. Celts establish the Kingdom of Noricum centred on Carinthia

15 BC. Roman province of Rhaetia includes North Tyrol and Vorarlberg

10 AD. Romans subjugate Noricum and establish the province of Pannonia

25 AD. Romans consolidate the *Limes* (fortified frontier) along the Danube from Passau to Carnuntum

304 AD. Christianity reaches the Danube

375 AD. The so-called *Völkerwanderung* (Great Migrations) begins with tribes arriving from the East

Mid-5th Century. The Huns penetrate and devastate Central and parts of Western Europe

488 AD. Roman withdrawal from Danubian territories. They take with them the remains of Austria's first saint, a Roman official revered as Saint Severinus, the Apostle of Noricum

791 AD. The Austrian region becomes the *Ostmark* of Charlemagne

800 AD. Charlemagne crowned Roman Emperor of the West

Babenbergs 976–1246

976 AD. Margrave Leopold of Babenberg is rewarded for military assistance by Emperor Otto II with territory named for the first time in a legal document as *Ostarrîchi* (Austria)

1156 Under Henry II of Babenberg, Austria becomes a hereditary duchy with Vienna as its capital

1192 Richard the Lionheart of England is arrested and imprisoned in Austria

1194 With ransom money raised, Richard the Lionheart is released from imprisonment and returns to England

1246 Frederick the Quarrelsome, the last of the Babenbergs, is killed fighting the Magyars

1252 Otakar II of Bohemia occupies the Duchy of Austria

Habsburgs 1273–1918

1273 Rudolf of Habsburg elected German King

1278 Rudolf of Habsburg defeats Otakar II of Bohemia on the Marchfeld, east of Vienna

1335 Expansion of Habsburg territory under Albert II to include Carinthia and Carniola

1358–65 Under Duke Rudolf IV 'the Founder', the University of Vienna is established.

1363 Rudolf IV obtains Tyrol and increases Habsburg territory in Vorarlberg

1452 Friedrich III (ruled 1439–93) is the first Habsburg elected Holy Roman Emperor (and the last emperor to be crowned in Rome)

1474 Completion of acquisition of Vorarlberg

1477 Beginnings of Habsburgs' 'marriage diplomacy'. Habsburgs acquire the Netherlands and Franche-Comté of Burgundy by marriage contract

1485–90 Matthias Corvinus, King of Hungary, occupies Vienna

1493–1519 Emperor Maximilian I establishes his court at Innsbruck

1499 Switzerland wins independence from imperial rule by defeating the Swabian League

1515 Double (proxy) marriage of Maximilian I's grandchildren to the heirs of the Bohemian and Hungarian thrones

1521 Martin Luther excommunicated. Later, at the Diet of Worms he is also made a political outlaw. The Reformation begins to spread throughout Habsburg lands. Lutheranism dominates in German-speaking urban or mining centres. Subsequently, Calvinism predominates in Hungary-Transylvania

1522 Separation of Habsburg Empire under Charles V into Spanish and Central European lines

1529 First Turkish siege of Vienna

1545–63 The Council of Trent attempts to reconcile Catholicism and Protestantism

1555 Peace of Augsburg. Subjects to follow the faith – Lutheranism or Catholicism – of their rulers

1570–1640 The Counter-Reformation attempts to reimpose Catholicism across Europe

1571 Don John of Austria inflicts major naval defeat on the Turks at Lepanto on the Gulf of Corinth

1583–1612 Emperor Rudolf II rules from Prague and makes it a centre of Mannerist art, the sciences, astronomy and the occult

1618 The Defenestration of Prague. Enraged Protestants eject King Ferdinand's hardline Catholic representatives from a window of the Hradčany Castle

1620 The Battle of the White Mountain marks a significant victory for the Counter-Reformation. The victory sparks the Thirty Years War in Germany (1618–48)

1622 Catholics regain control of Vienna University. Counter-Reformation making steady advances in most Habsburg lands from 1621

1648 The Peace of Westphalia ends the Thirty Years War and establishes (in principle) freedom of religion for individuals

1658–1705 Reign of the 'Baroque Emperor' Leopold I. Consolidation of Habsburg territories. Italian artists, architects and musicians dominate the culture of Austria

1679 Worst year of plague in Vienna ever recorded

1683 Failure of second Turkish siege of Vienna

1686 Expulsion of Turks from Buda

1699 The Peace of Karlovitz 'saves Europe' from the Turks

1701–14 War of the Spanish Succession following the extinction of the Habsburg line in Spain

1711–40 Emperor Charles VI. Baroque building boom in Austria led by great Austrian architects

1717 Prince Eugene of Savoy's brilliant campaign drives Turks back as far as Belgrade, Subsequently, Austria reacquires Hungary, Croatia and Transylvania

1740 Maria Theresa becomes Archduchess of Austria. Austria invaded by the Bavarian claimant to the imperial throne, while Frederick II of Prussia occupies (Austrian) Silesia. A French-led coalition moves on Austria / Bohemia

1745 Maria Theresa becomes Empress as consort of Francis Stephen of Lorraine, elected Holy Roman Emperor as Francis I

1780–90 Joseph II's 'enlightened absolutism' brings in social reforms such as the Patent (1781) and Edict (1782) of Tolerance guaranteeing religious freedom. Significant reduction of discrimination against Jews

1787 Mozart's opera *Don Giovanni* rapturously received in Prague

1794 Ludwig van Beethoven settles in Vienna

1804 Emperor Francis II brings into being (as Francis I) the Austrian Empire

1806 The Holy Roman Empire is dissolved by Napoleon

1813 Napoleon is defeated at Leipzig at the Battle of the Nations

1814–15 The Congress of Vienna. Conservative post-war settlement is orchestrated by Prince Metternich

1848 Revolutions in Europe and across the Empire. Francis Joseph becomes Austrian Emperor

1866 Defeat of Austrians by Prussians at Königgrätz in Bohemia and setbacks in Italy lead to the Compromise with Hungary (1867) and the creation of the Austro-Hungarian Empire

1873 Vienna's World Fair and its last cholera epidemic. First stock market crash.

1889 Crown Prince Rudolf and his lover Mary Vetsera commit suicide in the Mayerling hunting lodge

1898 Empress Elisabeth assassinated by an anarchist in Geneva

1908 Austria annexes Bosnia and the Herzegovina, the last extension of Habsburg territory

1914–18 World War I, following assassination in Sarajevo of Archduke Franz Ferdinand, heir to the imperial throne

1916 Emperor Francis Joseph dies

First Republic

1918–19 Collapse of the Habsburg Empire. Austria reduced to its present dimensions and forbidden by the victorious allies to merge with Germany

1920 Founding of the Salzburger Festspiele by Max Reinhardt

1922 Last Habsburg Emperor, Charles I, dies in exile in Madeira

1925 After prolonged hyperinflation, the Austrian currency is rebased and renamed the *Schilling*

1927 Police shoot eighty-nine rioters and the Palace of Justice burns down after the High Court acquits right-wing paramilitaries of killing two members of the Socialist Schutzbund. Tensions between right and left in Austria reach a high point

1933–38 Austria under clerico-fascist rule (*Ständestaat* – Corporate State), first under Engelbert Dollfuss (assassinated by Nazis in 1934), then under Kurt Schuschnigg

1934 Civil war in Austria

1938 Nazi troops occupy Austria, which becomes part of Germany (*Anschluss*)

1939–1945 World War II

Second Republic

1945–1955 Four allied powers (USA, USSR, UK and France) occupy Austria. The Marshall Plan (1948–1952) stimulates economic recovery

1955 *Staatsvertrag* (State Treaty) frees Austria from occupation and establishes a republican constitution. Austria declares (perpetual) neutrality

1970–1983 Era of Social-Democratic rule under Bruno Kreisky introduces radical social reforms and builds the welfare state

1986 Election of the former UNO Secretary General Kurt Waldheim as Bundespräsident reignites controversy about Austria's Nazi past

1989 Fall of the Iron Curtain

1995 Austria joins the EU

2000 Coalition between the Conservative People's Party and the far right Freedom Party under Conservative Chancellor Wolfgang Schüssel leads to temporary 'ostracisation' of Austria within the EU

2017–19 People's Party under Chancellor Sebastian Kurz again in coalition with the Freedom Party

2024 At a time of far right gains across Europe, the Freedom Party wins the most votes in the September elections.

2025 More than five months after the general election, a coalition of the conservative People's Party, the Social Democrats and the Liberal NEOS forms a government, thereby excluding the Putin-friendly Freedom Party.

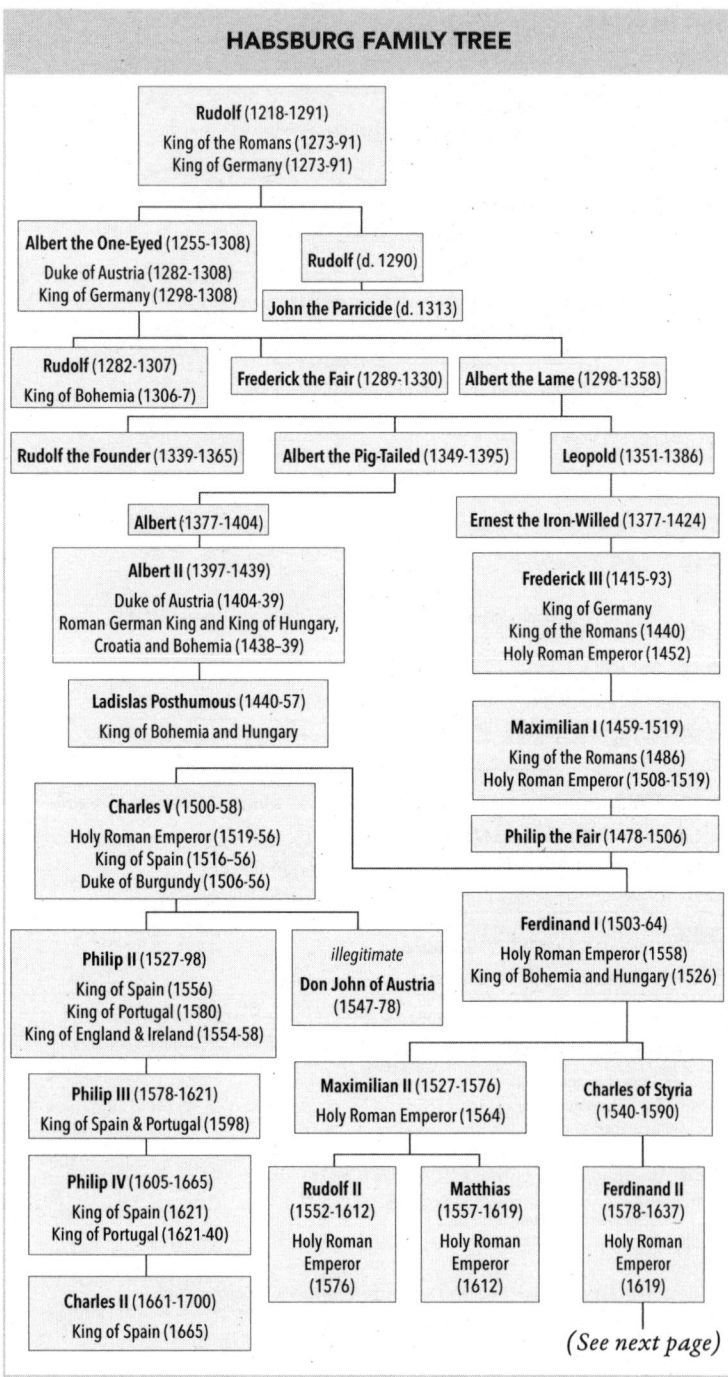

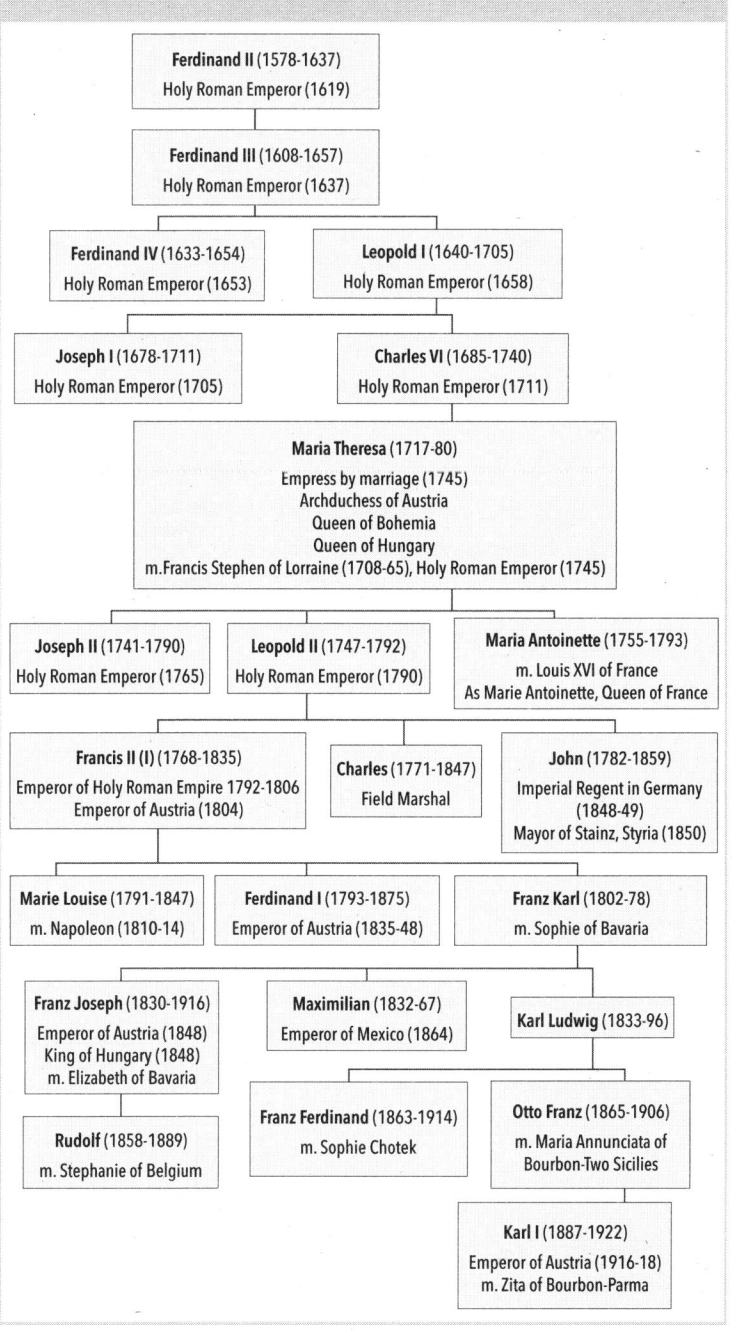

To the Reader: In the present text, English topographical names are used where there is one (e.g. Wien is called Vienna). German (and Czech, Hungarian etc.) names of persons follow the native tongue at first mention and thereafter the English is used (if relevant, e.g. Lajos / Louis). Many Habsburgs bore diverse titles. The title used is generally that of the highest rank attained, e.g. *Kaiser* (Emperor) or *Erzherzog* (Archduke).

The Austrian narrative offered here is both chronological and theme oriented. This means that certain peculiarities of Austrian history that merit more detailed examination, looking backwards and forwards in time, are treated in the text's accompanying boxes.

OVERLEAF: Part of Schwarzenbergplatz in Vienna, that had been renamed Stalinplatz in honour of the Russian liberators in 1945, has its name restored as the Russians prepare to leave in 1955.

WHAT THEY SAY ABOUT AUSTRIA...

'Austria has no equal among the nations.'
JOHANNES SPIESSHAYMER CUSPINIANUS, *Description of the Territory of Austria* (1553)*

'In other countries dynasties are episodes in the history of the people; in the Habsburg Empire peoples are a complication in the history of the dynasty.'
A. J. P. TAYLOR

'I am thrice homeless, as a native of Bohemia in Austria, as an Austrian among Germans, and as a Jew throughout the world.' GUSTAV MAHLER

'Who is talking about victories? All that matters is to survive.' RAINER MARIA RILKE

'We acknowledge all the facts of our history and the deeds of all parts of our population, the good as well as the bad. Just as we claim credit for our good deeds, we must beg forgiveness for the evil ones.' CHANCELLOR FRANZ VRANITZKY, Hebrew University, Jerusalem, 9 June 1993

---

* Cuspinianus actually only got as far as covering Lower Austria in his planned treatise on 'Austria', but evidently that was enough to convince him!

PRELUDE
SMALL COUNTRY, LARGE HISTORY

The North Korean Embassy, one of the country's biggest in Europe, is close to where I stay in Vienna. Every year, it holds an unintentionally and grimly hilarious celebration of the Kim dynasty, featuring grotesque videos of a flourishing – which is to say starving – nation, followed by a very generous buffet.

The North Koreans are here in such force because the city is home to influential multilateral institutions such as the UN and OPEC, whose deliberations the North Koreans monitor with Maoist zeal. Since the 1960s, Vienna has been transformed from something of a provincial backwater into a cosmopolitan metropolis for international organisations to rival Geneva.

This represents a remarkable comeback for a small country with a glorious history but a troubled recent past. It's alleged that when the Austro-Hungarian Empire was carved up into its remaining ethnic parts after World War I, Georges Clemenceau said that 'Austria is whatever's left over'. Diminished, yes, but not to be dismissed. Because Austria sits right at the heart of Europe – not just east and west, but north and south, too. By the time of the Cold War, Vienna may no longer have been the capital of a massive empire, but it had re-emerged with a new role: as a happy hunting ground for intelligence gathering and diplomatic back-channels.

Looking beyond politics, Austria has for centuries been at the centre of many of the continent's cultural and intellectual flowerings, from Baroque to Biedermeier to *fin-de-siècle*, from Mozart and Beethoven to Johann Strauss, from Gustav Klimt to Egon Schiele, Arthur Schnitzler to Robert Musil and Joseph

Roth, Ludwig Wittgenstein to Karl Popper to Hedy Lamarr. Even, if you like, to Harry Lime.

The pages that follow tell the story of Austria from its small beginnings through the Habsburg centuries up to the present day. It is the story of the rise and fall of one of the world's great empires – one of the few of which it was said 'the sun never set' – which held the core of European history for more than 500 years. The consequences of its break-up into nation states are still playing out today.

It is not, though, solely a story of securing territories through political and military might, but of spiritual conflict, of the Reformation and Counter-Reformation. From the east, too, the Habsburgs defended the Christian West against the onslaught of Islam, culminating in the defeat of the Ottomans in Vienna in 1683.

Later, it becomes the story of the emergence of a particular Austrian identity and the country's complex relationship with neighbouring Germany, from nineteenth-century dreams of *'Großdeutschland'* unity to the twentieth-century nightmare of nazification and unification with Germany. *'Finis Austriae,'* as

Sigmund Freud grimly recorded in his diary in Vienna on the day that Nazi troops moved in. Since the war, however, Austria has had to come to terms with its role in the Holocaust and has managed to find its rightful place in the postwar world.

Today Austria is a neutral nation, an EU member, but not in NATO. And yet with the 2022 Russian invasion of Ukraine that neutrality has come into question. Again and again, as we shall see, the history of Austria is not just fascinating in itself, but shines a light on the history of a whole continent.

A Note on the Federal Provinces

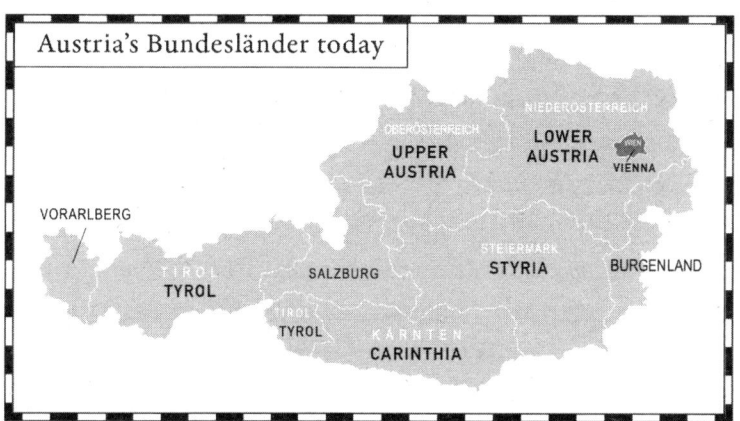

976	**Niederösterreich / Lower Austria** begins to come under the rule of the Franconian Babenbergs, whose seat was at Bamberg in today's Bavaria.
1156	**Wien / Vienna** becomes the centre of Babenberg rule when Heinrich II / Henry II, Duke of Austria, moves his court there.
1192	**Steiermark / Styria** becomes part of Babenberg Austrian possessions.
1276	**Styria** reacquired by Rudolf of Habsburg, the first of his line to rule in Austria. The duchy had been occupied by Ottokar II of Bohemia since 1260, who was defeated by Rudolf at the battle of Dürnkrut in 1278.
1281	**Oberösterreich / Upper Austria** confirmed as a Habsburg Crown Land
1309	**Vorarlberg** begins to pass under Habsburg control
1335	**Kärnten / Carinthia** becomes part of the Habsburg patrimony
1363	**Tirol / Tyrol** is acquired by Rudolf IV of Habsburg
1816	**Salzburg** becomes Austrian territory following the Congress of Vienna
1919	**Burgenland** added to the Austrian First Republic

Austria may be small but it contains multitudes. Today there are nine *Bundesländer* (Federal Provinces) and each has an individual historical and cultural profile, in some cases also a pronounced local dialect. Dialect is particularly marked in Vorarlberg in the far west, where it is Alemannic, and in Tyrol, where it is Bavarian with remnants of Alemannic in the north and Rhaeto-Romanic in the south neighbouring Italy. In nineteenth-century Vienna, some districts even had their own patois, often also reflecting the influence of migrant tongues from different regions of the Empire. For example, Favoriten was a region where the Czech bricklayers who built the city's Ringstrasse were mostly settled; as late as the 1930s, the local police on the beat were still obliged to have a mastery of Czech.

The constellation of provinces today dates from 1918, after the dismemberment of the Austro-Hungarian Empire following defeat in World War I. All except Burgenland, on the eastern border with Hungary, have deep roots in Austria and a history of considerable autonomy. For the Federal Government, they can still be obstreperous. They will crop up throughout these pages, and it is hoped that by the end of the book the reader will have gained some sense of their individual characters. A Tyroler's ethno-historical sense of himself, likewise a Styrian's, from the very heart of historical 'Inner Austria', will be markedly different from that of a Viennese brought up in the so-called urban melting pot of cultures.

CHAPTER 1

AUSTRIANS AND PRE-AUSTRIANS

Pre-Austrians

The Venus of Willendorf is a palaeolithic fertility symbol discovered in Lower Austria in 1908. Carbon dating estimates it to be around 30,000 years old and not made from local stone.

According to palaeontologists, we can thank the appearance of the Alps – which are considered young as mountains go – to geological events in the Cretaceous period, when dinosaurs were still around, and the Neogene period, when it seems they were not. During this unimaginably long period between about 144 million and 3 million years ago, the African plate of the earth's crust crept northwards, submerging part of the great ocean then separating Africa (Gondwana) from Eurasia (Laurasia). It collided with the Eurasian one about 30 million years ago. One result was the dissolution of the great ocean into the Mediterranean, Black and Caspian Seas; another was the uplifting of the earth's crust to create so-called fold mountains – among them the Eastern Alps in Austria. Curiously enough, the major theorist of the submersion and division of the original great Tethys Ocean, which he named in 1893 after the consort of the Greek god Oceanus, was the Austrian paleogeologist

Eduard Suess (1831–1914). Suess was such a pioneer that he has craters on the moon and Mars named after him.

Habitation in the Alpine valleys and foothills, and especially in the milder Danube valley, began early. The most important object in Vienna's Museum of Natural History is a stone statuette of a woman with vast pendulous breasts and a carefully sculpted vulva. She is known as the Willendorf Venus after where she was found in 1908 on the banks of the Danube in Lower Austria, and is estimated to have been fashioned 25,000 years ago, towards the end of the last Ice Age. But she cannot, alas, claim to be the first known Austrian, as she is not made from local stone. It seems she was brought from further afield.

Ötzi the Iceman

A more plausible candidate for the first Austrian, perhaps, is Ötzi, the mummified man who emerged remarkably intact from a retreating glacier and was discovered in 1991 by hikers in the Ötztaler Alps on the South Tyrol (Südtirol) border. At first, they thought he was a climber who had met with a mishap, but it soon became apparent that the ice had preserved a prehistoric corpse – that of a tribal leader, judging from his

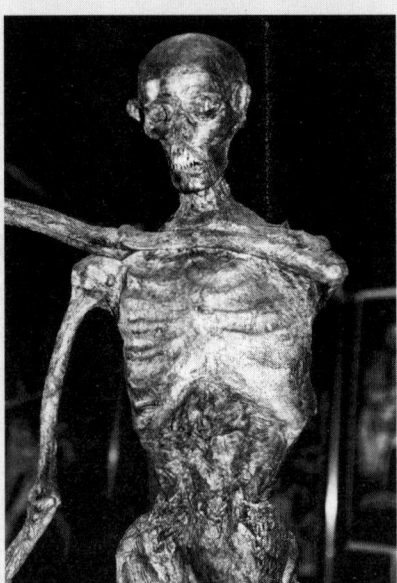

Ötzi the Iceman is Europe's oldest surviving naturally mummified human. He was found in the Ötztaler Alps in 1991.

dress and accoutrements. He may have been followed up the mountain from the Ötztal below by an assassin whose arrowhead left a wound in his left shoulder. Ötzi was killed in the late Stone / early Chalcolithic (Copper) Age, around 3,500 years before the birth of Christ. His DNA places him amongst early European farmers who migrated from Anatolia during the 7th millennium BC (one theory is that he was a high-altitude shepherd); and, likewise, DNA analysis in 2013 identified nineteen contemporary Tyrolean men who appeared to be descendants of Ötzi or his relatives. Analysis of his stomach contents show that Ötzi had quite a modern diet (meat, grains and berries) and even suffered from an increasingly prevalent modern ailment, namely lactose intolerance. It was also reassuring to see that he knew a competent tattooist.

Ötzi predates by about 2,000 years the Celts, Caucasian tribes who appear around 1200 BC in Austria (Celts is the Greek name; the Romans called them Gauls). Their sophisticated Iron Age culture flourished north of the Alps, in particular at Hallstatt on the shores of the Hallstätter See in Austria's Salzkammergut.* Hallstatt has lent its name to a late Bronze Age and early Iron Age culture that spread throughout Central Europe and into France between 1200 and 450 BC. Hallstatt itself also grew rich from its extensive salt mines.

Although the Celts were divided into many tribal groups, from around 200 BC there emerged something resembling a Celtic state named Noricum after its leading tribe; *regnum Noricum* covered much of today's Austria. In due course, under

---

* Salt was a valuable commodity in the Middle Ages. Salzkammergut means 'the salt domain', the revenues of which were later reserved to the Habsburgs as part of their privileges as Roman kings.

Emperor Claudius (AD 41–54), it became the first Roman province in Austrian territory. Roman Noricum encompassed what are today the Austrian provinces of Carinthia, Salzburg, Upper Austria, Lower Austria, Styria and part of Tyrol (plus a chunk of south-eastern Bavaria), so it is hardly an exaggeration to say that geopolitically Austria was born under Roman hegemony. With its salt, gold and iron reserves (*Ferrum Noricum* was crucial to Roman weapon production), Noricum was important to the Roman economy. In 181–180 BC, Roman colonists had founded the city of Aquilea at the head of Adriatic, the southern end of the historic Amber Road that ran all the way from the Baltic shore where the precious substance was collected. The route crossed the Danube at Carnuntum (between present-day Vienna and Bratislava), before continuing down through Pannonia to the Adriatic coast of Roman Italy. From there goods were carried on to eastern lands. It wasn't just amber: Noricum's own exports also benefited from Roman roadbuilding.

The Romans in Austria

Roman troops remained on today's Austrian territory for half a millennium. There was progress on infrastructure and border defence; baths and amphitheatres were constructed. A late Roman road map (AD c.365) known as the *Tabula Peutingeriana* illustrates the many settlements and facilities available along its routes.* The legionaries were officially not allowed to marry during their twenty-five years of service, but no doubt many unofficial liaisons were legitimised upon a soldier's retire-

---

* The roadmap was allegedly stolen from a library in Worms by Conrad Celtis, a humanist at the court of Maximilian I. At the time, the Habsburgs were keen to acquire artefacts that connected them symbolically to the Roman Empire, which had morphed into the Holy Roman Empire with Maximilian as its second Habsburg emperor. Today the map is held in the Austrian National Library.

ment. There was also substantial migration into Austria from Italy itself. By the time the Roman troops departed in the late fifth century, they left behind a largely romanised and ethnically mixed population.

Roman military camp and attendant civilian settlements were scattered across Austria. Two examples are Vindobona (the Roman name for Vienna) and the more important Carnuntum, some twenty kilometres to the east, a base for the legions and the Danube port for the Roman Pannonian fleet.

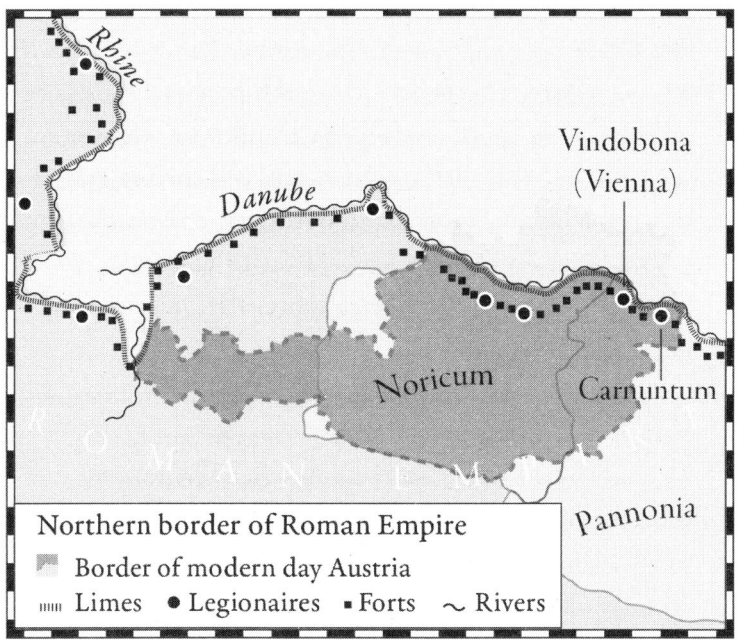

During its heyday, Carnuntum not only witnessed, in AD 193, the appointment by acclamation of Septimius Severus as emperor by legionaries, but for a time also hosted the philosopher emperor Marcus Aurelius (AD 172–175), who wrote part of his *Meditations* there. In AD 308, the town was the venue for a summit held by the retired Emperor Diocletian to try to force the four fractious members of the so-called tetrarchy to resolve their differences. As Emperor, Diocletian had realised that the empire had become too vast to be ruled by a single man, so had divided it into a Western and an Eastern part, each ruled by one senior and one junior emperor. A little more than 1,200 years later, the Habsburg Emperor Charles V (1500–58), having inherited possessions ranging from South America to the Eastern borders of Central Europe, would come to a similar conclusion.

Marcus Aurelius at Carnuntum

'Made in Carnuntum' are the closing words of Book II of Marcus Aurelius's *Meditations*, written during breaks in skirmishes with the warlike Marcomanni and Quadi tribes that would emerge suddenly from the forests across the Danube. The *Meditations* are stoic and elegiac in tone, recommending a preparation for death with a cheerful mind, 'since it is nothing but a dissolving of the elements of which each living creature is composed.'

For some 500 years, the northern boundary of the Roman Empire was formed by the Rhine's western and the Danube's southern bank, both of which were marked by fortifications known as the *Limes*. These consisted of palisades interspersed with watchtowers and small forts, the river affording the real protection against sudden attack. The watchtowers served as early warning positions, while the *castelli* were often crossing points for trade with the barbarians and so doubled as customs border posts. These great river boundaries have played a geopolitical role in Europe throughout its turbulent history up to the end of World War II, and remind us of Austria's long-standing position as European pivot, not only between east and west, but also north and south.

Saint Severin and Saint Florian

In the metaphorical search for the 'first Austrian', historian Stephan Vajda offers us a candidate in Saint Severin (Flavius Severinus), an immigrant Roman official who converted to Christianity and became a monk. In Noricum from 453, he founded a cloister and became Bishop of Lauriacum (Lorch), the garrison town near Enns in Upper Austria (the first town to be awarded 'city' status in 1212). Besides being a holy man who helped the poor and the starving, Severin performed the role of intermediary between the romanised population and potentially aggressive heathen tribes such as the Rugieri, Alemannen and Heruli. Given his remarkable ability to strike deals from a weak position, it may not be too fanciful to see Severin as an early exponent of the arts of diplomacy at which the Habsburgs (or their statesmen) later excelled. Perhaps this is why Vajda eulogises him as 'the first prestigious Austrian long before Austria existed'. When the legions finally withdrew across the Alps in 488, they carried the remains of Severin (d. 482) with them, later reburying him near Naples.

Severin lived long after Emperor Theodosius had made Christianity Rome's official religion. Saint Florian, who preceded him by almost 200 years, met a contrasting fate. A Romanised Austrian from Aelium Cetium (today St Pölten), he became a commander in the army and organised the first fire brigade. But in 304 he was martyred in the Diocletian purges and thrown into the Enns River with a millstone round his neck. Today Florian is one of the most widely revered saints of Austria, and his image is ubiquitous. As patron saint of chimney-sweeps, soap makers and firemen, he was someone you wanted on your side: 'O Holy Saint Florian, please spare my house, set fire to another one' goes one not-very-neighbourly prayer to the saint.[1]

The Great Migrations

> Two thousand years before the European Union, there was a common language and culture, a common currency, common trade agreements and a 'superhighway' for trade in the form of the Amber Road that ran through the whole of Europe and down to the Mediterranean.[2]
>
> Werner Freudenberger

The picturesque German phrase *Völkerwanderung*, meaning the Great Migrations (coined as *migration gentium* in the sixteenth century by the Viennese scholar Wolfgang Lazius[3]) is somewhat misleading to characterise the period between about AD 375 and 578. The first date marks the earliest onslaught of the Huns* into western Europe and the second the arrival of the North German Longobardi, who did indeed migrate southwards and gave their name to Lombardy. In between there was much opportunistic plundering before retreating to a heartland in the east or north of Austrian territory.

The fortunes of the Western Roman Empire in the north waxed and waned according to the competence of individual emperors, the vagaries of civil war and the movements of the peoples outside its borders, as diverse tribes and raiders arrived from the Asian steppe and displaced local populations. Often these incomers were partially integrated, for example by employing them in the Roman army – by the Empire's final years, emperors themselves could be of 'barbarian' stock. The overall tendency was Germanisation of what had been the Western Roman Empire, later the Holy Roman Empire. Nevertheless, the new rulers recognised the symbolic importance

---

* Originally the Huns were pastoral nomads, perhaps first emerging from the region of modern Kazakhstan.

of the old Empire, and embedded many of its administrative structures in the new order that emerged.

The period between the fifth and tenth centuries AD is popularly known, following Petrarch, as the 'dark ages'. This has been challenged by modern historians who point to the lack of surviving written records that might have shed light on those centuries, rather than simply a presumption of years of decline and decay. Certainly, Austria's oldest churches testify to early Christian foundation, such as Vienna's Romanesque St Ruprechtskirche (probably built around AD 740). Ruprecht himself was Bishop of Salzburg, but also patron saint of the merchants of Vienna's lucrative salt trade. (Salt was unloaded nearby from the Danube which, at that time, still washed against the inner-city walls.) Elsewhere, archaeological remains suggest a continuity of Romanised settlement.

The rise of the originally Germanic Frankish empire itself had its roots in an exceptionally able fifth-century commander of Roman forces, Childeric I. Then, as many Europeans are taught in school, the defining moment that symbolically ushered in the Middle Ages and marked the end of the 'Dark Ages' was the coronation of Charlemagne as Emperor of the Romans (*Imperator Romanorum*) by Pope Leo III in Rome on Christmas Day 800. Thereafter, the German kings were also 'Kings of the Romans', though Charlemagne, a political realist, preferred to style himself 'King of the Franks'. His rule extended over modern Germany, France, Belgium, Switzerland and nominally about half of Italy as well as parts of Spain.

Around this time, Charlemagne established an *Avarenmark* (Avar March), so-called because it was intended to be a bulwark against the latest incursions from the east by the Avars in the Carpathian Basin. The *Avarenmark* covered an area corresponding to south-eastern Bavaria and Austria, which had been increasingly settled by *Bajuvaren*, about whose origins there are at least thirty theories. All agree, however, that there is a connection to *Boiohaemum* (that is, Bohemia) and they were established as a leading (perhaps accumulative) ethnic group by the sixth century AD.

Like all others before and since, Charlemagne's empire declined after his death through imperial overreach, internal rivalries and the increasing belligerence of its neighbours. In the case of the empire's easternmost Austrian Ostmark, the major threat to its security came from plundering pagan Magyar armies. This only ceased after a savage defeat of the Hungarians by the German King Otto the Great in 955 on the Lechfeld near Augsburg. Following this, the Magyars were converted to Christianity under King Saint Stephen and his marriage to a Bavarian princess. Otto's prestige and that of Germany so increased that seven years later he was elected Holy Roman Emperor.

The Alps

The Alps cover sixty-two per cent of Austria; this is why the Austrian Schilling (before Austria joined the Eurozone) was dubbed the 'Alpine Dollar'. To the east, the Alps give way to the burgeoning Pannonian (Great Hungarian) plain. The River Danube, running west to east, divides Austria almost exactly along its centre. In Upper and Lower Austria, the granite Bohemian massif, known as the Bohemian Forest, intrudes from the north. Some 20 per cent of Austria is cultivable, while the Alpine foothills provide plenty of pasture. In summer, stock is driven from the valleys to the mountain pastures known as *alm*, this practice recalling an ancient semi-nomadic tradition. At least 40 per cent of the country is forestry, mostly on the mountains and hills.

In the past, habitation in the Alps was sparse and physical isolation meant that dress, customs, dialects and even lan-

A 1920s advertisement for tourism in the Tyrol Alps and Austria's highest mountain, the Großglockner. With the founding of the Arlberg skiing club in 1921, the sport caught on elsewhere in Austrian mountain resorts.

guages could differ between neighbouring valleys. Despite that, Austria has been a north-south transit land from earliest times. Several passes were known in antiquity to the Romans, but many others were only used by locals. The busiest today is the Brenner, between Austrian Tyrol and the Italian Bolzano province, and is the subject of endless international negotiation to reduce the impact of the massive daily throughput of carbon-emitting hauliers (more than 2 million lorries a year). However, a 55-km rail tunnel is under construction (completion is planned for 2032), and should radically reduce pollution, as well as halving the journey time from Innsbruck to Bolzano from 2 hours down to 50 minutes.

Copper mining was practised in the Alps by the Celts between the eighth and sixth centuries BC and salt, mined at Hallstatt for 7,000 years, was once produced at the rate of a tonne a day. Later the Romans extracted gold. Under the Habsburgs, silver mined in the Lower Inn valley at Schwaz in Tyrol was a huge source of income. In Styria, there is a huge iron ore deposit (the *Erzberg*) which is still worked.

Since World War II, the Alpine economy has sprung to life with massive extension of ski resorts (some places now have twenty hotel beds to every long-term resident). Inevitably this results in overtourism and environmental damage, against which there is something of a backlash. Winter tourism represents about 5 per cent of Austria's GDP. Balancing this winter crush is the European Forum Alpbach, a sort of Davos for the coming generation, held in the Tyrol in late August.

Not everything about the Alps is congenial. Avalanches regularly kill the unwary who ignore official warnings, snowboards have become a menace, and some unpleasant oligarchs have holed up there in fancy villas. A sporadic hazard is the *Föhn*, a warm wind swirling up from the Mediterranean and surging down the northern gradients into the rest of Austria causing very abrupt rises in temperature of 10 degrees or more. It's allegedly tough on the human body and psyche, resulting in irritation, inattention, traffic accidents, circulation problems and (for some) very nasty migraines.

CHAPTER 2

BABENBERGS AND EARLY HABSBURGS

The Babenbergs in Austria (976–1246)

The first recorded mention of *Ostarrîchi* – the Old High German name for Austria – occurs in a document concerning land transfer from the German Emperor Otto III to the Margraviate of Austria in 996.

In 1996, the picturesque townlet of Neuhofen an der Ybbs in Lower Austria was awakened from its perry-making slumbers. The occasion was Austria's millennium, and Neuhofen stood at the centre of the festivities because it was near here that, on 1 November AD 996, the German Emperor Otto III gave land to the Bishop of Freising, referring to the territory as '*Ostarrîchi*'. This being the first written source of a name resembling *Österreich*, Neuhofen is popularly referred to as the 'cradle of Austria'. The elevation of Austrian territory to a largely autonomous margraviate, and finally, in 1156, a dukedom, begins with this bestowal.

Following the defeat of the Magyars at the Battle of Lechfeld in 955, the Holy Roman Empire had re-established the Bavarian Eastern March (*Marcha Orientalis*), which included '*Ostarrîchi*', and which, from 976, was ruled by margraves from the House of Babenberg. The Babenbergs were connected to German emperors by marriage and also achieved an international profile through the marriages to three Byzantine princesses. However, they had to take extreme care not to back the wrong side in German imperial power struggles, of which there were many. Fortunately, only once did their judgement seriously falter: during the Investiture Controversy (1076) over who got to appoint bishops and others to high ecclesiastical office, when the Margrave of Austria, Leopold II (1050–95), unwisely sided with the Papacy against Emperor Henry IV.*[4]

The struggle between *imperium* and *sacerdotium* – between the empire and the church – would become a leitmotif of the Middle Ages and lasted up to the Reformation, indeed to the Enlightenment of the eighteenth century. Pope and emperor needed each other for legitimation, but each was inclined to encroach on the other's power. Through patronage, the German emperors, and likewise the Babenbergs themselves, ensured loyalty either by founding new monasteries or placing reliable people in charge of them. Essentially, the dispute was a power struggle between secular and papal privilege which became focused on ecclesiastical appointments.

However, bishops were powerful, with extensive lands and a large stake in local administration, and could also have great influence over the secular rulers who were theoretically set above them. Indeed, so powerful was Bishop Altmann of the Passau diocese, whose writ extended deep into Babenberg territory through the Danubian monasteries, that he was backed by Margrave Leopold II (1075–95) in his pursuit of Gregorian reforms. This eventually caused a break between Leopold and Emperor Henry IV, who promptly sent a Bohemian army that

---

* Henry IV of Germany was forced to seek absolution from Pope Gregory VII after being excommunicated in 1076. Allegedly, but implausibly, he stood for three days barefoot in the snow before the castle of Canossa until Gregory relented and lifted his ban. The sequel to this event is less well remembered: eight years later, after a second excommunication, Henry marched on Rome, deposed Gregory and installed Clement III as anti-pope, who duly crowned him. Gregory had been a bit too free with the two-edged sword of excommunication. But the effects of excommunication against towns, bishops, monarchs etc. were often mainly symbolic and represented a law of diminishing returns.

laid waste to a large swath of Babenberg territory. Ultimately, the Concordat of Worms (1122) theoretically resolved matters between emperors and the papacy by allowing the Pope to select the local religious officeholder, who was, however, obliged to swear an oath of fealty to the secular ruler.

Leopold II's son, Leopold III (1073–1136), was renowned for his piety. He was once considered a candidate for the office of Holy Roman Emperor (he declined) and was later made Patron Saint of Austria. He founded two of Austria's most impressive monasteries at Klosterneuburg (on the outskirts of Vienna) and the beautiful Cistercian Heiligenkreuz in the Vienna Woods (Wienerwald). As the name implies, Heiligenkreuz (Holy Cross) claims to possess a fragment of the True Cross which Leopold V (1157–94) brought back from the crusades. Leopold himself is perhaps the only one of the line whose

Remodelled in the seventeenth century, Klosterneuburg Abbey was founded in 1114 by Leopold III of Babenberg, who later became the patron saint of Austria.

name pops up in English histories. He had the effrontery to kidnap the crusading king Richard I (the Lionheart), while Richard was travelling incognito through the duke's lands.

Richard the Lionheart

The story goes that Blondel, Richard the Lionheart's minstrel, travelled Austria playing outside the windows of castles where his master was rumoured to be held. One day Richard heard Blondel playing outside Dürnstein Castle and in return sang the song's second verse.

Over the years, accounts of the kidnapping and ransom of Richard the Lionheart (Coeur de Lion) have accrued some colourful features reminiscent of the *Braveheart* school of history. What we definitely know is that, while on crusade in 1191, Richard offended the Babenberg Duke Leopold V by tearing down his banner after the successful siege of Acre. In addition, he was suspected by the German Emperor Henry VI of involvement the following year in the assassination of his kinsman, Conrad of Montferrat, in the Holy Land. When stranded at the head of the Adriatic on his voyage home, Richard knew that he was a wanted man moving in imperial territory. Disguised as a pilgrim, he made his way overland, but was apprehended at an inn on the outskirts of Vienna. He was imprisoned in the picturesque, but doubtless far from comfortable, Castle of Dürnstein in the Wachau region of the Danube.

The ransom for Richard was allegedly 100,000 Silver Marks, to be divided equally between Emperor Henry and

Duke Leopold. To raise this sum, it required, among other things, all the church silver of England to be melted down and despatched to the kidnappers. When the ransom was paid, Richard returned to England where in March 1194, in an effort to erase the shame of his imprisonment, he was crowned for a second time.

In Austria, the enormous ransom money that Leopold had received enabled him to improve and better fortify several cities, including Vienna. Equally significant was the founding of the town of Wiener Neustadt on the road to the Semmering Alpine pass to support trade with Venice. Venetian trade indeed boomed in the ensuing epoch, compensating for hazards on the so-called 'dustless highway' of the Danube. In recent years, the chicanery on the river had degenerated to outright piracy. One estimate claims that between Linz and Vienna there were some seventy-seven *Mautstationen* where the local bigwigs – secular or clerical – extorted a toll.

Babenberg power continued to grow through the second half of the 12th century. In 1156, the Babenberg Margraviate was elevated to a dukedom, with Duke Heinrich II (Henry II) – known as '*Jasomirgott*' after his favourite epithet 'So help me God' – moving his court to the expansive Am Hof ('at the Court') in Vienna. A year earlier, he had founded Vienna's Schottenkirche (Scottish Church) and Benedictine monastery – actually Irish, rather than Scots, because Ireland was at that time known as *Scotia maior*.

The *Privilegium minus* of 1156, signed in Regensburg, freed the Babenberg dukes from a number of obligations to the emperor, which thereafter kept them (mostly) out of dynastic quarrels in Germany and ensured the succession, also in the female line. In addition, it released them from military obligations not affecting the integrity of Austria. In return, claims of the Babenbergs to the Bavarian dukedom were finally abandoned. In 1192, towards the end of Leopold V's rule (1177–94), Styria finally came under Babenberg control

From Babenbergs to Habsburgs

The Babenbergs died out when the last duke was killed fighting the Hungarians in 1246. Their legacy, though, was a prize worth having. By now, Vienna was a wealthy east-west trading entrepôt, due not least to the incredible con trick of the Staple Right (promulgated in the *Leopoldinum* of Leopold VI in 1221). This compelled incoming traders to offer their goods for a set period exclusively to the Viennese, the latter having rights to sell them on at profit. After three months, traders had to export unsold wares on payment of an exit tariff.[5] Landmarks in the inner city of Vienna still today recall this lively trading – for example the Regensburgerhof for merchants from Regensburg and the Tuchlauben where cloth was auctioned.

Ulrich von Liechtenstein's poems of courtly love tell of his unlikely exploits that singularly fail to impress the objects of his desires.

Styria was rich in minerals, the salt trade prospered and there was a well-developed wine culture, too. Finally, Vienna had also become a glittering centre of the arts, famous for its *Minnesänger* – protagonists of courtly love and its attention-seeking stunts. For example, Ulrich von Liechtenstein (c.1200–74) paraded around Austria dressed as Venus and performed in tournaments, or so he claimed in his fictional autobiography *Frauendienste* (*In the Service of a Lady*).

Unsurprisingly, the glamour of the Babenberg court and the rich mineral resources in the land – fruit that seemed ripe for the picking – attracted attention from covetous neighbours. In 1252, the 23-year-old second son of Wenceslas I of Bohemia, Otakar (soon to be Otakar II Přemysl and a candidate for the Holy Roman imperium) married the sister of the last Babenberg. She was more than twice his age when he began a 26-year reign in Austria. Otakar was not universally welcome but, through a mixture of diplomacy and war, managed to become Duke of Austria from 1251, Duke of Styria from 1260 and, nine years later, Duke of Carinthia and landgrave of Carniola. In Vienna at least, his reign was considered a golden age since he did a great deal for the city, such as continuing the construction of the Stephansdom (St Stephen's Cathedral) and the ruler's seat of the Wiener Hofburg. He also financed reconstruction after a great city fire and established the first citizens' hospital.

In 1250, the Holy Roman Emperor Frederick II died from dysentery. Within four years, his Hohenstaufen dynasty had fallen and the empire subsequently remained without an emperor for more than twenty years. Then, in 1273, the *Kurfürsten* (electors) chose a new 'Roman King' – the former emperor's godson. This Emperor Elect (which he remained until his death) was Rudolf of Habsburg, a Swabian Count with extensive lands in Alsace and in what is now Switzerland. Few of the electors, who were jealous of their own power and privileges, would have imagined that the Habsburg line was about to embark on a journey through history that would last for more than 600 years. Fewer still could have believed that the dynasty would at one time aspire to domination of much of Europe and even a continent, South America, which they didn't know existed.

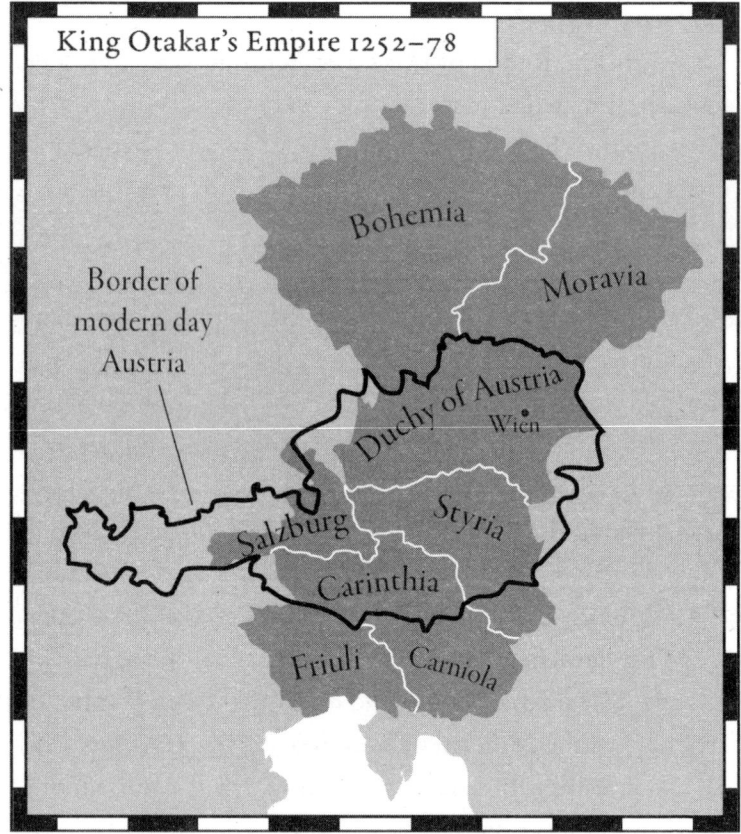

Rudolf of Habsburg, Roman German King

The seat of the Habsburgs was Habichtsburg ('Hawk Castle')* overlooking the Aar River, a tributary of the Rhine. The castle was allegedly built on a rocky outcrop where the founder of

---

* Linguists can be tremendous spoilsports and some maintain that the oldest record refers to '*Havichsberch*' (1108), from Middle High German *Hav* meaning 'ford', so suggests a river crossing, not a hawk.

the line retrieved one of his falcons that had gone missing. It would be appropriate that the Habsburgs, skilled at mythologising their house, should begin with a myth, a myth greatly embellished over the years and apotheosed in the nineteenth century by Franz Grillparzer in his patriotic play *The Rise and Fall of King Otakar*.[6]

Nevertheless, Rudolf of Habsburg (1218–91) was considerably underestimated at first. A competent and, when necessary, ruthless soldier, he was a skilled diplomat and was remarkably frugal compared with many of his spendthrift successors. Like his godfather Frederick II, he was for a while excommunicated for taking the wrong side in one of the endless disputes between the German king and the papacy. However, says Benjamin Curtis, he also 'combated private feuds, abolished illegal tolls... and travelled about Germany destroying robber knights and their castles.... In 1289, he had twenty-nine malefactors executed for flouting imperial law, then displayed their heads before Erfurt's town gates.'[7] He gradually eroded Otakar of Bohemia's grip on the Austrian lands and finally smashed him at Dürnkrut on the Marchfeld north-east of Vienna. Otakar died on the battlefield (allegedly assassinated by one of his own men) and it is said that Rudolf had his corpse put on display for thirty days in the Minoritenkirche next to the Hofburg. Was this out of respect for a ruler the Viennese had admired, or a warning to the city's dwellers?

Grillparzer's great play was first performed in 1825 (it was originally intended to be about Napoleon, but seeing as the Austrian emperor's daughter had recently been forced into a dynastic marriage with Napoleon, the playwright reconsidered). It contains the famous *Lobgedicht an Österreich*, a paean of romantic nationalism, beginning with the words '*Es ist ein schönes Land...*' ('It is a beauteous land...'). When the play was staged during the Nazi period, a Nazi spy indignantly reported that this passage elicited spontaneous applause. You can see why, because Grillparzer, a great Austrian, had written slyly about undesirable German (Prussian) influence on his homeland. Perhaps, he writes, there are more supposedly learned heads in Germany, but the Austrian maintains his 'clear and candid vision', his good sense and 'may God preserve his spirit of youthful contentment and may he prosper when others lose themselves in folly'.

> ### A Rubble of Titles
> Habsburg dynastic history is a story of power accumulation, setbacks, survival and revival. Sorting its multifarious players out individually is quite difficult and the multiplicity of titles – Duke, Archduke, King of the Romans (or Roman King), German King, Roman German King and Holy Roman Emperor – may seem baffling for the uninitiated.[8] Fear not: in this text we will follow individual Habsburgs using their most important title in each case – usually Emperor. For example, the biographical lexicon of the Habsburgs lists the Habsburgs' greatest survivor of the late Middle Ages, Friedrich III (1415–93 as Holy Roman Emperor, previously 'Friedrich IV as Roman German King (if Friedrich the Handsome is counted in)' and 'Friedrich V (as Duke of Styria, then (Arch)duke of Austria)'.[9] There are so many recurring family names that the early compilers of the dynastic tree resorted to colourful tags: the four sons of a fourteenth century Leopold are listed as Wilhelm the Courteous, Leopold the Fat, Ernst the Iron and Friedrich ('Freddy') of the Empty Pockets. Perhaps not accidentally, Leopold and Friedrich had been the commonest names of the Babenbergs.

A further complication is the tendency to partible inheritance – dividing the Crown Lands between siblings – of which the complex interaction between the 'Albertine' and 'Leopoldine' lines in the fourteenth century is the most salient example. Primogeniture – in which the firstborn inherits the title and the bulk of the estate – was not definitively established until the Pragmatic Sanction issued by Emperor Charles VI in the early eighteenth century to protect the inheritance right of his daughter, Maria Theresa. (Charles, by the way, was Charles II as King of Bohemia and Charles III as King of Hungary and – separately – of Spain.)

The extraordinary rubble of titles read out when Emperor Francis Joseph's corpse was waiting to be admitted to the Capuchin crypt in 1916 (including such rather unlikely ones as 'King of Jerusalem') testify to their amazing dynastic reach over 600 years. This recital did not satisfy the Capuchin priest at the door until at last, in answer to his repeated question 'Who craves admittance?' the correct reply was supplied, namely 'a humble servant of God'.

Albert the One-Eyed and Albert the Lame

Rudolf's successor was Albrecht I (Albert I, 1255–1308), chosen as German King in 1298, whose alarming one-eyed exterior proved quite a good guide to his tough character. (The loss of the eye was a result of a cure for poisoning that involved suspending him upside down to drain out the poison, but the effect of which was to induce a blood clot in the eye. History does not relate what happened to the doctors recommending this cure.) Albert faced opposition on many fronts, not least for his plans to make the office of German king hereditary. His ambitions, however, met with an abrupt end when his discontented nephew, Johann (John, known as 'Parricida'), ambushed and murdered him in 1308. Although murder was hardly uncommon in the Middle Ages, regicide was an outrage with particular symbolic and religious significance, and the Habsburgs now began to lose caste in the eyes of the imperial *Kurfürsten* (electoral college) which chose the Holy Roman Emperor.

A further problem came in the partition agreement signed at Neuberg in Styria in 1379, setting in law the separate Albertine and Leopoldine lines of inheritance for Austrian lands, with the Leopoldine line itself later splitting into Tyrolean and Styrian territories. Apart from the internal turmoil that this tended to create, the Habsburgs were under pressure from the Swiss Confederation. Founded in 1291, this was fast becoming the expression of a common Swiss identity – and in due course the Swiss cantonal state. In 1415, the Swiss were to appropriate the Habichtsburg, marking the symbolic end of Habsburg influence in Switzerland.

There was some revival under Albert II (1298–1358), known as 'The Wise' (which he was) and 'The Lame' (despite the customary suspicion of poisoning, examination of his remains have determined that he suffered from crippling rheumatoid arthritis). An able administrator and conciliator, he is sometimes regarded as the true founder of the Austrian state, his goal being to achieve 'one people, one ruler, one house'. It was his son, however, the dynamic and wildly ambitious Rudolf IV, who was to be the dynasty's next shooting star.

Rudolf IV, 'The Founder'
Rudolf IV (1339–65) took up the reins of power at the age of nineteen in 1358 and although he only lived for seven more years, he made a vivid impression on Austrian history, particularly, but not only, for his splendid forgeries. The son-in-law of the Holy Roman Emperor Charles IV, who ruled from Prague,

Rudolf ruthlessly prosecuted the Habsburg interest. In fact, he was so ruthless that Charles sought to limit the Habsburgs' influence by making sure that they were excluded from the list of electors who would select future emperors.

Rudolf was also something of a populist, proclaiming that 'the entire fame and power of a government rests on the firmly founded contentment of its subjects'. This was not mere bluster – he removed tax privileges from the aristocracy and the educated elite, while students at the university that he founded in Vienna (1365) enjoyed unaccustomed protection from rapacious landlords. The university itself was modelled on Charles IV's great Karolinum in Prague. And just as Charles built out St Vitus Cathedral in Prague, so Rudolf built out the Vienna Stephansdom, in 1359 laying the foundation stone for the architecturally stunning South Tower.

Rudolf is perhaps best known for two successfully bold coups. On learning in 1363 that the young Tyrolean Count Meinhard III was on his deathbed, Rudolf made a winter's march over the Alps to enforce a disputed Habsburg claim to succession of Tyrol and fend off a similarly prompt attempt by the Bavarian Wittelsbachs. He then colluded with Meinhard's mother, Margaret, in forging a document that made the Habsburg claim superior.

Margaret was a strong-willed woman, much vilified by her enemies, who referred to her as 'Margarete Maultasch' – 'Margaret Mouth Pocket'. The opprobrious nickname not only implied that she was disfigured, but followed a classic misogynistic pattern, portraying her as ugly, yet bewitching. It was rumoured that she was possessed of a voracious sexual appetite that destroyed her lovers (*Maultasch* also being at that time vulgar slang for vagina). She had, in fact, divorced her first, singularly unpleasant, younger husband on the grounds of alleged impotence. She disposed of him by the simple expedient of shutting him out of their castle, before subsequently marrying a Bavarian Wittelsbach. After the agreement with Rudolf, she followed him back to Vienna, where she lived an isolated existence, carefully watched and even prevented from returning to Tyrol after Rudolf's death.

Rudolf's alert diplomacy had brought him a key geopolitical territory for the Habsburgs, linking the southern territories to their western ones of the German *Vorlande* (Habsburg possessions in Germany). Moreover, Tyrol was a land fabulously rich in silver, gold and copper mines.

Rudolf's second coup was the *Privilegium maius*, one of the most spectacular forgeries in European history. Rudolf had the seals removed from the *Privilegium minus,* which had been granted to the Babenbergs by Frederick Barbarossa in 1156, and recast the document as an impressive legitimisation of the Habsburgs ancient lineage, stressing thereby their entitlement to power in the Reich. Cleverly, the deed's five 'charters' interspersed genuine documents with those cooked up in Rudolf's chancellery, which improbably included letters from Julius Caesar and Nero awarding privileges to a land clearly implied as Austrian territory. Charles IV was decidedly sceptical and, for verification, passed some of the documents to Petrarch, the Italian scholar and poet. His verdict was, at least, concise. 'The man who fabricated these is an arch-rogue ['*Erzschelm*', playing on '*Erzherzog*', meaning 'archduke'] and the man who believes them is an ass.' But they largely served their purpose.

Albert V

A long period of partition and rivalry followed Rudolf's death in 1365 until Albert V (1397–1439) took over as Austrian duke in 1411, subsequently being elected King of Hungary in 1437.

A year later, he was crowned King of Bohemia, becoming also Holy Roman Emperor elect, but he died before he could be crowned. Thereafter, Habsburgs were to retain the elective imperial title, with one short break, until its dissolution in 1806.

Albert was an energetic church reformer who ruled with such a firm hand that, according to the fifteenth-century chronicler Thomas Ebendorfer, gold could be transported openly and safely throughout Austria. Unfortunately, Albert's rule was also marred by the *Wiener Geserah* ('Vienna Gesera', 1420–21), the first of many pogroms against the Jews in Habsburg realms in which property and money were plundered under the guise of religious concerns and false accusations. Jews, barred from many professions in Christian Europe, were obliged to work in marginal occupations such as moneylending, considered a sin by the medieval Church and so not 'permitted to Christians. As a rule, attacks on Jews, including the *Wiener Geserah*, took place when a ruler had borrowed too much money from Jewish lenders and was looking for an easy way out of his debts.

One of Albert's excuses for the expropriation and torture of Jews was the false allegation that they were in league with the Hussites, an increasingly aggressive proto-Protestant group in Bohemia inspired by the theology of the English reformer John Wycliffe (c.1328–84). Their leader Jan Hus was executed for heresy in 1415 but the movement continued to spark violent attacks on Catholic Austrian territory, prompting the pope to launch an anti-Hussite crusade in 1420.

To the Hussites and the Jews would soon be added a third category of Habsburg enemy: the Ottoman Turks.

CHAPTER 3

THE HABSBURGS AS HOLY ROMAN EMPERORS

The Great Survivor

The last Holy Roman Emperor to be crowned in Rome (1453), Frederick III was the greatest survivor of his dynasty, outliving his many enemies.

While campaigning against the insurgent Turks in Hungary in 1439, Albert V died of dysentery. He was succeeded by his second cousin, Frederick of Styria, who, as Friedrich III (Frederick III) (1415–93), would become one of the longest reigning, most enigmatic (and maligned) Habsburgs. In 1452, Frederick was the last Holy Roman Emperor to be crowned in Rome. Often depicted as indolent, Frederick was a diabetic who eventually had to have a foot amputated in what was hailed as surgical triumph, although unfortunately the patient died ten days later. Despite being mocked as the *Erzschlafmütze* ('Arch-nightcap') because of his evident physical torpidity, Frederick got through an astonishing amount of work himself, alongside sending commissioners across his empire to compile reports and initiate reforms. He himself stayed at home for his own security, suffering the indignity of once being besieged in the Vienna Hofburg by his own power-hungry brother. Meanwhile, he was faced with having most of Austria occupied by King Matthias Corvinus of Hungary.

The importance of Frederick for Austrian history is threefold. Firstly, he institutionalised the idea of Austrian exceptionalism, insisting also on the superior rank of archduke for members of the dynasty, for which Rudolf the Founder had wrung reluctant concession from Charles IV. Secondly, he succeeded, after often staring disaster in the face, in outliving all his enemies and rivals, and effectively ending the Habsburg version of the English Wars of the Roses between the Albertine and Leopoldine lines. These wars had reduced much of Austria to near economic ruin in the previous half century. Lastly, with the advantageous betrothal of his son Maximilian to Maria of Burgundy, he not only laid the groundwork for Habsburg accession to the richest territory of north-western Europe (including the Netherlands), but also for the brilliant marriage diplomacy of his line that was to prove more successful than for any other dynasty.

AEIOU

The enigmatic AEIOU monogram of Frederick III was carved onto all his buildings. There are innumerable interpretations as to its meaning.

A man of Renaissance learning, Frederick III busied himself, among other things, with the esoteric. On his magnificent red marble tomb in Vienna's Stephansdom (construction of the tomb began in 1467, more than twenty years before he died) is engraved the enigmatic acrostic AEIOU. It appears on all buildings associated with him. But what do these vowels stand for? More than 300 possible meanings in three languages have been suggested, but most historians have settled on *Alles Erdreich ist Österreich untertan*. This tallies with the Latin *Austria est imperare orbi universe*: 'The whole world is subject to Austria'. The historian Richard von Kralik (1852–1934), a great proponent of the Austro-Hungarian monarchy, found the motto appropriate because Austria was 'the only world power that over centuries took on the task of giving an overarching rule of law to peoples of diverse languages and cultures'. Although one could say the same of, for example, Russia, that country's rule was less based on legitimacy through kingship or imperial rights like the Habsburgs, but rather on conquest and suppression. Austria today is a small neutral country; Russia reverts to its traditional role and methods.

The Last Knight of the Middle Ages

Maximilian I by Albrecht Dürer. Although a gifted soldier and generous patron, Maximilian proved to be an extravagant, reckless emperor.

Frederick III's son Maximilian I ruled very much in the spirit of AEIOU, even though he had to spend much of his life fighting to retain his territories. He was the first ruler to appreciate the public relations potential of printing, long known in China in various forms, but made more economic and efficient with metal moveable type invented by Johannes Gutenberg of Mainz in the mid-fifteenth century.

Maximilian was a prolific author or commissioner of self-glorifying texts – the one apostrophising his journey to marry Maria of Burgundy being cast in a form of heroic biographical fiction similar to that of the eccentric *Minnesänger* Ulrich von Liechtenstein. In reality, this journey was not a string of Herculean trials of strength, but a month-long progression of pageant and feasting. He summoned the scholar Conrad Celtis to Vienna and made him his chief laureate, but some forty other poets were also honoured. Between them, they created a small industry in imperial eulogy.

The alignment with the greats of antiquity, however, was not accidental. Maximilian, like Rudolf before him, was obsessed with an ancient lineage extending beyond the customary Trojan origins beloved of European rulers to figures as distant as Noah. Arranged around Maximilian's magnificent cenotaph in the Hofkirche at Innsbruck stand twenty-eight over-size bronze figures – the so-called *Schwarze Mander*, the 'Black Men'. What Martin Rady calls the 'self-promoting bricolage of history and genealogy', these are mostly representative of Maximilian's forebears and relations, together with the more significant Habsburg spouses, such as Elisabeth of Hungary, wife of Albert II, the first Habsburg King of Hungary; Maximilian's own wife, Maria of Burgundy; plus the slightly terrifying mother of Frederick III, Zimburgis of Masovia. This Polish princess was reputed to be so strong she could drive nails into walls with her bare hands. More to the point, the much-cited protruding lower lip of the Habsburgs is thought by some to derive from her, although surviving portraits do not suggest this.

Among the *Schwarze Mander* are a few figures evidently added to impress as spiritual forebears, such as Clovis I, the Merovingian King of the Franks, and even England's King Arthur. As was typical of many Habsburg enterprises, the *Schwarze Mander* was an unfinished, or perhaps eternal, project – the original idea had been to include the Roman emperors and one hundred saints venerated by the dynasty.

Maximilian I fought seventeen military campaigns with mixed success. After the death of his beloved wife, Maria of Burgundy, who fell from her horse when pregnant in 1492, he did manage (with great difficulty) to secure the rich Burgundian Netherlands. He held on to the Austrian (later the Spanish) Netherlands, despite being kept hostage in Bruges, and obliged to watch his officials tortured and executed in front of him. In northern Italy, he was less successful in rivalling the French.

In the end, his diplomatic – which is to say marriage – strategy was probably his greatest achievement. He married his son Philip the Handsome and daughter into the Spanish royal line in 1496–97, respectively to the daughter and son of Ferdinand and Isabella of Aragon and Castile. Then, in 1515, his grandchildren were betrothed to the children of Wladislas Jagiello, King of Bohemia and Hungary. The remarkable success of this dynastic planning meant that his successor, Charles V, with land reaching across Europe and the Americas, inherited the unique legacy of the 'empire on which the sun never set'.

The extraordinary tomb of Maximilian I in the Innsbruck Hofkirche consists of a multitude of black bronze statues (the *Schwarze Mander*) tracing Habsburg lineage, and therefore their legitimacy, back to antiquity, including Habsburg-related saints, Roman emperors and even legendary figures such as England's King Arthur.

The Fuggers

Like most Habsburgs, Maximilian was perpetually short of cash for his wars, his profligate celebrations and the necessary outlay on bribes. He was rescued by the Augsburg brothers Ulrich and Jacob Fugger, investment bankers who had taken over most of the Medici assets as the Italian banking dynasty declined. The Fuggers earned vast sums of money from their copper cartel, gold and silver mining concessions, and even from a cut on the sale of papal indulgences. It's a poor joke, but the 1367 Augsburg tax records show that the original name of the family was Fucker: *Fucker advenit* – 'Fucker has arrived'.

Jakob Fugger by Albrecht Dürer. The house of Fugger was the principal supplier of credit to Maximilian, becoming the largest trading bank in Europe.

In reality, Jakob, as the richest man in Europe whose net worth has been calculated at $400 billion today, or 2 per cent of the then European GDP, poured money into charitable institutions, such as housing, which in some form still exist today. For Maximilian I, he financed wars and the expensive marriage pacts, but refused the preliminary bribing of cardinals when the Holy Roman Emperor took it into his head that he would like to be pope. Far more ruinous, anyway, was the huge sum of more than half a million Gulden needed to grease the palms of the *Kurfürsten* (Imperial Electors) to ensure they elected Maximilian's grandson Charles as Emperor.

The relationship was eventually one of mutual dependence, a bit like that of today's most reckless megabanks and the US or UK governments – too big to fail and too big to jail. Having invested so much money in him, Fugger certainly could not afford to see Maximilian fail.

Meanwhile, Maximilian directed much of the profits from mines in the Habsburg lands to Jakob's coffers. For example, 50 per cent of revenue from Tyrol's copper and silver mines went to the Fuggers, 18 per cent to Maximilian and 32 per cent to the mining contractor.[10] The emperor raised Jakob to the nobility, an unheard of honour for a merchant, and it helped that the Fuggers remained firmly Catholic as the Reformation broke out. It is hardly an exaggeration to say that the Fuggers financed the rise of the Habsburgs to world power.

Charles V, Holy Roman Emperor

> I sought the imperial crown, not that I might rule over more realms but to provide for the well-being of Germany and my other kingdoms, to create and preserve peace and harmony throughout Christendom and to bend its forces against the Turks. My many treaties have been broken through the passions of unpeaceable men. On errands of war and peace I have therefore had to travel nine times to Germany, six times to Spain, seven times to Italy, ten times to the Netherlands, four times to France, twice to England and twice to Africa. God is our God, thanks be to him, even in misfortune.
>
> Charles V

These words were spoken by a gout-ridden Charles V (reigned 1519–56), who had inherited a sprawlingly vast empire stretching from Transylvania in the east to South America in the west, and from the Low Countries in the north to Italy in the south.

Charles V had to make concessions to Protestants with the Peace of Augsburg, establishing the principle that populations should follow the confession of their ruler, either Catholic or Lutheran (but not Calvinist).

He was giving an account of his reign at Brussels when preparing to relinquish his crown and retire to quarters in a monastery. His career is as good a representation as any of the notion of Austrian exceptionalism which underpinned imperial rule and its combination of idealism and realpolitik.

The Fuggers did their work well and Charles V became Holy Roman Emperor in 1519, making him on paper the most powerful European ruler since Charlemagne. Between them, his predecessors had managed to establish an element of bureaucratic governance and systematic legal process in the somewhat ramshackle structures of the empire, although the emperor's demands and sanctions often remained largely symbolic in the face of local particularism. All the same, his reign was a watershed in European history. The Habsburg Empire split in two – on the one hand, a Spanish branch that was to last until 1700; on the other, a Central European/German branch that included Hungary, Bohemia and substantial parts of Germany and Italy, besides, of course, the hereditary core lands. The German branch lasted in various constellations until 1918.

While Charles ruled in Spain and was Holy Roman Emperor, his brother Ferdinand was appointed to rule the Eastern part of the Empire. It is worth noting that, in addition to the rule of the two brothers, their four married-off sisters had made the dynasty the most well-networked in European history. Mary married Lajos (Louis), Jagiello King of Bohemia and Hungary. He died at the battle of Mohács (southern Hungary, 1526), which opened the way to 150 years of Turkish occupation of most of Hungary, but also to Habsburg rule in the non-occupied regions. Louis' grieving widow was made Regent of the Netherlands (1531–58), an office she filled with dignity and shrewdness. Charles and Ferdinand's sister Eleonore was first Queen of Portugal, but quickly widowed and then married Francis I of France. She was followed by Katharina as another Habsburg Queen of Portugal. Lastly, the unlucky Isabella (known as Elisabeth) became Queen of Denmark, Sweden and Norway. Nor should one forget that Charles V's son, Felipe II (Philip II) of Spain, was, by right of his wife – *jure uxoris*

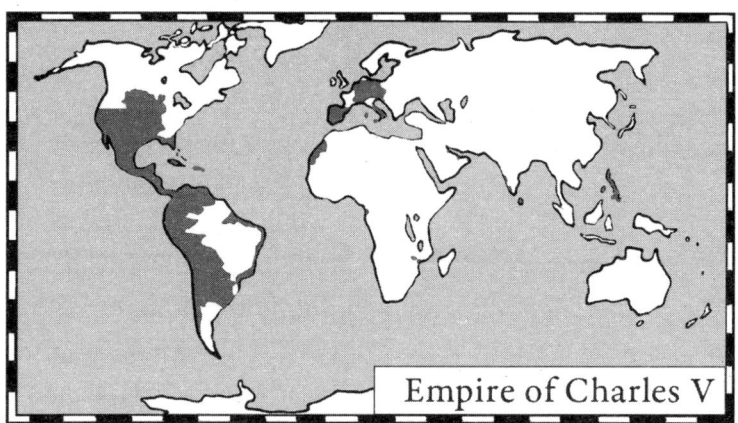

The phrase 'an empire on which the sun never sets' was coined for Charles V's Habsburg Empire.

– legally king of England (as distinct from a mere consort) through his marriage to Queen Mary (Tudor) of England from

1554 until her death in 1558. It is only through a number of accidents (principally the disaster of the Armada in 1588) that Britain is not a Spanish-speaking province.

> ### The Holy Roman Empire 800–1806
>
> Except in his own dynastic lands, the emperor had no direct claim on the vast majority of the Empire's inhabitants that lived under the authority of one or more of the territorial lords... imperial estate members distinguished between the Emperor and the Empire. They were loyal to both, but their ties to the emperor were personal, whereas [those] to the Empire were collective and corporate.[11]
>
> Peter Wilson

Voltaire wrote in 1756 that the Holy Roman Empire was 'neither Holy, nor Roman, nor an Empire'. Was he right? The remark is both true and untrue. The Holy Roman Empire is generally considered to originate with Charlemagne, King of the Franks, crowned Emperor of the Romans by Pope Leo III on Christmas Day, AD 800, in the old St Peter's Basilica in Rome. Having the blessing of the Pope was reciprocally valuable. The assertion of symbolic power bolstered the moral authority of the Pope and the Roman Church versus Constantinople and the Eastern Orthodox Church. Orthodox Christians naturally believed that authentic Christianity resided with them, since Constantine had moved the capital of his Empire to the East and re-founded Byzantium as Constantinople in AD 330. In the West, it was therefore initially important that papal coronation underpinned the legitimacy of kings.

Since the office of 'Holy' Roman Emperor was elective, it was permanently subject to politicking, not to mention bribery of the electors. These were, with a few exceptions like the king of Bohemia, German princes or members of the ecclesiastical hierarchy in Germany. No doubt Voltaire was right that, even if the office was 'Holy', the means of getting it definitely were not.

Inevitably, the Holy Roman Empire became entangled with two perennial controversies: firstly, the rights of secular rulers to appoint persons to high ecclesiastical office (the Investiture Controversy of the late eleventh to early twelfth century); and secondly, the struggle for domination in Europe between the French and the Germans. The Holy Roman Empire was a German entity, and even if for a period the French managed to keep their tame pope at Avignon (1309–76), no French king was elected emperor, although Charles IV tried. And even Henry VIII of England had a tilt at it.

The papacy had strengthened its position by means of an eighth-century forgery known as the Donation of Constantine, which asserted the Roman Church's authority over the old Roman Empire's western territories. Nevertheless, power struggles amongst contenders for papal election continued to have a direct effect on the balance of power in Western Europe. To that extent, Voltaire was right to say that the 'Roman' part of the title was not entirely plausible, although, until the Reformation, the Christian West did usually recognise papal authority and the legitimacy of rulers it supported.

The great achievement of the Habsburgs was to make the office of Holy Roman Emperor effectively hereditary from the time of Friedrich III, the last Emperor to be crowned in Rome by the Pope (1452). Charles V was the last actually to be crowned by the Pope (in 1530 in Bologna). The Pope did crown Napoleon as Emperor *of the French*, but even that under duress.

> Even so, the imperial title remained elective and cost the dynasty a fortune in bribes. So Voltaire's jibe that the 'Empire' was no such thing has considerable force, but is again only partly right. Imperial power was to a degree both symbolic and built on custom, tradition and legal relics, matters that were sorted out after 1663 in endless negotiation between stakeholders at the Regensburg Perpetual Diet. In addition, imperial power was based to a certain extent on direct rule by the Habsburgs, typically in territories where they were also kings (e.g. Hungary and Bohemia, although on paper both countries long enjoyed a 'right to resist' kings they did not like).
>
> Historian Martin Rady, concluding his remarks on the empire, states that 'generations of public lawyers puzzled over the Holy Roman Empire and whether it constituted a monarchy, an aristocracy, a common body made up of sovereign parts, or indeed something that altogether defied categorization, being in the words of one influential commentator "abnormal and freakish".'[12]

Having abdicated in 1555, Charles ended his days three years later as a contemplative living adjacent to the Extremaduran Monastery of San Jeronimo at Yuste. He spent his time in a room bizarrely lined with clocks that required constant attention so that their ticking should harmonise – 'But at my back I always hear / Time's winged chariot hurrying near' as the English poet Andrew Marvell was later to put it.

The emperor reportedly kept three seminal works by his bed: the Bible, Machiavelli's *The Prince* and Baldassare Castiglione's philosophical work *Il Cortegiano* (*The Book of the Courtier*). These reflect key aspects of his strategies and tactics for governance: his conviction that the imperial mission was to protect the Catholic faith, his sometimes desperate twists and turns employed to accomplish that, and his appreciation of a civilised court. This last was important to Charles, who avoided humiliating enemies defeated by his periodically effective generalship. For example, he ordered alterations to a celebratory picture of the Battle of Renty (1554) which showed the French in flight, protesting that they had in fact made 'an honourable withdrawal'. In any case, the battle and its sequel had ended in defeat for Charles.

There were contradictions inherent in all this – the emperor who ordered a cloak to be provided for a shivering South American native brought to his presence and gave orders that the indigenous peoples should be well treated was also held responsible for the infamous Sack of Rome in 1527. Ironically, this was chiefly carried out by 14,000 mutinous Protestant German mercenaries under the command of a renegade Frenchman and against Pope Clement VII – the pope had sided with Francis I of France who was seeking to gain control of Italy. Charles maintained that he had by no means ordered this and the army was supposed only to threaten the city to bring Clement to order. Be that as it may, the carnage was, in the words of historian David Eggenberger, 'reminiscent of the barbarian pillages 1,100 years earlier and thousands of Romans were massacred'.[13] The population was reduced from 55,000 to 10,000 through slaughter, famine and plague; churches, monasteries and palaces were pillaged. The split between Protestants and Catholics deepened from doctrinal dispute to hatred and violence. Despite his rank, the emperor, who ruled half of the planet, proved to be in this case helpless. Charles V, in some respects, bestrode the world like a colossus; yet he also was the victim of imperial overreach, his reign marking the inevitable slow pivot from expansion to gradual decline, from attack to defence.

Austria and the Netherlands

The Netherlands – today's Belgium and Holland – were the richest part of Burgundy, which itself was the richest agrar-

Hans Makart's sensational historicist picture, painted in 1878, celebrates the glory days of Habsburg rule as the young Emperor Charles V processes into his Netherlands territories in 1520. The painting caused a scandal as the faces on the scantily dressed ladies in the foreground were allegedly recognisable as well-known beauties of Viennese high society.

ian part of western Europe and a hugely important commercial hub. The Netherlands may have been a long way from the other Habsburg heritage territories in Austria itself, but they were of vital economic and geostrategic importance. At the same time, they turned into the vortex in which a violent and highly symbolic struggle between Catholic Habsburg Spain and the aspirant Calvinist Dutch state was engaged.

Originally fiefs of the emperors, the Netherlands became a directly ruled Habsburg possession as a result of Maximilian I's marriage to Mary of Burgundy (1477) and following the death of her father, the Burgundian Duke Charles the Bold. Maximilian had to fight hard to hold on to it, likewise subsequently the Spanish Habsburg line, which lost a large chunk that became the autonomous Dutch provinces. Maximilian's grandson Charles V, who was brought up in the Netherlands and whose first language was French, restructured and extended the region in 1549 as the Seventeen Provinces of the Netherlands, with a Royal Governor (*Statthalter*) based in Brussels.

> To God I speak Spanish, to women Italian, to men French, and to my horse – German.
>
> Charles V

When Charles abdicated in 1555, the Netherlands ceased to be Austrian ruled and was turned over to the Spanish line. Philip II of Spain then began his bloody and ultimately futile war to eradicate the reformed faith and revert the country to Catholicism. This proved to be a foretaste of the politico-religious struggle for Europe that was to come, culminating in the following century with the appalling attrition of the Thirty Years War.

In 1585, following the assassination of the rebellious Dutch leader William the Silent (William of Orange), the Dutch-speaking provinces gained *de facto* recognition of their autonomy, while the other provinces (roughly today's Belgium) remained under Spanish Habsburg rule. Interestingly, Elizabeth I of England was offered the crown of the newly independent (and Protestant) Dutch colonies, which, as Robert Tombs puts it, 'she prudently declined'. Elizabeth did make the provinces somewhat symbolically an English protectorate and sent over Robert Dudley, Earl of Leicester, as governor-general. However, Leicester only lasted three years.

The Spanish Habsburg line died out in 1700, their demise sparking the War of the Spanish Succession (1701–14). Resolving this conflict, after the Treaty of Utrecht (1713), the Spanish Netherlands reverted to rule by the Austrian Habsburgs. This lasted until 1795, when Napoleon usurped it. After the 1815 Congress of Vienna and until Belgium became an independent state fifteen years later, the territory was briefly part of a united Kingdom of the Netherlands with Holland. In 1831, Leopold, Queen Victoria's uncle of ill repute, became the first king of the Belgians.

CHAPTER 4

PROTESTANTS AND THE EMPIRE

The Reformation

Martin Luther by Lukas Cranach c.1532. Luther's rendering of the Bible into German helped open the way to a scripture-based relationship with the Almighty less constrained by the straitjacket of Church dogma.

On 31 October 1517, Martin Luther (1483–1546), an Augustinian friar, allegedly nailed his *Ninety-five Theses* disputing orthodox Catholic doctrines to the door of All Saints' Church in Wittenberg in Saxony. This date is conveniently taken to mark the onset of Protestantism, although some historians dispute as to whether the event happened at all, or if it did, whether it was genuinely an act of defiance rather than an invitation to debate.

Either way, the Reformation was a watershed in European history, mixing political rebellion (both of local princes against emperors and of peasants against princes) with demands for reform of a seriously, and sometimes grotesquely, corrupt Catholic establishment. Ultimately, it redrew the map of European power relations as between the Protestant north and the Mediterranean littoral. France was an exception, having a strong Protestant presence until the expulsion of the Huguenots in 1685, while Transylvania practised confessional toleration, and the Swiss Confederation, too, remained divided between Catholics and Protestants.

All this was a complex process, not simply a reaction to the scandalous way in which the Papacy monetised the sale of indulgences in a manner similar to local borough councils today that farm out the collection of parking fines to private firms with target revenues. Ostensibly the money went to the building of the new St Peter's in Rome, but a great deal ended up in enhancing the material grandeur of popes and cardinals. The most notorious seller of indulgences in Germany coined the slogan 'when the offering falls in the glass, the soul leaps to heaven'. Martin Luther's own Archbishop in Brandenburg bribed an agent in Rome to help him collect income-yielding benefices, a practice against ecclesiastical law and known as simony. In order to escape the consequences of this sin, he paid substantial sums both to Popes Julius II and Leo X, and was duly rewarded with the requisite indulgences, which basically meant that he jumped the queue for the exit from Purgatory.

The political scientist Alan Ryan argues that the Reformation broke out when it did because of the alignment of two parties hostile to the papacy for different reasons. The first were the financially straitened but warring western European monarchs who resented the papacy's wealth. The second were the general public who found the papacy morally, spiritually and theologically wanting. 'The decisive factor,' writes Ryan, 'was the readiness of secular authorities to take control of the religious life of their own states.'[14]

The Surging Protestant Tide

In 1521, Charles V summoned an already excommunicated Martin Luther to attend an imperial diet in the city of Worms (the Diet of Worms) to renounce or reaffirm his views on the Catholic Church. There, the two debated, but, refusing to recant, Luther was now also made a political outlaw by Charles.

No matter, the emperor had conspicuously failed to strangle Protestantism at birth. Indeed, there was a distinct danger towards the end of his reign that the Electors of Germany would become in the majority Protestant and elect a Protestant Holy Roman Emperor, a horrifying prospect for both the papacy, the priesthood and the Habsburgs. As early as 1521, a papal envoy estimated that nine-tenths of the Germans sympathised with Luther's ideas. So did many of their princes, though not always openly, the only staunchly Catholic ones being in Bavaria and Austria. However, even that did not mean the populace in those duchies necessarily agreed with their rulers.

By the 1530s, the Protestants were in the majority in the diets of both Upper and Lower Austria. Iconoclasm was taking hold and there were reports of Protestant knights riding their horses round the aisles of Vienna's Stephansdom, beheading votive statues with a swipe of their swords. In the Netherlands, the situation was particularly dramatic with the *Beeldenstorm* (1566) that saw massive destruction of images in Catholic churches.

In the light of this, one can see that the ageing emperor's scheme, whereby his son Felipe (Philip) II and his own brother Ferdinand I should alternate in the imperial office, only increased the danger for the empire. The last thing the German princes wanted was 'Spanish' rule. In the event, the 'Austrian' Habsburg, Ferdinand I, was elected emperor in 1558 by the usual means and was obliged to pursue a conciliatory course with the heretics.

Although Ferdinand had tried to impose a ban on Luther's teaching 'on pain of death' in 1527, he realised that he desperately needed the financial contributions of the Protestant nobles to fight the Turks. The latter conducted their first siege of Vienna in 1529 in the wake of the wipe-out of the Hungarian and Polish army at Mohács in southern Hungary. For Ferdinand, antagonising Protestants would be a recipe for civil war and disaster. The Diet of Worms had become a Can of Worms. It was therefore a result of Ferdinand's efforts (though declared in his brother's name) that the Peace of Augsburg (1555) was achieved under the motto of *Cuius regio, eius religio* – 'whose land, his religion'. This established the principle that the inhabitants of an individual territory in the empire should follow the confession of their rulers (although those unwilling to do so could emigrate to a more congenial jurisdiction).

Some historians see this as the birth pangs of the modern sovereign state, although it did not solve the intractable problem that both sides believed they were in the (absolute) right and Charles himself regarded the agreement simply as *reculer pour mieux sauter* – a strategic withdrawal. Such attitudes were to ignite years of warfare in the Netherlands, while the Peace of Augsburg itself was to be overturned in the following century when almost the whole of Europe became engulfed in the Thirty Years War.

Defeat and Retaliation: the Counter-Reformation

One of the many interpretations of the enigmatic AEIOU motto of Friedrich III, is *Austria erit in orbe ultima* – 'Austria will survive all others on earth'. The history of the Counter-Reformation may lend support to that conceit. By the end of the sixteenth century, it appeared that Protestantism had swept the board in the German-speaking territories. As late as 1600, it is believed that at least 50 per cent of the Viennese were still Protestant, despite vigorous attempts to reverse the triumphal course of heresy. A pivotal moment had occurred in 1525 when the Grand Master of the Teutonic Knights (who were out of a job when no longer required for crusades and had been deployed to convert the Baltic tribes to Christianity) converted to Lutheranism. The Grand Master founded the Duchy of Prussia, Europe's first Protestant state, after an accommodation with King Sigismund of Poland. The Hohenzollern Prince-Electors of Brandenburg became the Prussian rulers in the seventeenth century and the Elector of Brandenburg declared himself 'King in Prussia' in 1701.

In these developments lay the seeds of a Protestant Prussian militarism that increasingly challenged the Habsburg Catholic hegemony. It was to expand through the reign of Friedrich II ('the Great') with the three partitions of Poland in the eighteenth century, and then by means of Bismarck's expulsion of the Austrian Empire's influence from Germany in the nineteenth century. Its apotheosis was the proclamation of the Prussian Empire at Versailles in 1871 after the French had been humiliated in the Franco-Prussian War.

Maximilian II – Machiavellian Cunning or Balancing Act?
Ferdinand I, who died in 1564, sub-divided the eastern Habsburg Empire among his three sons. Maximilian (Emperor 1564–76) ruled in Hungary (the western and northern peripherals not under Turkish occupation), Bohemia, Upper Austria and Lower Austria. Charles ruled Inner Austria (Styria, Carinthia and Carniola) from Graz. Ferdinand received Tyrol and Vorarlberg, as well as some Habsburg possessions in the Swabian Rhineland. Although the rulers were Catholic, the Diets of these territories were mostly Protestant.

Like several other Habsburgs, Maximilian II was conversant with the languages relating to his imperial position – German, Latin, Italian, French, Spanish, Czech and Hungarian. He was also in favour of religious tolerance; indeed, his first tutor had been a former pupil and later friend of Martin Luther. This, along with his easy-going manner, strong attachment to Renaissance humanism and a moderate humanist-tinged attitude to the religion of Erasmus (c.1466–36), led to rumblings amongst the hard-liners that he was a closet Protestant. 'I've seen a number of things that make me greatly suspicious that you, Maximilian, would fall out from our religion and go over to the new sects,' his father Ferdinand had written to him; 'God grant that this is not so and that I have falsely suspected you.'[15]

High-ranking Catholic prelates detested Maximilian and during one undiagnosable illness he thought that a cardinal with whom he had been negotiating had initiated a plot to have him poisoned – something not unknown in papal politics. He also communicated with confidantes in invisible ink for fear of compromise. On his deathbed, he refused the Catholic sacrament of extreme unction, sticking to an earlier claim he had made: 'I am neither Catholic nor Lutheran. I am a Christian.' He intensely disliked the Spanish rigour and militant Catholicism of his cousin, Philip II in Spain. However, a bigoted Spanish wife Maria, who was also his cousin, was wished on Maximilian at the age of seventeen and she ensured that their children would be educated in Spain, with subsequent consequences for the re-Catholicisation of Austria during the Counter-Reformation.

In the meanwhile, he had to navigate the turbulent fall-out from the Council(s) of Trent, whereby the Catholic hierarchy attempted to regain the initiative against Protestantism, reforming the Church but preserving the fundamental sacraments and doctrines of the apostolic faith. The Papacy was generally keen to thrash out the issues with input also from Protestants, but the Roman Curia was rigidly opposed and the papacy itself was determined to avoid the appearance of bowing to demands from secular rulers.

The Council of Trent

Held over twenty-five sessions between 1545 and 1563 in Trento, northern Italy, the Council of Trent aimed to confirm the unalterable precepts of the Roman Catholic faith while reforming other aspects. Varying numbers of bishops attended individual sessions but Protestants, who had hoped to be invited, were permitted to attend only one session in 1552, although certainly Protestant doctrinal issues were discussed and disputed throughout.

The Catholic Church's response to the insurgent Protestant Reformation, the Council of Trent led to much needed reforms to stamp out corruption, clarify doctrine and liturgy, and introduce the German Catechism.

The ruling popes did not attend in person and some of them were a good deal more tolerant than the hardliners at the Council – for example Pius IV reacted to the increasing religious tolerance in Transylvania with the resigned observation that 'heretics are, after all, Christians'.* In 1564, however, a year after the Council completed its work, Pius

---

* This pragmatic flexibility was to culminate in the Edict of Torda, 1568, which officially recognised Lutherans, Calvinists and Unitarians alongside Catholicism and is regarded as the earliest official sanction of religious diversity in Europe.

> issued the Tridentine Creed, which was followed, six years later, by the codification of the Tridentine Mass by his successor Pius V. This mass would remain the Catholic Church's primary liturgy for the next 400 years.
>
> The Latin Vulgate – a fourth-century Latin Bible – was declared the authentic form of the scriptures, but other translations were tolerated as long as they did not 'distort' the Greek and Hebrew originals. The more liberal popes often had Protestant Bible translations in the vernacular in their private libraries. All this was the blueprint for the recovery of the Church's authority. It was to be achieved by force where necessary (the Holy Office or Inquisition was established in 1542), but mostly by activism, preaching and strict adherence to orthodoxy in liturgy, sacraments and dogma. The moderation of both Charles V and Ferdinand I (who suggested abolishing the celibacy of the clergy, from which, then as now, so many scandals arose) was brushed aside. The battle lines for the Counter-Reformation were now drawn.

The starting gun for the Counter-Reformation in Austria can be said to have been fired when Maximilian's brothers, Charles of Inner Austria and Ferdinand of Tyrol, met the Duke of Bavaria in Munich in 1579. Together they planned a rolling reversal of the religious freedom that the diets, through obduracy and persistent legal challenges, had obtained for themselves. They had to proceed with caution, since Maximilian had extracted an immense number of ducats from the Upper and Lower Austrian Diets in return for granting religious freedom. As the ducats were Venetian standard gold, these monies would be equivalent to hundreds of millions of pounds today.

While the Habsburg dukes, archdukes, kings and emperors clawed back concessions, the Catholic Church itself was, by the end of the sixteenth century, on the front foot: well-organised, substantively reformed and messianic in mood. Its most intelligent protagonists had realised that Luther's concepts of 'the priesthood of all believers' and 'justification by faith through Grace' were potentially socially revolutionary, as well as theologically reformist, ideas.* It was clear that a hierarchical, authoritarian and often greedy or corrupt institution had to find a way of relating to the laity directly, and mobilising them for the faith. Protestantism seemed to offer people a more direct stake in their religion. More especially, its appeal to local, particularist or even ethnic feelings provided a weapon for rebarbative regional diets in their struggles with the imperial centre.

The effectiveness of the reconquest of hearts and minds in Austria was very largely due to two orders, the Jesuits and the Dominicans, who might vulgarly be described as the good cop, bad cop duo of the Counter-Reformation. Jesuits brilliantly appealed through spectacles, architecture, art, drama, literature, music and, above all, education. In 1622, a milestone was passed when they regained control of the University in Vienna. Such as it was, they already largely controlled primary and secondary education. In every corner of culture, and thus in every corner of the vulnerable mind, the Jesuits were present while also often being the spiritual-cum-political advisers behind the scenes to the Catholic rulers. Dominicans, the *canes domini* (Hounds of the Lord), on the other hand, were the enforcers.

---

* Luther himself became alarmed by the dangerous alignment between Protestant dissidence and the peasant rebellions that were a recurring phenomenon in Germany. The most brutal was led by Thomas Müntzer, a former protégé of Luther, who commanded an unruly revolt of peasants, miners and the poor which greatly alarmed him. Indeed, Luther referred disparagingly to the 'murderous mob of peasants' and feared the consequences for social order until Müntzer was arrested and beheaded in 1525.

They were in charge of the heretic-punishing Inquisition, and of the Index of Prohibited Books. They were also the most formidable preachers, like St Dominic himself, appealing to the innermost anxieties and guilt of their potentially transgressive congregations.

In Vienna's old town centre, there are two striking churches quite close to each other: the Jesuitenkirche (Universitätskirche) and the Dominikanerkirche. The former was redesigned in Baroque manner by Andrea Pozzo, who had worked on the Chiesa di Sant'Ignazio Loyola in Rome. On the other hand, the Dominikanerkirche's Baroque facade announces its doctrinal adherence with its statues of two great Dominican doctors of the church: Albertus Magnus (the polymath who incorporated Aristotle into Christian thought) and his pupil Thomas Aquinas, the latter arguably constituting the theological backbone of Catholicism.

At the same time, a 'monastery offensive' swept the Habsburg lands, recalling a similar wave in the Middle Ages, but now with foundation or refoundation, as well as reform, of monasteries and schools by Augustinians, Capuchins, Franciscans and Piarists. All these had charitable, including educational, functions. They represented a sufficiently impressive transformation to inspire the aphorism 'Österreich ist klösterreich' – a pun that means Austria is rich in monasteries.

The Fraternal Strife of the Habsburgs

Before the Counter-Reformation really took hold in Austria under Ferdinand II, there was a transitional and confessionally ambivalent period under Rudolf II (1576–1612). He became emperor in 1576 and ruled from Prague from 1583, the last of the dynasty not to rule from Vienna. The problems with the Protestant Estates that beset Vienna were, if anything, even more formidable in Prague, where the Bohemian Protestant nobility were in the ascendant, most of them Hussite Utraquists or otherwise Lutherans.

Who were the Utraquists?

Utraquist Protestants (those who advocated that the laity receive the Eucharist in both kinds – bread and wine – as opposed to Catholic practice of bread only) were the dominant force of the proto-Protestant Hussites. Their leader, Jan Hus, had been burned at Constance in 1415, despite the safe passage guaranteed to him by Emperor Sigismund for his attendance at the Council of Constance. The Hussites' doctrines were greatly influenced by the English religious reformer John Wycliffe (c.1328–84), who had fiercely attacked corruption in the Church and challenged the authority of the papacy. The same Council had ordered that the works of Wycliffe be burned and his remains removed from consecrated ground.

Hussites, however, thrived and provided Europe with its first Protestant king, the Czech Jiří z Poděbrad (George of Poděbrady) who from 1458 reigned in Bohemia for thirteen years. He proved to be a pragmatist and a visionary for a pan-European alliance beyond confessional sectarianism. On one occasion in 1462, he even rescued Emperor Friedrich III from a rebellious mob stirred up by his jealous brother, Albert VI, who was besieging the Vienna Hofburg.

Rudolf II was a depressive bisexual oddball fascinated by astronomy, alchemy and the occult – all of these considered mainstream science at the time. Rival Christian denominations were welcomed to his court, as well as some plausible charlatans who claimed to have discovered how the philosopher's stone turned base metal into gold or silver. His benign attitude to Judaism stands out for the age as unusually enlightened. Moreover, he was one of the greatest Habsburg patrons; polymaths thronged his palace, among them the English occultist John Dee, the Danish astronomer Tycho Brahe and Johannes Kepler, who completed much of Brahe's work plotting the movements of the planets. In terms of fine art, Rudolf assembled the greatest collection of northern mannerist painting, and the mannerist painter Giuseppe Arcimboldo made his portrait in his bizarre style, depicting the features of the emperor's face as various vegetables and fruits signifying Vertumnus, the Roman god of the seasons.

Rudolf had a *Wunderkammer* (Cabinet of Curiosities) for the scientific presentation of specimens, particularly gemstones, and kept exotic animals. Allegedly a tiger and a lion roamed freely in the Prague castle precincts – at any rate, Rudolf's account books record large sums of compensation paid to courtiers or their dependants who had the misfortune to be attacked or eaten.

In a eulogy to the golden age of creativity under Rudolf II, Italian painter Giuseppe Arcimboldo allegorically depicts the emperor as Vertumnus, the Roman god of the seasons, plants and growth.

Rudolf's political and military initiatives, particularly the long Turkish War (1593–1606), were a failure and he sank more and more into depressed passivity. Consequently, it was decided to replace him with his younger brother Matthias, who proved to be equally unsuccessful. Indeed, the playwright

Grillparzer would later paint a decidedly unflattering portrait of Matthias in his historical drama *Ein Bruderzwist im Hause Habsburg* (*Fraternal Strife in the House of Habsburg*, 1848, first performed in 1872).

Apart from his military failures, Matthias was over-reliant on his wily and eventually over-mighty adviser Cardinal Melchior Khlesl, whose enemies managed to have him held captive for a while on trumped-up charges in the Castel Sant'Angelo in Rome. Khlesl is remembered, and not with affection, for his decision in 1596 to extirpate Protestantism in Upper Austria with the help of Spanish veterans of atrocities in the Netherlands. They were, he explained, 'braver, and more experienced in robbing, looting and fighting'.[16] In reality, Khlesl, a Catholic convert, was an opportunist who as often advised appeasement as he did violent methods. Matthias, on the other hand, has gone down in history as a prize bungler with doubtful loyalties.

On Matthias's death in 1619, the way was open for a Habsburg emperor cut from very different cloth: the King elect of Bohemia, Ferdinand, of the Styrian line of Habsburgs. Europe was about to become embroiled in a long war of unbelievable brutality.

Ferdinand II and the Thirty Years War

The prelude to Ferdinand II's reign was ominous. One of the many grievances of the Bohemian Protestants was a dispute over the demolition of Protestant churches built on land that belonged to a Catholic abbot and to the Archbishop of Prague. Matthias had handled it ineptly so that the Bohemians angrily invoked Rudolf's Letter of Majesty issued in 1609, which they said guaranteed rights that were now being trampled upon. They accordingly convoked an assembly at Prague in May 1618 at which two officials representing the emperor, along with their secretary, were thrown out of the palace window during an argument – the notorious Defenestration of Prague.* Despite falling 56 feet, they landed largely unharmed on the castle rubbish tip. According to the official account, this was because a passing flight of angels intervened to ensure a soft landing. Delightfully, their secretary Fabricius, who was also defenestrated, was subsequently ennobled with the title Baron von Hohenfall – 'Baron High Fall'.

The notorious Defenestration of Prague. The emperor's representatives, sent to negotiate in a property dispute between the Catholic and Protestant establishments, were thrown from the windows of Prague Castle.

Following Matthias's death, Ferdinand barely survived his inauguration as emperor when Lower Austrian nobility, sympathetic to the Bohemians, threatened him in the Vienna Hofburg. Worse was to follow when Bohemian nobles deposed

---

* In fact, this was the *third* Hussite attempted defenestration in Prague, there having been one in 1419 in Nové Město (the New Town) Town Hall, and another in 1483 in Staré Město (the Old Town) Town Hall; in both cases the intended victims were the mayor and his officials. They illustrate how deeply embedded Protestantism allied to Bohemian nationalism had become over a short period of time, and how seriously the Habsburgs underestimated it.

him and invited Frederick of the Palatinate (married to a daughter of England's James I) to be their Protestant king. At this point, the Catholic League rallied and Philip III of Spain offered to send a fleet – he shared Shakespeare's belief evident in *The Winter's Tale* that Bohemia had a sea-coast.

In the end, a 30,000-strong army was mustered and inflicted a devastating defeat on Frederick at the Battle of the White Mountain (8 November 1620). Large numbers of Bohemian Protestants were expropriated and their lands given to Habsburg-loyal Catholics. The process was pretty indiscriminate, however, and re-Catholicisation ended in the emigration of some 150,000 Czechs, the loss of Bohemia's elective rights in the imperial caucus and the removal of the Bohemian Chancellery to Vienna. Bohemia effectively became a Habsburg hereditary territory like any other, provoking thereafter Czech national(ist) historians to refer to the onset of three centuries of 'Darkness' before the restitution of their state and its ancient liberties.

Ferdinand's piety bordered on zealotry (he prayed seven times a day and attended Mass twice), but the most inflammatory part of his policies was his determination to break Protestantism in the lands that he ruled as emperor. To this end, he rowed back both on concessions made by his predecessor-but-one, Rudolf's Letter of Majesty of 1609, but also on his own undertakings. When he felt strong enough, he issued his Edict of Restitution (1629), returning to Catholic ownership any properties that had moved into Protestant hands since the Peace of Augsburg seventy-four years earlier. In Central Europe, this proclamation is roughly analogous to Louis XIV's later Revocation of the Edict of Nantes (1685) in a bid to rid France of Protestants. By the time of Ferdinand's Edict, Europe was more than a decade into the Thirty Years War.

The Thirty Years War (1618–48)

> When the leaders speak of peace, the common folk know war is coming.
>
> Bertolt Brecht

Most of Europe's history could be viewed as continuous warfare interspersed with fairly brief periods of peace. However, the Thirty Years War has acquired an ominous status in the history books because it drew in almost all the countries of Europe, as well as places where there were European interests overseas. Its devastation was appalling, perhaps 8 million dead (up to 1.8 million of them military casualties)

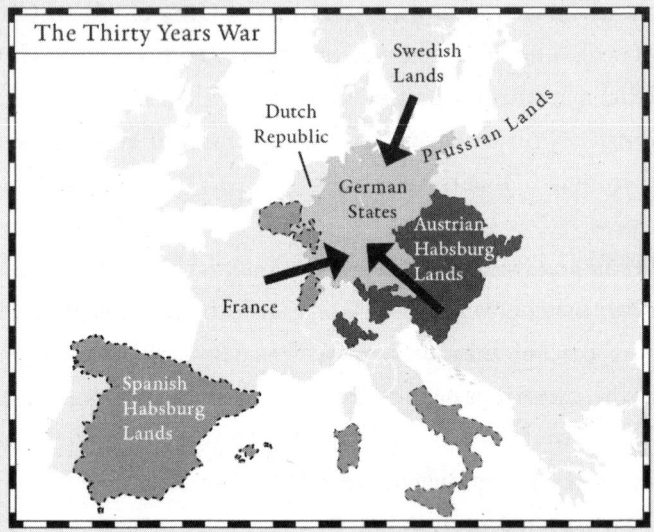

and European populations in some areas reduced by half through famine, plague, other diseases or the barbarities of war. Unpaid armies mutinied and occasionally soldiers changed sides – even the great General Wallenstein's soldiers sometimes deserted or went on a plundering rampage – or died in their scores in winter quarters through cold, illness and under-nourishment.

The conflict has impinged on modern sensibilities as the first 'global war' before the twentieth century, not least through Bertolt Brecht's masterpiece of alienation theatre *Mother Courage and her Children*. The play, today not often performed but considered by some critics as the greatest of the twentieth century, surrealistically depicts the way in which war has reduced human beings to amorality through the need to survive – 'Grub first, then morals' is a famous Brecht aphorism. Mother Courage is an anti-heroine who sells the goods from her provisions cart to different warring factions but loses her children to the conflict. The piece is inspired by the satirical and scurrilous work *Die Landstörtzerin Courage* (1668–69), part of a cycle of stories written by Hans Jakob Christoffel von Grimmelshausen, who himself fought on the imperial side in the Thirty Years War. The conceit of Grimmelhausen's so-called *Simplicissimus* satire is that frightful events are described with faux-naivete. Brecht added his own flavour of nihilistic cynicism in what was primarily an anti-fascist cabaret-style drama of the interwar Weimar Republic. By the time he wrote *Mother Courage* in 1939, Brecht was in Sweden in exile from Nazi Germany.

There were four main phases of the Thirty Years War:

1618–25: war in Bohemia and the Palatinate
1625–29: the intervention of Denmark
1630–34: the intervention of Sweden
1635–48: the intervention of France

The Austrian heartland was economically hit, but somewhat less affected by the physical horrors of war than German territory, while the still independent Prince-Archbishopric of Salzburg managed to stay out of the war altogether. Even so, there was a serious peasant rebellion in Upper Austria in 1626 and by 1648 a Swedish army had intruded on the Habsburg core lands nearly as far as Vienna.

The Thirty Years War ended with the Peace of Westphalia in 1648, bringing peace through complex negotiations among numerous interested parties. This first multinational settlement among equals (each delegation had to enter the

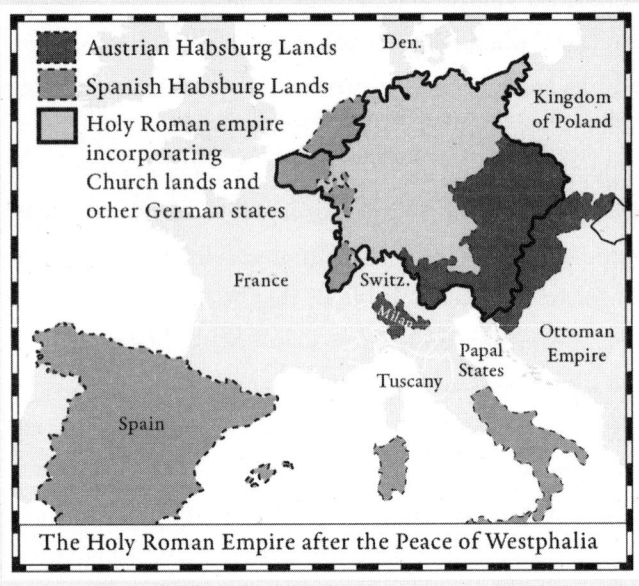

The Holy Roman Empire after the Peace of Westphalia

conference rooms by a different door at the two venues) has tempted historians to herald it as the birth of the sovereign nation state. This supposedly enshrines the inviolability of sovereign borders, a principle that has been honoured more in the breach thereof. Nevertheless, it remains an aspiration of international relations that is still cited in political science (for example by the late Henry Kissinger) as the 'Westphalian System'. In early modern Europe, whole populations might be shifted from one ruler to another through the vagaries of dynastic bedchambers or an agreement signed on their behalf at a treaty, perhaps one concerned with an issue in which they had no stake and still less say. This was particularly so in the context of the Austrian Habsburg Empire. Examples of arbitrary disposal include the removal of the ruler of the Palatinate by Ferdinand II to give to the staunchly Catholic Maximilian I of Bavaria, and the Duchy of Mecklenburg being handed to Ferdinand's warlord Wallenstein.*

The Holy Roman Empire was a different sort of animal from states where religious faith and statehood in Europe were becoming largely synonymous – for example, the Lutheran Scandinavian nations, the Calvinist Dutch Republic, England with its move towards an established state religion of Anglicanism, or alternatively the Catholic states of the Mediterranean littoral. By contrast, Bohemia had lost its ancient autonomy completely and the Habsburgs were now to embark on integrating a fiercely independent-minded and confessionally mixed Transylvania, which they regarded as legally in their empire by virtue of their possession of the Hungarian crown.

The war had also highlighted the complex interaction between religion and national identity, something that was to grow in importance over the coming centuries. The principle of sovereignty, of course, cut both ways: the imperial Habsburgs now had diminished influence over their German territories which had become sovereign and Protestant (notwithstanding that the imperial Diet was

---

* Wallenstein, correctly Albrecht Eusebius von Waldstein, Duke of Friedland and Mecklenburg, Prince of Sagan and Glogau and Admiral of the North and Baltic Seas, was a Catholic convert who saved Ferdinand's bacon in the Danish war. He was later dismissed by the emperor due to intrigues in the Viennese War Council and the intense jealousy of less successful generals. Later still, Ferdinand had to reinstate him, but finally had him murdered (1634) for allegedly holding secret peace negotiations and generally abusing his powers.

moved to Catholic Regensburg, just beyond the hereditary crown lands). On the other hand, they insisted all the more on their sovereignty in lands where they were both emperor and king (Bohemia and Hungary) or Austrian Archdukes (the core lands of hereditary Habsburg rule).

CHAPTER 5

INTERNAL AND EXTERNAL ENEMIES

Leopold I and the Struggle against the Turks
The Thirty Years War gobbled up the energies of two emperors: Ferdinand II and Ferdinand III (1637–57). It weakened Europe economically, militarily and politically, something that did not go unnoticed by a renascent Ottoman Empire. For a century, the latter had been in possession of the greater part of Hungary and regularly launched further probes northwards and westwards in the campaigning seasons. Transylvania was an Ottoman vassal state, although enjoying wide autonomy under its able Protestant leader, Gábor Bethlen, who was also supported by Protestant England. Bethlen was much involved in the earlier phase of the Thirty Years War, making repeated attacks on imperial troops in the Czech lands and on what is now Slovakia.

Winston Churchill once told a colleague: 'You have enemies. That is good. It means you stand for something.' This is a compelling *mot*, but there is a danger that the politician or statesman can come to be defined by their enemies. The Habsburgs had to tread a thin line between conciliation and savagery, for example the gruesome execution of leading Bohemian rebels on the Old Town Square in Prague and the prolonged exhibition of their heads. These executions included such *Grand Guignol* touches as cutting out the tongue of a particularly eloquent Protestant preacher as he was led to execution.

While the heretics were being slaughtered, Ferdinand was at the Styrian shrine of Mariazell praying for the souls of those executed. Some might see this as an example of the famed Habsburg *pietas Austriaca* – Austrian piety – if not perhaps the later much proclaimed *clementia Austriaca* – Austrian clemency. The siege and sack of Lutheran Magdeburg in 1631, where more than 20,000 inhabitants were slaughtered or died in the fire, suggests savagery rather than mercy.

Under Ferdinand III's successor, Leopold I (1657–1705), the Protestants – the most formidable of the enemies of what the dynasty stood for – were not defeated but contained. Ever since the Czech Hussites had launched attacks on Lower Austria in the fifteenth century, and up to the Peace of Westphalia in 1648, Catholicism had been under serious threat. Now there were attacks from the so-called *kurucok* bands of Hungarian Transylvanians (between 1670 and 1711), who were opposed to Habsburg rule and consisted mainly of Protestant lesser nobility and serfs, though one of their leaders was a Catholic prince.

Counter-reformatory doctrine, therefore, counted three great enemies of the true faith as an ongoing threat to the Church and consequently the state: the heretical Protestants, the infidel Turks and the irredeemable Jews. This last obsession very nearly proved Leopold's undoing.

The Jews and Austria

A passage leads from the north-west corner of the Am Hof square in Vienna to the Judenplatz. As stated, there is a reason why the Jewish ghetto was originally next door to the Babenberg court: the Jews, who gradually filtered into Austria from about 1200 onwards, required the sponsorship and protection of the ruling house in a frequently hostile environment. They were active in credit finance – forbidden to Christians and called usury (*Wucher treiben* in German, with the implication of profiteering).

The freedom that their non-Jewish ducal or noble protectors gave to the most able Jews, in particular to set ruinously high interest rates on loans,* was one cause of distrust and envy. When they later enjoyed imperial protection, they prospered, sometimes with non-Jewish business partners, and there were periods when there were so many Jews settling that Austria was dubbed by some *Judaeis Apta* (The Land of Judah). However, when supervision of the Jewish settlement was handed over or back to a local magistracy, the resentment of their alleged privileges among local burghers became rampant. To that was added increasing pressure from papal synods to penalise and marginalise Jews. The justifications for this were long-standing claims of both collective and inherited 'guilt' for the betrayal and murder of Christ, hatred-inspiring attitudes that have morphed into Jewish conspiracy theories of the twentieth and twenty-first centuries.

The precariousness of the Jews' position is underlined by the remains of a synagogue on the Judenplatz, destroyed in the first great pogrom of 1420–21 (the *Wiener Geserah*) under Albert V of Habsburg. The official grounds for attacking the Jews and compelling Christian baptism were suspicions that they were collaborating with the other arch enemy, the Hussites. Other accusations, such as desecration of the Host – the bread used in Mass – were added, all of which afforded justification for torturing Jews to find out where their treasures were. Many refused enforced baptism and a large number starved themselves to death in the syna-

---

* Hans Tietze in his classic study of *Die Juden Wiens* (1933, reprint Atelier 1987), speaks of eight pennies per pound per week in one case, an APY (annual percentage yield) of 173 per cent. When a pogrom in 1338 in Lower Austria was quashed before it took hold in Vienna, the Jewish community, as a gesture of gratitude, lowered the rate to three pennies per pound per week, an APY of 65 per cent. Such high rates reflected the very real risk of default (to say nothing of plunder or expropriation if the political wind changed) but were naturally regarded as extortionate.

gogue. Others were put on a rudderless boat on the Danube and made it down to Pozsony (today Bratislava) in Hungary, where they were taken in, while more than 200 were burned alive on the Erdberg, now a suburb of Vienna.

Over the years, however, Jews returned to Austria and again received imperial patronage as long as they paid ever rising taxes to the exchequer. This irony – that Jews were hated and resented, yet desperately needed for the economy – is recurrent in Central European history.

The next large-scale expulsion of Jews after the 1420s *Geserah* came more than 200 years later under Leopold I. Allegedly, he was pressured by his fanatically Catholic Spanish wife, who herself was under the influence of her confessor and his enforcer, Cardinal Kollonitsch. Kollonitsch was a military man who was not ordained until 1668, when he was thirty-seven, and yet was made a bishop the following year. His religious zealotry may be inferred from his expulsion in 1675 (with the enthusiastic collaboration of the Primate of Hungary, Archbishop Szelepcsényi) of forty Hungarian Protestant pastors who were sent to the Neapolitan galleys. After long negotiations to free them had proved fruitless, they were rescued by a Dutch flotilla. This was as nothing compared to the embarrassment the misstep caused Leopold himself, who was obliged to reverse the sentence on the pastors. Amongst other diplomatic embarrassments, Charles II of England had raised funds to free them. Those who survived the ordeal (several did not) returned eventually to Debrecen via Switzerland, Germany or Holland.

In 1670, Leopold gave the Jews, about 1,500 of whom had settled on the Danube flood plains known as the Unterer Werd (today Vienna's Leopoldstadt), an ultimatum to leave the city. It may have played a role that 1670 was a bad year for Leopold. The recently completed grand extension to the Hofburg burned down. Wars on both eastern and western

Austreibung der Juden im Jahre 1670
Kupferstich

The expulsion of the Jews from Vienna in 1670. Leopold ordered a church, the Leopoldskirche, to be constucted on the site of the synagogue. Since revenue from Jewish taxes was essential for imperial budgets, within a few years some Jewish bankers were being invited back.

fronts were not going well. There was renewed rebellion in Hungary. And the people were discontented due to a deteriorating economy not helped by the emperor's wild extravagance. If in doubt, blame the Jews. Clearly God wished to indicate that the presence of Jews with significant privileges in the city was an offence that needed to be corrected.

In the event, the expulsion proved to be disastrous. Jewish property was seized, but at the same time, the enormous tax revenue that had been forced out of them now dried up, as did credit and investment. Elaborate face-saving manoeuvres were required over the next decades (in 1671 Jews were likewise driven out of Lower Austria) to readmit at least wealthy Jews. As a further humiliation, Leopold was obliged to repair his budget with Dutch and British subsidies (aimed

> at keeping up a front against the French). Both arch-enemies – Protestants and Jews – seemed to have had the last laugh, although at great cost.

One might think that in view of such misjudgements, Leopold's forty-seven-year reign would be accounted a failure. In fact, the opposite is the case, demonstrating the extraordinary survival capacity of the Habsburgs. This was despite the delicate balancing act between French aggression to the west and Turkish aggression, plus Hungarian rebelliousness, in the east. With the Hungarians, it was a war of attrition culminating in their last great revolt led by Ferenc Rákóczi III during the first decade of the eighteenth century. In the end, Leopold I succeeded in achieving what Ferdinand II had managed in Bohemia: the *de facto* recognition of Habsburg succession rights in Hungary through the abolition of the *ius resistendi* – a constitutional 'right to resist' – that had so bedevilled his predecessors.

The position of the empire in Europe now rested on Westphalian principles, which in effect meant a restoration of the Peace of Augsburg's *cuius regio, eius religio* ('whose land, his religion'). The sovereignty of Protestant states within the empire was underlined and Protestant Sweden's war gains even included a seat at the Imperial Diet. The independence of Switzerland (neutral during the Thirty Years War) outside the empire was formally recognised. The Holy Roman Empire no longer represented an exclusively Catholic bastion, but an agglomeration of sovereign states with certain common interests, chiefly the containment of France under the extremely unscrupulous and aggressive Louis XIV (1643–1715). The Austrian rulers had so far failed in the counter-reformatory absolutism espoused by Ferdinand II and Ferdinand III, yet remained important and totemic figures (but not without certain legal powers) in the

European balance of power – something that was vital to their successors' resistance to the Turkish threat.

By contrast, except in Eastern and Upper Hungary, the Counter-Reformation in directly-ruled Habsburg lands was completed with the aid of charismatic teachers and preachers, plus propaganda, processions and spectacle to draw in the *Pöbel* – 'the populace', if behaving well; 'the rabble', if not. The most famous and notorious of the preachers was Abraham a Sancta Clara, whose diatribes against Jews and Protestants were designed to demonstrate that the terrifying plague of 1679 was God's revenge on wicked apostasy, toleration of Jews and decadent living.

Plague Years

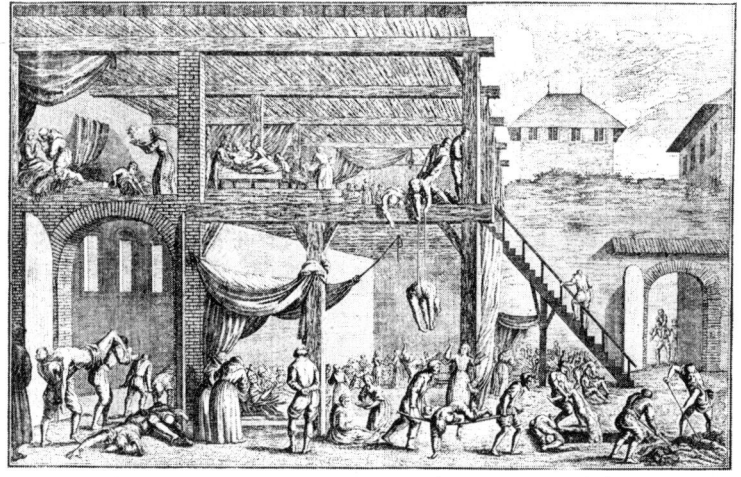

In Vienna, plague recurred so often that it became known in other parts of Europe as the 'Viennese death'.

Recent research of a grave in Lower Austria suggests that plague was present in Austria as early as the Bronze Age. Comprehensive records of it in Vienna, however, date only from the Middle Ages, notably the great Bubonic plague of 1348 – the Black Death. Plague remained recurrent in Europe, often connected with the movement of troops or goods, the warehousing of which attracted rats, such as at a trading hub like Vienna. Because primitive hygiene and inadequate infrastructure was aggravated by population growth, plague became rampant at the end of the seventeenth century in Vienna – and elsewhere in Central Europe, where it was known as 'the Viennese Death'.

A Walloon doctor, Paul de Sorbait, was appointed chief medical officer by Leopold I and worked assiduously against the plague. Despite his implementation of a *Pestordnung* (a sort of early version of lockdown), wacky advice was ubiquitous. Edward Brown, an English traveller, reports seeing a man in Vienna drinking blood from the decapitated head of a recently deceased plague victim in the hope of acquiring immunity (the same basic idea as vaccines, but perhaps a little less sophisticated). Wash-and-drink-urine cures were also popular. Stirring the air was thought to disperse the infection, so church bells were constantly rung, while songbirds were released from their cages and chased round the room. Stinking billy goats were introduced into dwellings to repel the disease with their smell, though more likely it drove the inhabitants out. In 1679, the plague reached a peak in Vienna when 76,000 people died. The last serious outbreak was recorded in 1711–13.

A Viennese folk hero of the time was the drunken bagpipe player Augustin, who is mentioned disapprovingly in one of Abraham a Sancta Clara's texts. Leaving

A nine *Schilling* memorial postage stamp from 1998 depicting Vienna's legendary bagpiper and folk singer Augustin.

a tavern well refreshed, Augustin made his way homewards but unfortunately near the church of St Ulrich fell into a pit dug for plague corpses. Still playing on his pipes to attract attention, Augustin was discovered the following morning when the city workers arrived to throw lime on the bodies. Pulled out of the pit just in time, he went on his way to continue his riotous living until the plague had receded. He thus became the symbol of the invincible Wiener, *der geht nicht unter* – 'who never submits' – one who survived not only the well-merited wrath of God, but even (arguably worse) the attempt by the municipal bureaucracy to bury him. A few lines from a reimagined version in modern English may serve to evoke the bleakly sardonic tone of the original:

> *Augustin, my friend*
> *Wine and whores must end,*
> *What's broken will not mend,*
> *Nothing's left to spend.*
> *Best-fed men in Wien*
> *Got poor like Augustin;*
> *Greedy, fat and mean,*
> *Better times they'd seen –*
> *Times riotous before*
> *The plague was at the door.*
> *Now Wien's a stinking nest*
> *Of corpses laid to rest.*

The Siege of Vienna, 1683

Leopold bolted from the plague in 1679, as did others who had the resources. Four years later, he had to bolt again, this time to Passau – but for a very different reason. The Turks had finally reached Vienna with an army of some 100,000 men, including a mixed bag of Tatars and Thököly's Transylvanians, plus a full complement of eunuchs, concubines, musicians, slaves, falcons, leopards and 16,000 head of cattle to keep them fed. They besieged the city for two months while Charles of Lorraine

The Battle of Vienna 1683 by Martino Altomonte (1657–1745). Polish winged hussars help turn the tide against the Ottoman Turks.

waited for reinforcements to his army for the counterattack. That eventually consisted of Protestants from German states (and thereafter even Swedes), as well as the Catholics of the Holy League – but not the French. Despite Pope Innocent XI's call for Christendom to be defended, Louis XIV was busy in Alsace, which he had just annexed, and French military sappers had been at the Ottoman court to inform on imperial defensive weaknesses, some of them accompanying Kara Mustafa Pasha's army to Vienna.

But even the successful Holy Roman army was papering over cracks – there were disputes over who should have the lion's share of the booty (the Poles got it), how to foot the enormous bill for the relief army (the Pope stumped up large sums), and, even during the relief force's approach, Protestant Saxons were subjected to abuse from the Catholic locals and consequently refused after the initial victory to continue pursuit of the Ottomans.[17] A late arrival came in Jan Sobieski of Poland, who nevertheless insisted on leading the decisive final charge of thousands of Polish lancers careering down from the Kahlenberg on the western edge of Vienna and putting the Turks to flight. That said, his looting soldiers were none too popular and the locals sometimes shot at them until Count von Starhemberg, the commander of the Vienna defence, put a stop to it.

Apart from the Pope's call to arms, the victory was a tribute to Leopold's diplomacy in bringing fractious elements together to save Vienna and pay for the campaign. When the emperor arrived back a day or two later, Sobieski (who had not been above financing Hungarian *kurucok* rebels in the past) greeted him ceremoniously at Schwechat with the grandiloquent (but not entirely unironic) words: 'I am honoured to have rendered Your Majesty this modest service.'

Ugly little Leopold with his protruding lower lip and Habsburg jaw, his indecisiveness and preference for risk avoidance, had shown once again how the Habsburgs were rescued by their enduring instinct for survival. The Turks now began a long retreat from Europe, chased, following the liberation of Buda and Pest in 1686, by Eugene of Savoy right down to Belgrade. Soon an air of triumphalism inserted itself, expressed in the exuberant counter-reformatory culture of the Baroque.

Culture of the Word, Culture of the Senses

It is a truism that Protestantism hugely benefited from the innovations of the printing industry. Tracts and Bibles could be printed *en masse* and also quickly distributed *en masse*. Literacy, likewise, advanced, enabling more people to have direct access to the key sources of their faith and in their own language. Luther's German Bible was a bestseller of its day. Published in 1522, it sold 200,000 copies during his lifetime. Looking beyond the excesses of its violence, bigotry and iconoclasm, Protestantism was potentially also therefore a political liberation for individuals. They could now consult their consciences privately – which might tell them something different from ideas and interpretations hitherto exclusively the preserve of an ecclesiastical hierarchy in symbiosis with a political one.

The new way of thinking, which had germinated in the great intellectual flowering of the Renaissance, has been dubbed by the philosopher Michael Oakeshott as 'the morality of individualism'. Clearly this looks forward to the Enlightenment's increasingly secular view of the world, although the view of sociologist Max Weber, long influential, that Protestantism was the engine of modern capitalism has now largely been abandoned.[18] Protestantism's most positive influence was arguably catalytic, presenting a challenge to the established Church, goading it into reform and, as it were, into improving its offer. Baroque was the improved offer, a *Kultur der Sinne* – culture of the senses – to counter the *Kultur des Wortes* – culture of the word.

CHAPTER 6

BAROQUE CULTURE

The Counter-Reformation Mobilises the Senses

Cultural historians have named the period from around the 1590s to the 1730s the Age of the Baroque. This highly emotional and sensual style emerged with different regional versions across Europe. What makes it especially remarkable in the Habsburg Empire is that Baroque art flourished even during an almost permanent state of war. This contradicts the maxim that amidst the weapons, the Muses are silent! Baroque penetrated all the arts: architecture, sculpture, painting, music and poetry. The Church and the Viennese court were the seminal patrons of Baroque arts. Some Habsburg emperors, for example Leopold I and Joseph I, were themselves gifted composers.

The Italians brought Baroque to Austria, constituting the first two generations of masters in the fine arts, although the Spanish influence was also strong. Towards the end of the seventeenth century, and especially after the Turkish wars, local artists (mainly trained in Italy) assumed the leading role, establishing a kind of vernacular synthesis of all influences from abroad. After 1700, there emerged a Golden Age of Austrian Baroque *par excellence*. Many years later, this became a source and inspiration for creating a local artistic Austrian identity – for instance with the twentieth century libretto by Hugo von Hofmannsthal for Richard Strauss's opera *Der Rosenkavalier* (1911) set during the time of Maria Theresa (1740–80). The running joke of Strauss's *Ariadne auf Naxos* is that the unfortunate performers of the court opera must curtail or hurry through their masterpiece in order not to interfere with the scheduled fireworks – those being one of the most crowd-pleasing elements of Baroque spectacles.

Propaganda for some, Entertainment for others

Baroque culture also used words to good effect, but chiefly as drama. The Tyrolean Nicolas Avancini (1611–86), the leading Jesuit dramatist patronised by the court, wrote in Latin and for a university audience, but other writers adroitly included folk references (as Abraham a Sancta Clara did), vulgar jokes and knockabout comedy, together with scenic effects (ships sailing on water, horse ballet, fireworks) in order to draw in the public. As early as 1608, a *History of St Leopold*, with 106 speaking roles, had been staged in the open air on Am Hof. It attracted a huge crowd, who stuck it out for six hours despite being periodically soaked by passing rainstorms.

Later, the shows became incredibly elaborate in terms of *mise en scène*; nor was theological didacticism obligatory for the plot. *Il pomo d'oro* (*The Golden Apple*), for example, was

The ruinously spendthrift Leopold I commissioned the spectacular operatic entertainment of *Il Pomo d'Oro* to celebrate his marriage to his Spanish cousin, Margarita Teresa, in 1666.

an operatic collaboration between the composer Antonio Cesti, lyricist Francesco Sbarra and the sculptor/engineer

Ottavio Burnacini, written to celebrate the marriage of Leopold to Margarita Teresa.* Leopold himself is thought to have contributed music. It was performed in 1668 and the theme, supposedly flattering to the bride and ending with unblushingly obsequious eulogies of the peerless dynastic titan and his spouse, was the ancient Greek story the Judgement of Paris. The opera was so long (sixty-five scenes) that it had to be performed over two days. This was not quite bread and circuses, but fulfilled a similar role in diverting the people from their discontents and reminding them of the illustrious generosity of their rulers. The show swallowed 350,000 Gulden, with the cost of stolen plates alone reaching 900 Gulden.

The Italianisation of Culture

It will have been noted that all the creators of that huge undertaking of visual, verbal and musical splendour, *Il pomo d'oro*, were Italian. Whether sacred or profane, much of the Austrian Baroque was the work of Italian masters. Even the two greatest architects of Austrian extraction had trained in Rome: Johann Bernhard Fischer von Erlach in a circle where Bernini was the leading light; Johann Lukas von Hildebrandt with Carlo Fontana. Hildebrandt was also a military engineer who worked with the age's greatest general, Eugene of Savoy, to build Vienna's most impressive palace, the Belvedere. Fischer von Erlach's Viennese masterpiece is the Karlskirche, while in Salzburg he built the Holy Trinity Church (Dreifaltigkeitskirche) and the Collegiate Church (Kollegienkirche). Italian architects were

---

* Margarita Teresa was Leopold's second wife and his niece from the Spanish Habsburg line. She always addressed her husband as 'uncle' and was much indulged, as it was hoped she would quickly produce an heir. She appears as a pretty little blonde child in Velázquez's *Las Meninas*. When she arrived at the Hofburg in 1666, she was just sixteen.

themselves active in the Austrian duchies, particularly in Styria, while somewhat better-known masters, such as Vincenzo Scamozzi and Santino Solari, worked in Salzburg. In Vienna,

Vienna's most impressive Baroque church, the Karlskirche, was completed in 1737. The narratives on the columns in front recall the deeds of San Carlo Borromeo, a leading figure of the Counter-Reformation.

we find names like Tencalla, Carlone and Canevale, as well as Italian Baroque painters and, in particular, the great sculptor Lorenzo Mattielli (1687?–1748).

> ### The Cult of St John of Nepomuk
> In Vienna's Peterskirche, you can see perhaps Mattielli's greatest work, an elaborate gilded recreation of the drowning, on the orders of Wenceslas IV, of the Bohemian St John of Nepomuk (Czech: Svatý Jan Nepomucký, c.1345–93) in the River Vltava. Nepomuk was a favourite in the Counter-Reformation's pantheon of saints. As the patron saint of bridges, statues of him may be seen next to river-crossings all over Austria. His, however, is not a Habsburg-oriented cult so much as a symbol of *ecclesia triumphans*. According

to legend, Wenceslas IV unjustly martyred Nepomuk, the Queen's confessor, for not revealing her confessions to him (he suspected she had a lover).* His martyrdom is therefore a stinging rebuke to the secular power when encroaching on the sacred rights of the Church. Nepomuk is thereby the eternal guardian of the Seal of the Confessional. He is the protector against floods and drowning, of course, but, more importantly, the martyr who stands against calumnies and conspiracy. He therefore offered something for the laity that was both morally vivid and theologically orthodox, which even the greatest verbal fireworks of the Protestant Culture of the Word (*Kultur des Wortes*) was hard-pressed to match. In fact, Bohemian Protestant writers vehemently maintained that his legend had simply been cooked up by the Jesuits.

The Italians dominated the music scene, too, providing several *Kapellmeister* (Masters of the Court Music) for the Habsburgs. During the late Renaissance, the Ducal court at Graz had brought Italian musical influence into Austria, employing Orlando di Lasso (c.1532–94) among others as a prolific composer for his court's sacred and profane music. In Vienna, Antonio Cesti (1623–69), Antonio Caldara (1670–1736) and Marc'Antonio Ziani (1653–1715) made their mark. The most prominent Austrian composer and musical theorist of the day was Johann Joseph Fux (1660–1741), but even he shared the office of *Kapellmeister* with an Italian. Fux, who produced the

---

* The real cause of the conflict between the monarch and Nepomuk appears to have been a dispute about the appointment to the abbotcy of the rich Abbey of Kladruby, whose wealth Wenceslas coveted, and Nepomuk's recalcitrance in respect of his wishes. In St Vitus Cathedral in Prague, there is a magnificent silver and gilt monument to Nepomuk by Joseph Emanuel Fischer von Erlach, son of the architect Johann Bernhard Fischer von Erlach. The whole story of Nepomuk reeks of the ancient investiture controversies, but has also become entwined in Bohemian nationalism.

standard work on counterpoint (*Gradus ad Parnassum* – 1725), had studied in Italy and been strongly influenced by the music of the sixteenth century Italian composer Palestrina.

The quarrelsome musician Nicola Porpora (1686–1768) was turned down by Karl VI (Charles VI), but Joseph Haydn studied under him, lived at his Viennese lodgings, as well as accompanying him on tour as valet and accompanist. Haydn said of him:

> There was no lack of *Asino, Coglione, Birbante* [jackass, arsehole, scoundrel], and pokes in the ribs, but I put up with it all, for I profited greatly from Porpora in singing, in composition, and in the Italian language.

The most celebrated Italian musical imports were the *castrati*, who were performing in Vienna as late as the reign of Charles VI. Some were capable of sexual intercourse despite their surgical intervention and were considerably sought after by aristocratic ladies who fancied an affair with a handsome Italian without the danger of pregnancy. All of them were indeed Italian (including one – Gaetano Guardagni – who ensured that Gluck's opera *Orpheus and Eurydice* became a smash hit). Haydn, who had a fine soprano voice as a boy in the Stephansdom choir, was recommended for castration by the superintendent, but his father seems to have intervened.

The most famous Italian composer to seek work in Vienna was Antonio Vivaldi (1678–1741), whose work was greatly admired by Charles VI. Unfortunately, his would-be patron died just before Vivaldi could take up his position and the composer died impoverished shortly after his arrival in Vienna. He was buried next to the Karlskirche.

Following the sensationalist film *Amadeus*, based on Peter

Shaffer's play, which retells an unsubstantiated rumour regarding the death by poisoning of Mozart, everybody has heard of Antonio Salieri (1750–1825). He was director of the court opera when Mozart was enjoying huge popular success, so the two were indeed rivals, although the slightly younger man had also been Salieri's pupil. In truth, Salieri was hugely affected by the unjust rumours that he had a hand in his colleague's death and this contributed to his nervous breakdown later in life. Mozart was not appointed *Kapellmeister* as might have been expected and is quoted as observing somewhat loftily of the remuneration for the job of *Kapellmeister*, 'It is too much for what I would do and not enough for what I could do.'

Spain is Lost, Baroque Splendour Lives on
Leopold I died in 1705 to be succeeded by his eldest son, the promising but short-lived reformer Joseph I. When Joseph died of smallpox six years later, he was succeeded by his younger brother Karl VI (Charles VI) (1685–1740), known as the last of the Spanish Habsburgs, in that he had tried to enforce his claim to the Spanish throne on the death of his cousin in 1700. He succeeded only in ruling briefly in Catalonia.

Charles was cordially disliked in Austria, not only because of his passionate homosexual affairs but more especially because he enforced rigid Spanish etiquette at court and affected Spanish dress. His Spanish inclinations may also be seen in his projected version of the Spanish royal residence Escorial to be built at Klosterneuburg, just upriver from Vienna. Unfortunately, his wars, largely unsuccessful, virtually bankrupted the state treasury. Despite that, the construction of grandiose Baroque palaces during his reign showed that the nobles had money enough, partly from the vast tracts of land reclaimed after the defeat of the Turks. The sharp-eyed philosopher Montesquieu noted this contradiction on a visit to Vienna in 1728, remarking ironically, when he first saw Eugene of Savoy's Belvedere, what a splendid land it must be where the subjects lived better than their monarch.

Charles was able to exploit for propaganda purposes the allegories and symbolism that formed part of the Baroque idiom. Vienna already had a magnificent and intricately symbolic column memorialising the plague. Designed in 1693 by eight leading artists and sculptors including Burnacini and Paul Strudel, it combined a thanksgiving for divine delivery from the affliction with heraldic shields as symbols of the trilateral *Hausmacht* of the dynasty – that is, the hereditary lands of Austria, Bohemia and Hungary. The trilateral dynastic governance dovetails with emblems of the Holy Trinity (*Dreifaltigkeit*), the column's official name. A dramatic relief by Fischer von Erlach on the south side shows Leopold kneeling in humble thanksgiving on behalf of himself and his people.

In Vienna, Charles added two more statements of divine power and his correspondingly divine mission. The first is the astonishing Hofbibliothek (Court Library) with its 200,000 books and manuscripts, which is also a pantheon of his great forebears. Not accidentally, it recalls Maximilian I's expression of the same idea in Renaissance style – the *Schwarze Mander* in the Innsbruck Hofkirche. Just as Maximilian's tomb was to be the central focus of the Hofkirche, so a life-size marble statue of Charles VI stands at the centre of the Hofbibliothek. And just as Maximilian had liked to create genealogies and parallels reaching back to antiquity, so Charles is presented here as the Hercules of the Muses. The dramatic painting of the cupola above him anticipates his apotheosis with accompanying allegorical allusions.

The second triumphal monument is Fischer von Erlach's

great Karlskirche, named not after Charles himself but after San Carlo Borromeo (1538–84), who had ministered to plague victims in Milan between 1567 and 1579. Construction started in 1713 to mark deliverance from the last plague pandemic that had just ended in Vienna. The ascetic Borromeo was a towering figure in the Church. A man of immense intellectual and physical energy, he successfully combatted Protestant ideas at the Council of Trent, two sessions of which he personally organised. In particular, he was assiduous at visiting the most remote parishes of his diocese and enforcing much needed reform, since many were regarded as having become idle, ignorant and debauched, besides shamelessly cashing in on indulgences. Forceful reform, though, proved not to be without its dangers. Carlo was lucky to survive an assassination attempt by a faction called the *Humiliati*, a penitential order doing well out of the vices that he was determined to purge.

Charles VI, depicted here, commissioned Vienna's magnificent Hofbibliothek (Court Library) in 1722. Celebrating the Habsburg dynasty, its central Grand Hall features statues of many of its rulers.

The two Trajanesque columns fronting the Karlskirche are unique in Baroque architecture, their spiralling friezes depicting the life and good works of the saint. But they are also symbolic of Habsburg dominance, or would-be dominance, as the leading Christian power of Europe: twin reminiscences of

Charles's motto *'constantia et fortitudine'* ('constancy and fortitude', i.e. 'through perseverance and courage').

The symbiosis of the two Charles, the zealous religious reformer and the mission-inspired emperor, is achieved, as so often with Habsburg mythologising, through antique reference. The columns symbolise, on the one hand, the Pillars of Hercules giving on to the Atlantic at Gibraltar and thereby recalling Charles VI's lost Spanish realms; and on the other, the two bronze columns, Boaz and Jachin, which, according to the Bible, fronted the temple of King Solomon himself. The German philosopher Leibniz worked out this complex scheme of allusions, which would naturally have been more evident to scholars of the day than to the masses. Divinity and majesty, the imperial and the sacred, the profane and the spiritual, all come together in this heart-stopping visual display of late Baroque symbolic monumentalism.

Egon Friedell's Baroque

> Then came the Baroque with its double reversal of the idea of worldliness. It first rejected the world as mere dream. But since at the same time it affirmed the dream as the only reality, it again returned to the world in a roundabout way. Thus it became the philosophy of the most worldly worldliness, since it rejected every accountability on the grounds that the world is just a dream. So arose that odd mixture of withdrawal from life and love of life, of submissiveness and pride, of incense and musk.
>
> Egon Friedell

CHAPTER 7
ENLIGHTENED ABSOLUTISM

Top-Down Enlightenment

One day in October 1740, an already feverish Charles VI went out on a duck shoot, returning later to his palace soaked and shivering with cold. For dinner, he was served his favourite dish of Catalonian mushroom stew. Unfortunately, some poisonous mushrooms look a lot like the edible sort. Charles was given the wrong sort (malicious tongues said on purpose) and, after great suffering, died two days later.

Austria's first reformer of the Enlightenment, Maria Theresa ruled as sovereign in the Habsburg territories while her husband, Francis Stephen of Lorraine, busied himself repairing the Habsburg finances.

His eldest daughter, Maria Theresia (Maria Theresa), succeeded to the hereditary lands. However, she was immediately besieged on all sides, including by rulers who had recently validated her accession by signing the Pragmatic Sanction (1713)* that Charles had pressed upon them. Nothing more endorses Edward Gibbon's view of history as 'little more than the register of the crimes, follies, and misfortunes of mankind' than what ensued. Friedrich II (Frederick II) of Prussia, whom Maria Theresa magnanimously described as a 'monster' but many Germans prefer to think of as the enlightened 'Frederick the Great', immediately seized Silesia from Austria (December 1740). The French, unable to resist a chance of carving up the empire, invaded the Austrian Netherlands and Lombardy with their own and Spanish troops. Karl Albrecht (Charles Albert), the Prince Elector of Bavaria and a kinsman of Maria Theresa, decided he had a better claim to the imperial title than she did, and also invaded his Austrian neighbour (July 1741). He made good his claim and was elected Holy Roman Emperor, the only break in the Habsburgs' long tenure between 1452 and 1806.

Charles Albert ruled from 1742 until his death three years later. Thereafter, Maria Theresa's husband, Franz Stephan (Francis Stephen) of Lorraine, along with their descendants, re-established the grip of what was now the dynasty of Habsburg-Lorraine. To achieve this, however, Francis Stephen had to give up his own title to Lorraine, which the French wanted. On the other hand, Francis Stephen was a descendant of the Medicis and so when the Medici line became extinct, the Habsburgs were compensated through him with the Duchy of Tuscany. The views of the peoples of these lands were, of course, not required.

---

* A Pragmatic Sanction was merely a fancy name for an imperial decree made without the approval of the Electoral Diet. Charles VI hoped thereby to ensure the succession in the female line and the unity of the Habsburg patrimony.

The Army inherited by Maria Theresa

> Who would believe that there was not the slightest attempt to achieve uniformity among my troops! Every regiment had its own separate drill on the march, on manoeuvres, on deployment. One fired in quick time, another in slow time; the same terms and words of command meant different things to different regiments. No wonder the Emperor was beaten all the time during the ten years before my accession, no wonder the state in which I found my army was indescribable.
>
> Maria Theresa

Assailed on all fronts, Maria Theresa displayed the courage, tenacity and diplomatic skills that have made her something of a romanticised heroine. Her main coup was to appear before the Hungarian Diet at Pozsony (today Bratislava) in September 1741 and appeal to the Hungarian nation (in Hungary the nobles legally and constitutionally *were* 'the Hungarian nation') to support their newly elected queen. This they did on receipt of guarantees for their privileges, especially tax exemption. At the same time, Austria began receiving generous subsidies from the British, whose main interest was to maintain the balance of power in Europe (by which they usually meant 'keeping the French down'). Between 1742 and 1745, when Charles Albert died, Maria Theresa rallied and re-equipped her armies, which achieved notable success on the battlefield. She could not, however, dislodge Frederick II of Prussia from Silesia, which was economically of vital importance to her realms.

She subsequently faced more military challenges in the pan-European, indeed quasi-global, Seven Years War (1756–63), in which the British deserted her,* preferring a Prussian alliance. Austria had now decided to neutralise the French danger, in part through a dynastic alliance, which led to her daughter, Maria Antonia (Marie Antoinette), being despatched aged fourteen to marry Louis XVI and her subsequent guillotining during the French Revolution.

Maria Theresa's never-ending quest for national security then led to the most questionable act of her reign. As Benjamin Curtis puts it with brutal frankness, 'as a way to prevent Catherine the Great of Russia from preying on Habsburg territories', she approved a plan, cooked up by her son and co-regent Joseph in collaboration with Frederick II of Prussia, for the three countries 'to prey on Poland instead'.[19]

This was the first of three cynical partitions (1772) of that unfortunate land, from which Austria gained Galicia and much of southern Poland excluding Cracow. This and a later arrangement with the Turks to acquire the Bukovina meant that the Habsburgs had acquired one of the poorest parts of Eastern Europe together with a mixed population of Ruthenians (that is, Ukrainians), Poles and 200,000 Galician Jews. It is doubtful if all this was in 'Austria''s economic or indeed political interests – and most certainly no compensation for the loss of Silesia to Prussia.

Mother Hen and The Bull in a China Shop

In the mid-eighteenth century in Austria, the old style of divine monarchy gave way to the notion that the ruler was the servant of the people, rather than the other way round. Partly, this involved a more specifically Austrian sense of identity and, correspondingly, less emphasis on the Holy Roman Empire, a body which was already looking anachronistic. Tellingly, in moments

---

* It should be said that Kaunitz, her first minister, had already embarked on a policy of rapprochement with France, which was incompatible with British interests.

of bad conscience, Maria Theresa regretted the carving up of Poland since, after all, it was a sovereign state. The spirit of the Peace of Westphalia of 1648 recognising territorial sovereignties was not quite dead, notwithstanding the generally Gibbonian picture of greedy, duplicitous and often amoral rulers indulging in their own parody of what the English philosopher Thomas Hobbes (in the context of civil war) had called 'the war of all against all'.

Jesuit-educated, Maria Theresa was deeply conservative but generally not a reactionary, except in a few areas like anti-Semitism. (She insisted that a partition be erected between herself and unbaptised Jews appearing before her to deliver a petition.) In 1782, she even expelled her former Jesuit mentors who had become somewhat inebriated with their power, almost as a state within a state. The expulsion ended the Jesuit stranglehold on education and the resulting gap was largely filled by the moderate Order of Piarists.† They began teaching in the Vienna Josefstadt at what is still today a venerable *Gymnasium* (grammar school), although brought under state control in 1870.

In 1774, primary education became obligatory for six to twelve-year-olds, a reform that followed the Prussian model. It was generally unpopular as children were needed for other things at home. The primary schools were henceforth to ensure competence in the three Rs (reading, writing, numeracy, plus instruction in the Catholic faith), while the children of bourgeois families had access to secondary schooling in languages, basic agriculture and crafts, housekeeping and Latin. The reform thus laid the essential educational foundation for a modern state.

---

† Order of Poor Clerics Regular of the Mother of God of the Pious Schools, founded in 1617 and dedicated to education, with many illustrious Catholics later teaching in it. It also offers specialised instruction for the disabled or mentally impaired.

Maria Theresa's Enlightened Advisers

Maria Theresa's greatest skill lay in her eclectic choice of gifted advisers, of whom the four most prominent were Haugwitz, Kaunitz, Sonnenfels and Van Swieten.

Friedrich Wilhem von Haugwitz, a Saxon, was the chief minister who espoused the philosophy of efficient and centralised administration known as Cameralism (*Kameralismus*), which improved both bureaucracy and tax revenues.

He was later outmanoeuvred by another able politician, the Bohemian Prince Kaunitz, architect both of the French dynastic alliance and of Austria's participation in the partition of Poland.

Joseph Freiherr von Sonnenfels, meanwhile, was a baptised German Jew who became head of the Academy of Fine Arts. He advised on legal and social matters. It is largely due to him that torture was abolished both in Austria and the Duchy of Tuscany – at that time ruled by Maria Theresa's third son Leopold of Habsburg. As a member of the Illuminati and a Freemason, Sonnenfels was strongly influenced by the philanthropic legal framework developed by the great Italian jurist Cesare Beccaria (1738–94). In opposing the death penalty, he advanced the unanswerable rationalist argument that it deprives the state of a lifetime of free forced labour.

Dutchman Gerard van Swieten was Maria Theresa's personal physician. He reformed medicine in Austria, while also being in charge of censorship (replacing the Jesuits) in which capacity he acted liberally. His son was a friend and patron of Beethoven and Mozart, both of whom broke taboos in staging works that could be deemed critical of authority. Last but not least, Van Swieten combatted the belief in vampires then prevalent in some areas, and even persuaded his empress to rescind convictions for witchcraft.

Seeing herself as mother to her subjects, Maria Theresa felt that her maternalistic measures should be regarded as for the people's own good. Martin Rady writes that, along with banning lead drinking mugs for her subjects, she:

> cajoled and nannied them into good behaviour, forbidding them from blowing post horns at night, requiring tobacco pipes to be fitted with lids, banning candles from barns, prohibiting advertisements for arsenic.

Even her Chastity Commission,* the object of much ridicule by subsequent historians and an irritation for Casanova who was slightly inconvenienced by it in his Viennese manoeuvres, was partly designed to raise standards of behaviour amongst the elite as an example to the rest.

Despite Francis Stephen's wandering eye, Maria Theresa remained devoted to her husband. Her essential magnanimity may be seen in her gesture at his funeral when she approached his then mistress and remarked 'I know full well what we have both lost.' She understood that it was usually counter-productive to confront deeply embedded traditions and ancient privileges head on, unlike her son Joseph II, who issued streams of decrees that disregarded social context, including severe punishments for masturbation in the cadet schools.

Chastity Commission and antisemitism notwithstanding, 'Enlightened Absolutism' began under Maria Theresa and encompassed social and financial as well as administrative reform. Due to the genius of Francis Stephen, the ever-sagging finances of Austria at least improved and for a few years

---

* In Vienna, a city of some 200,000 inhabitants at this time, it was estimated that there were 10,000 'common' and 6,000 'higher' prostitutes, the former treated as criminals, the latter as varyingly prestigious *grandes horizontales*.

miraculously showed a surplus. By entrepreneurial investments in landed estates and the establishment of a textile industry and potteries, as well as exploiting his armaments contracts, Francis Stephen was able to lend his wife vast sums of money needed to keep the ship of state afloat, while at the same time forcing a curb on public spending.

However, Maria Theresa's son and co-regent Joseph, who became emperor on his father's death in 1765, wanted to go further and much faster than his mother. His policy aims were ostensibly just – diminishing the power of the landed nobles to screw unpaid labour (the *robot*) out of their peasants *ad infinitum*; reducing the vast number of monasteries associated with the contemplative, and arguably non-productive, religious orders ('wealthy and useless' Gibbon had dubbed them in Byzantium, while Voltaire summed up their activity in his own day as 'I live, I eat, I digest'). Joseph abolished the torture of suspects (which Maria Theresa was in favour of – how else was one to get the truth out of a suspect who was clearly guilty?). Last, but very much not least, came the Toleration Patent in 1781 that allowed Protestants and Eastern Orthodox Christians free exercise of their religion and, with an amendment the following year, likewise extended conditions of toleration for Jews.

> ### *Medical Matters*
> Scientific medicine in Austria goes back to Rudolf IV and the founding of the University of Vienna, with a medical faculty, in 1365. The study of anatomy was introduced by the Paduan Galeazzo di Santa Sofia in 1404, who made the first dissection in Austria (at the time only allowed on the bodies of executed criminals). It wasn't until the eighteenth century, however, that the empress's physician Gerard Van Swieten

and his fellow Dutchman Anton de Haën became the first to teach students *in situ* with patients.

Joseph II's opening of the *Allgemeines Krankenhaus* (General Hospital) in 1784 was a milestone. The nineteenth century would see the first ophthalmic clinic, rapid improvements in

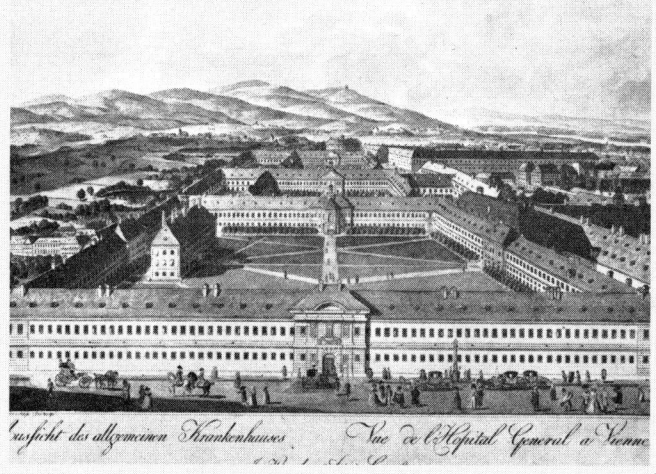

The Vienna General Hospital, which housed Europe's first mental asylum, was the foundation of the Viennese Medical School. It became one of the most sophisticated in Europe.

diagnosis and the first modern surgery under Theodor Billroth. In addition, in obstetrics Ignaz Semmelweis became known as 'the saviour of mothers' by revealing that the normally fatal puerperal fever could be prevented by physicians using simple hygiene. Although rigorous new diagnostic techniques attracted the usual naysayers (e.g. the Viennese joke about obsession with persistent diagnosis and re-diagnosis that ends with the punchline: 'I diagnose that the patient is dead'), the pragmatism of Van Swieten prevailed. He once sat with an overweight Maria Theresa and filled a pail with exactly the same helpings of each course she ate, then showed her the pail, observing 'That is why your Majesty is unwell'.

Joseph's success was mixed. The *robot* – the obligation of annual days of unpaid labour for the landlord – was harshest in Hungary, and so most resistance came from Hungarian landlords opposing Joseph's efforts to reduce it. Understandably so, given the assurances made by Maria Theresa when she'd needed the help of the Magyar nobles. Joseph refused to be crowned in Hungary and ruled by decree through commissars, which brought the country close to rebellion. He had more success with monastic 'reform', liquidating 140 monasteries in 1782, and so freeing up 1,484 monks and 190 nuns to do something he regarded as more useful. The Toleration Patent allowed almost all non-Catholic Christians freedom of worship, provided their 'prayer-houses' were inconspicuous.

A splendid piece of Habsburg publicity showing Joseph II lending a hand to Moravian peasants by ploughing a furrow.

As for the Jews, in exchange for their faith being tolerated, they lost the self-governance of their communities, had to pay a city tax, had to send their children to primary schools to be educated in German, and were obliged to take German family names. Orthodox Jews were inclined to refuse this, so officials dished them out names anyway for their record-keeping – hence the proliferation of surnames like Gelb (yellow), Grün (green), Schwarz (black) and Weiss (white); or, if the official was in a more playful mood, Grünspan (verdigris), Mandelbaum (almond tree) and Rosenzweig (rose twig).[20]

Joseph saw himself as the rational man incarnate and his critics as irrational, although he was not without self-irony. For example, he once snapped 'I am not a religious relic' at a startled petitioner who tried to kiss his hand.

When Joseph decided that wood was being wasted on coffins, he devised a new type with trapdoors on the under-side – a so-called *Klappsarg*. The corpse could then be carried with appropriate pomp to the cemetery and the coffin's contents deposited with due decorum into the grave. Job done, wood saved for the next one. Who could object to that? Well, the Viennese for a start, who greatly valued the proper obsequies ('*a schöne Leich*' – literally 'a lovely corpse' in the city's dialect) and found the idea offensive and irreverent. The outcry was such that the emperor eventually had to withdraw his decree, grumbling the while about his superstitious subjects. In fact, on his deathbed he felt obliged to withdraw the majority of his innumerable decrees, while others were repealed by his successor Leopold II. Joseph liked to present himself as servant of his peoples, as in the inscription above the entrance to Vienna's Augarten,* which he opened to the public in 1775. In truth,

---

* *Allen Menschen gewidmeter Erlustigungs-Ort von ihrem Schätzer*' ('A place of recreation dedicated to all the people by one who esteems them'). Nearly a decade earlier, the better-known Prater park had also been opened to the public. On that occasion, an aristocrat had complained of the indignity of having to share a space with persons of inferior rank, to which the emperor replied: 'If I was obliged only to share the space frequented by my equals, I should have to live in the Capuchin crypt' (i.e. where the tombs of the Habsburgs rest).

though, he felt even more obliged to save the same people from themselves – and was not about to tolerate what he regarded as ill-informed attitudes.

Cleaning up after Joseph

Joseph's brother, Leopold II (1747–92), who succeeded him in 1790, had been more successful in implementing enlightened reform as Grand Duke of Tuscany, where he is known as Pietro Leopoldo. Under his benign rule since 1765, he had, writes David Gilmour, 'attacked monopolies and encouraged free trade, built roads and bridges, made taxes both lower and fairer and reduced the public debt.' He also attempted valiantly to drain the Maremma's malarial marshes, and with the Milanese writer Cesare Beccaria, 'drew up a penal code that made Tuscany the first state in Europe to abolish the death penalty and burn the gallows' – both measures considered amazingly audacious in the rest of Europe.[21] They noted that these milder and more rational new laws startlingly reduced the crime rate, a sign that the abolition of torture did not endanger the public peace.

Leopold, however, would only serve for two years as Holy Roman Emperor. He died, at the age of forty-four, in 1792. During his reign, he was most preoccupied with cleaning up the administrative mess left by Joseph and with the threats to his empire coming from the worsening revolutionary conditions in France.

CHAPTER 8

NAPOLEONIC WARS AND THE BIEDERMEIER AGE

Austria Succumbs to Bonaparte
The clichéd narrative in regard to Leopold II's successor, Emperor Franz II (Francis II) as Holy Roman Emperor (1792–1806) and Francis I as Emperor of Austria (1804–35), is that he was a dim reactionary. Historians seldom miss a chance to deplore his suspicion of new technology, the 'police state' organised by his chancellor, Metternich, or his ultra-conservative views (as in his 1821 address to teachers: 'There are new ideas around, that I cannot, and never shall, approve... keep to what you know').

This litany was born out of the liberal opposition of his day, whose aims were admirable in many ways but which in Central Europe became the incarnation of modern nationalism. One should also bear in mind that he took office in the shadow of the French Revolution that butchered his aunt Marie Antoinette. Metternich's adroit policy on behalf of his emperor is too often or too glibly dismissed as 'reactionary'. Until 1848, it proved highly effective.

The truth is a great deal more complex, even if it irritates his critics to discover that the Emperor Franz himself was quite popular with his subjects. In Vienna, he held open sessions where people could air their problems (he had mastery of Viennese dialect, which went down well). During the cholera epidemic of 1831, instead of fleeing the metropolis as would have happened in the past, he made a tour of hospitals. He travelled quite frequently over his dominions and lived frugally, projecting an image, that was largely true, of himself hard at work on public affairs. The emperor had become his own senior civil servant.

Francis I was noted for his attention to bureaucratic detail and his determination to suppress revolutionary activity. This depiction shows him as the first bureaucrat of his people seated at his Biedermeier desk in the Hofburg.

The Wiener Klassik

From the Josephin period (1765–90) onwards, German music began to displace the Italian hegemony in Austria, culminating in a great flowering of Romantic and late Romantic music (Schubert, Brahms, Bruckner and Mahler) in the second half of the nineteenth century. The bridge between stiff Baroque *opera seria* and a more limpid and melodious style was made by Christoph Willibald Gluck (1714–87), who settled in Vienna in 1752 as Maria Theresa's court composer. Those who know nothing else of Gluck will probably be familiar with the sublime aria *Che farò senza Euridice?* from his opera *Orfeo ed Euridice* (1762).

However, the so-called *Wiener Klassik* – Viennese classical era – really comes to maturity with the work of Joseph Haydn (1732–1809), a significant part of whose career was spent as *Kapellmeister* to Prince Eszterházy at Kismarton (Eisenstadt) and Fertőd in western Hungary. Haydn's many operas have mostly faded from the repertoire, but his wonderful oratorios (for example, *The Creation*, 1798) and chamber music (for example, the stunning *Die sieben letzten Worte unseres Erlösers am Kreuze*) have not.* Early on, he spotted Mozart's genius and was devastated by his friend's early death at the age of thirty-five. In addition, he wrote the melody for the first *Volkshymne* or imperial anthem, beginning with the words 'God preserve, God protect our Emperor' (*Gott erhalte*, 1797) – equivalent to the English 'God save the King', which was, in fact, partly a model for the imperial anthem. Unfortunately, the tune is now better known as accompanying *Deutschland, Deutschland über alles*, Germany's national anthem.† Since 1946, Austria has its own national anthem with words by Paula von Preradović. This eschews bombast in favour of the honourable suffering and endurance of historical Austria thought to be more appropriate in the post-Nazi era.

Wolfgang Amadeus Mozart (1756–91) was a protean master of every musical genre of his time (we lack only a trumpet concerto), a child prodigy astutely marketed by his musician father, Leopold Mozart. Originally in the service of the Prince Archbishop of Salzburg, Hieronymus von Colloredo, who treated him as a servant and seated him at dinner 'among the cooks and the valets', Mozart escaped (literally being kicked out of the archbishop's entourage by a lackey) and embarked on a career producing some of the finest music ever written.

---

* Haydn's *The Seven Last Words of our Saviour on the Cross*, composed as an orchestral work (1786) and adapted to a string quartet (1787), which is how it is now most often played. The 'seven last words' are taken from the gospels.
† One should perhaps stress that, since the 1950s, only the third stanza of the *Deutschlandslied*, with its abstract references to unity, law and freedom etc., is now sung on official occasions. The other two stanzas are considered too reminiscent of Nazism.

Enduring success was, however, by no means assured and it is worth contrasting the prolific Mozart with the most successful contemporary composer of opera, Josef Adolf Hasse (1699–1783), who wrote more than sixty operas and yet today is almost forgotten except to musicologists. In fact, Mozart often referred to Baroque and Rococo ornamentation in his music, combining such elements with his own inventive and melodic harmonies. He was writing in an age where the misbehaviour or abuse of privilege by the nobility could be lampooned (if somewhat cautiously) on stage, as in *The Marriage of Figaro* or *Don Giovanni*. At the same time, a changing audience for opera might be accommodated with buffoonery or comical characters, typically in his *Singspiel* (dialogue interspersed with musical numbers, usually comic) such as *The Magic Flute*, which is now regarded as a quintessentially Viennese creation.

Mozart travelled Europe as a child prodigy with his composer father. His output was phenomenal (more than 800 works), particularly considering he was only thirty-five when he died.

The apotheosis of the *Wiener Klassik* and its opening towards Romanticism may be seen in the music of Ludwig van Beethoven (1770–1827). A German born in Bonn, he was retained in Vienna from 1800 by the generous patronage of his aristocratic admirers. Beethoven was a champion of liberation and famously dedicated his *Eroica* (1803–04) symphony to 'Bonaparte', only to scratch out the dedication when Napoleon, hitherto First Consul of France, declared himself emperor. Beethoven flew into a rage, exclaiming:

> So he is no more than a common mortal! Now, too, he will tread under foot all the rights of Man, indulge only his ambition; now he will think himself superior to all men, become a tyrant!

The symphony itself – Beethoven's 3rd – marks a musical transition from Classic to Romantic.

Due to its proliferation of talent (composers and performers) across all genres, and despite the operatic prestige of Paris and Milan, Vienna was established as the European 'capital of music' in this period, a position it effectively retains, despite political upheavals and war, even today.

The Fear of Revolution

That Emperor Francis II was conservative was hardly surprising. He came to power in 1792 at twenty-three years of age, his aunt Marie Antoinette was guillotined a year later in the French Revolution. He would have been intimately aware of the indescribable barbarities to which a supposedly civilised people could descend – not only the mass guillotining of innocent people, but also the emergence of psychopaths akin to today's terrorists. For example, there was Jean-Baptiste Carrier, who between 1793 and 1794 drowned 4,000 alleged counter-revolutionaries in the Loire and boasted 'we shall turn France into a cemetery rather than fail in her regeneration'. Francis decided to make it his business that such things were not going to occur on his watch and he acted accordingly.

Like the other Habsburgs who showed unexpected resilience

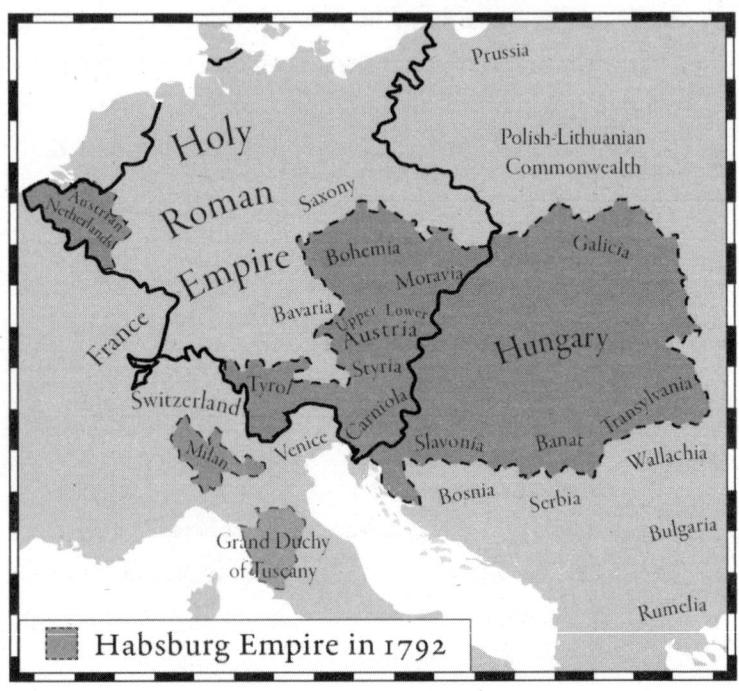

Habsburg Empire in 1792

against the odds, Francis proved to be a long-distance runner, ruling for forty-three years. Maria Theresa had lasted for forty years, Leopold I for forty-seven, Frederick III for an incredible fifty-three years, not to mention Franz Joseph's future tally of sixty-eight years. Long reigns were no guarantee of stability, but they did buttress and nourish the Habsburg myth of a god-appointed mission. Between them, Francis and Metternich did, in fact, achieve considerable stability for some two decades after the Congress of Vienna closed the Napoleonic wars, a period known as the *Vormärz* ('pre-March'), that is, up to the outbreak of the revolutions across Europe in March 1848.

However, right from his accession, Francis knew all too well that he was facing formidable odds. The first two decades of his reign were devoted to damage limitation against the spread of the French Empire, efforts which largely failed. The Austrians lost to the French at Austerlitz (1805) which led to the Confederation of the Rhine, a buffer state between France and Austria with Russia that was the final nail in the coffin of the Holy Roman Empire. The battles lost seemed unending and even the victory over Napoleon achieved at Aspern outside Vienna by Archduke Karl (Charles) in 1809 was reversed two months later at Wagram.

Vienna was occupied twice by French troops (1805 and 1809), who pointedly stabled their horses in churches and behaved with conspicuous arrogance. They saw themselves, after all, as the liberating, rationalist, universalist and secular vanguard of modernity. In 1796, Napoleon had proclaimed to the people of Italy that he would 'respect your property, your religion and your customs'. To his troops, however, he had promised something different: 'rich provinces, opulent towns, all shall be at your disposal; there you will find honour, glory and *riches*' (italics added).[22] Sitting next to an Italian Contessa after invading Italy, Bonaparte (who himself was descended from minor Tuscan nobility named Buonaparte) exclaimed that '*gli Italiani sono tutti ladroni!*' ('Italians are all thieves!'). The Contessa was unfazed, offering the punning retort: '*Tutti, no – ma buona parte, sì.*' ('Not all – but a good part of them.'*)

Well aware of the tendency of Napoleon's troops to loot as they liberated (like the Russians at the end of World War II), Austria played for time. In 1804, Francis had himself proclaimed Emperor Francis I of Austria, a tactical response to Napoleon being declared Emperor of France. Then, on 1 August 1806, a

---

* An alternative version of this anecdote attributes the aphorism to the sculptor Canova responding to a fellow artist's claim that '*Tutti i francesi sono ladri*' ('All French people are thieves!') when Napoleon set about the wholesale looting of Italian artworks for the Louvre. Despite profiting from Napoleonic commissions, Canova was furious about such impieties as the removal of the bronze horses from San Marco in Venice to Paris. Of course, the bronze horses had themselves been looted by the Venetians from Constantinople...

herald appeared on the balcony of Am Hof, not accidentally also the location of the first Babenberg court of 1156, and announced the demise of the Holy Roman Empire after 1,006 years. This was a move designed to protect what had always been a German empire being transferred wholesale to the French.

Napoleon had forced the Pope to crown him (or rather to watch and approve as he crowned himself) as Emperor of the French in 1804. This self-proclaimed title he retained, the necessary regalia for a coronation as Holy Roman Emperor having prudently been removed to the east, ultimately to Temesvár (Timișoara) in Transylvania. Napoleon's army got as far in East Central Europe as Győr (1809) in western Hungary. The subsequent attempt to take Russia in 1812 was to prove the beginning of the Corsican despot's downfall, although they did manage to take Moscow.

The Austrian Empire, as it finally had become *de facto* and *de jure*, was by now in a desperate state militarily and financially, maintained once again substantially by English subsidies designed to prop up the opposition to Britain's over-mighty neighbour. In 1811, Francis declared bankruptcy, reneging on 80 per cent of the state debt, which had a devastating impact on businesses and agriculture. The final indignity had been the forced marriage of Francis's daughter Marie Louise to Napoleon in 1810, an attempt to forge an alliance with France and keep Austria's position as a major European power intact. Marie Louise bore Napoleon a son who was given the title of the Duc de Reichstadt by Francis in 1818. Another title, King of Rome, was bestowed on him by Napoleon in an attempt to elbow his way into the legacy of the Holy Roman Empire.

The Duc was more or less locked up in the palace of Schönbrunn in Vienna for fear he would be able to unleash more mayhem as claimant to imperial office as Napoleon II.

Fortunately, he died of tuberculosis at the age of twenty-one, although he did bear the imperial title for a few days in 1815, before his father, defeated at the Battle of Waterloo, was obliged to abdicate unconditionally, which meant including his descendants. Nevertheless, the Duc's cousin was later to take power in France as Napoleon III. In a puzzling gesture, Hitler was to have the Duc's remains returned to France in 1940 and placed in the Pantheon, although the heart and intestines, following Habsburg burial ritual, remained respectively in the crypt in the Augustinerkirche and the Ducal crypt of the Stephansdom in Vienna.

The marriage of Marie Louise and the careful watch kept on Napoleon II were organised by Francis's chief minister: Klemens Wenzel Nepomuk Lothar, Prince of Metternich-Winneburg zu Beilstein (1773–1859), commonly known as Klemens von Metternich or Prince Metternich. Appointing him foreign minister in 1809, then chancellor from 1821, were undoubtedly masterstrokes by the emperor, since he proved to be, by common consent, the master diplomat of the age, bringing Austria from a weak position of near ruin back to the centre of European power politics.

Metternich the Puppet-Master of Realpolitik

> The word 'freedom' means for me not a point of departure but a genuine point of arrival. The point of departure is defined by the word 'order'. Freedom cannot exist without the concept of order.
>
> Prince Metternich

Metternich can best be understood as a man brought up with Enlightenment values who, however, realised that such values could only be made permanent through realpolitik.

From the assessment by Henry Kissinger through that of historian Alan Sked and on to the definitive work on him by Wolfram Siemann,[23] this is the underlying theme of Metternich's contemporary rehabilitation from the odium often poured on him by historians. His policies, though outwardly Machiavellian and obscure, were guided by three principles: firstly, to have a clear aim, which was to have peace in Europe through the balance of powers; secondly, a clear strategy to achieve that through diplomacy, manipulation and manoeuvring, with the avoidance of war where possible; and thirdly, to be the best informed statesman of Europe through censorship, a network of informers at home and connections all around Europe (which included shameless practices such as opening diplomatic mail).

To statesman Klemens von Metternich, 'freedom' could not exist unless it was based on 'order'.

Metternich had spent some time in England and was particularly impressed by Edmund Burke, most obviously by the latter's foresight in regard to the then forthcoming barbarism of the revolution in France. But he also admired Burke's framing of the balance between freedom and order in England by means of shared power through king, Lords and Commons. As ambassador in Paris, Metternich had listened for an hour as Napoleon, trying to impress a polished aristocrat, could not resist boasting of his plans. 'I was brought up in military camps,' Napoleon said, 'and know nothing but military camps, and a man such as I am does not give a **** about the lives of [*se foutre de la vie de*] a million men.' Metternich was deeply shocked by the French military hero's callousness.

The Congress of Vienna

Somewhat ironically, the disastrous French invasion of Russia in 1812 was initially accompanied by more than 30,000 'auxiliary' Austrian troops under Prince Schwarzenberg, as France and Austria were officially allies. After the French defeat at the Battle of The Nations at Leipzig in 1813 (the Austrians having in the meanwhile ditched the French alliance), Napoleon was deposed and despatched to the island of Elba.

The master of ceremonies at the Peace Congress was Metternich. His aim was to produce an outcome that restored the *status quo ante* in respect of the balance of European powers in a Holy Alliance of monarchies. An important aspect of this was the invitation to France to participate on equal terms, thus avoiding the humiliation of the defeated side (as would a century later have such devastating consequences in European history). Talleyrand, instigator of the coup to remove Napoleon (and the erstwhile recipient of bribes from Metternich when the latter was Austrian Ambassador to France) represented France. Following Napoleon's attempt to retake France and his ultimate defeat at Waterloo in 1815, France was restored to her 1790 boundaries.

From Austria's point of view, the outcome of the settlement was better than might have been expected. She retained all her core territories, but lost the Austrian Netherlands, which were to become the monarchy of Belgium in 1830. On the other hand, she was ceded Lombardy-Venetia inclusive of Dubrovnik. Cadet line Habsburgs continued to rule in

Tuscany and Modena, while Marie Louise, now divorced from Napoleon, ruled Parma in northern Italy with her new lover. Austria did not even entirely lose its traditional leader-

Habsburg Empire in 1815

ship role in Germany, remaining the nominal head of a German Confederation of thirty-nine statelets and four free cities. This relic of the Holy Roman Empire was designed to contain Prussia and obstruct German unification under Prussian rule. The Confederation was, however, weak and unwieldy, unable to broker the inherent rivalry between a strengthening Prussia and weakening Austria.

The Congress had been a great party. One characterisation of it ran:

> The Tsar of Russia falls in love for everyone; the King of Prussia thinks for everyone; the King of Denmark speaks for everyone; the King of Bavaria drinks for everyone; the King of Württemberg eats for everyone ... and the Emperor of Austria pays for everyone.
>
> Prince de Ligne (who also remarked that 'the Congress is not getting on; it is dancing')

Metternich continued to work on conservative monarchical defences against revolutionary aspirations, notably with the much-excoriated Carlsbad Decrees of 1819 which applied across the members of the Confederation. They were principally aimed at student *Burschenschaften* (Fraternities), one of whose members had caused widespread outrage by assassinating the writer August von Kotzebue in March 1819. Strict limitations were put on both membership and activities of the Fraternities, while professors with radical inclinations were to be removed, as well as tight censorship imposed both on the press and in academia. Criticism of Metternich for being obsessed with terrorism is somewhat disingenuous. There were plenty of trigger-happy radicals around.

The Legacy of Enlightened Absolutism

At this point it is worth stepping back and surveying to what extent the Austrian Empire had moved from monarchical absolutism and towards the more responsive arrangements that modern democracies now take for granted. Under the 'enlightened absolutism' of Maria Theresa and Joseph II, a process of centralisation had begun which was designed to reduce or remove the power of the nobility's vested interest. Joseph had visited Bohemia and seen the abuse of the *robot* system. Indeed, a propaganda flier had been issued showing the emperor himself ploughing a furrow.

Between them, mother and son had instituted reforms to education and the criminal justice system that aimed to curb immunities from prosecution (known as 'benefit of clergy' for the church, plus various forms of seigneurial privilege) and so move towards a dispensation that made their subjects nearly, or at any rate more, equal before the law. Torture had been abolished in 1776 and the death penalty in 1787.

While Joseph's posture of being *volksnahe* ('in touch with the people') was sometimes sabotaged by his peremptory and authoritarian manner, he was prepared to take on privilege and even once put some especially recalcitrant nobles on a chain-gang sweeping Vienna's streets.

Under Francis I, the introduction of an *Allgemeines Bürgerliches Gesetzbuch* (ABG – General Civil Code – 1811) instituted citizens' equality before the law. Rudimentary pension systems were introduced, hospitals founded (or charity care for those unable to afford them) and there was even financial support for impoverished students.

Even before the ABG was introduced, Austria, neither before nor during Metternich's government, ever had anything like the 1794 law of 22 Prairial in France whereby:

> mere criticism, or even suspicion of criticism or lack of support for the regime could bring a guilty verdict. And the only punishment was death. Francis I insisted that the Austrian Jacobins who were arrested in 1794 were all given a fair trial in accordance with established Austrian jurisprudence.[24]
>
> Alan Sked

Censorship was most observable in the theatre, about which Austrians were passionate. Johann Nepomuk Nestroy (1801–62), the most popular writer and performer of satirical comedy, would often get round it by ad-libbing, usually in dialect, which was hard for the censor to follow but immediately recognisable by his audience. Nestroy said:

> The censor is a pencil turned into a man or a man turned into a pencil, a fleshly line under the product

of the intellect, a crocodile lying on the banks of the streams of ideas that bites off the heads of the writers swimming in them... Censorship is the younger of two disgraceful sisters, the older one being the Inquisition. Censorship is the living admission of the higher-ups that they can only stamp on dumb slaves, but cannot rule free peoples.[25]

The reference to the '*Bürger*' (citizens) in the ABG civil code is crucial. The so-called Biedermeier period (1815–48) – named after a gently satirised petit-bourgeois character Gottlieb Biedermeier who first appeared in a humorous column in Munich's *Fliegender Blätter* newspaper in 1855 – sees the embourgeoisement of Austrian society proceed apace. Politics being taboo, the bourgeoisie settled (perhaps not too unwillingly) for 'inner emigration', 'happiness in a quiet corner' and the cultivation of the family and its innocent pursuits. This produced a flowering in the arts reflected in the glowing familial paintings of Friedrich von Amerling, Ferdinand Georg Waldmüller, Josef Danhauser, among others, as well as in the elegant comfortable furniture that eschews the showy Baroque virtuosity of the seventeenth and eighteenth centuries.

Metropolitan Biedermeier life is typically emblematised in the largely apolitical *soirées* of Franz Schubert (1797–1828) and friends, known as *Schubertiads*. However, plenty of drink was taken at these gatherings and in 1820 the paranoid Vienna police broke up a meeting and prosecuted one of the members for subversive activity, also severely reprimanding Schubert for allegedly using opprobrious language against officials. In truth, Schubert's depressive life was in many ways as tragic as his composition was prolific: 1,500 works, particularly of *Lieder*, including the brilliant cycle *Die Winterreise*, 1827, and chamber music, the *Forelle* (*Trout*) quintet being one of the most famous in the genre. Yet he only ever managed to stage a single full performance devoted to his works – in 1828, the year of his death from typhoid. He was thirty-one.

In 1857 came Adalbert Stifter's novel *Der Nachsommer* (*Indian Summer*), a *Bildungsroman* ('Coming of Age Novel') reminiscent of Goethe. A classic of *Biedermeier* quietism – that is, displaying a calm acceptance of external events – it's a retrospective and nostalgic work written a decade after the 1848 revolution. At once profound and naive, it evokes a world where *unum est verum pulchrum et bonum* – 'each of us is unique, truthful, beautiful and good'. Aesthetic beauty and morality are fused, while lives dedicated to personal intellectual enrichment are reconciled with diligent commercial pragmatism.

Economic Modernisation and Archduke John

Beginning around 1825, commercial activity rose with the industrialisation of Austria, mainly in the textile industry and making use of steam power. Steel production in Carinthia and Styria began to modernise, and foreign investors were drawn in. In 1829, two Englishmen founded a Danubian steamboat company with the unforgettable name of the *Donaudampfschiffahrtsgesellschaft*, saying which correctly is considered a test today of proficiency for learners of German.

Archduke Johann (John), Francis I's brother, had retired to Styria and acted as its unofficial regent. John had actively opposed Francis's disastrous treaty – having been defeated by Napoleon – ceding Tyrol to Bavaria in 1809, and which prompted the English *Gentleman's Magazine* to write:

> This Treaty is certainly one of the most singular documents in the annals of diplomacy. We see a

> Christian King, calling himself the father of his people, disposing of 400,000 of his subjects, like swine in a market.

A great Styrian local patriot who married the comely postmistress at Aussee, John was astonishingly active in founding bourgeois institutions and enterprises. These included an agricultural association with many branches (including his own model estate and winery), a museum, college, savings bank, fire insurance company, library and archive.

The underside of the Biedermeier idyll may be summed up by a single statistic, namely that in Vienna in 1834 there were ten illegitimate to every twelve legitimate births.[26] The drift to the city as industrialisation increased produced housing shortages and urban poverty. Meanwhile, the rising educated middle class had caused a mass of under-employed students – traditionally the kindling for a revolutionary flare-up. That occurred all over Europe, but especially in France, Germany, northern Italy and the Austrian Empire.

The 1848 Revolution

The historian Wolfram Siemann puts the 1848 revolutions down to:
> unfulfilled bourgeois demands for political participation; the aspirations for national self-determination and independence; the distress in the pre-industrial crafts; the effects of overpopulation and proletarianisation in the major cities and in many rural areas.

Add in poor harvests and radicalised students and you have the ingredients for revolution.

The iconic picture overleaf of the 1848 revolution shows

unemployed men, for whom a Rhineland city's 'make work' contract has run out, petitioning for its renewal. The 'revolutions' of 1848 were not always so respectful, and the extent of

Johann Peter Hasenclever's *Labourers before the City Council* (1848)

social misery was illustrated by the demonstrations sparked first in Paris and immediately followed across most of Europe. The participation of the intellectual elite of the variously threatened monarchies (87 per cent of the hastily convened Frankfurt Parliament for the German Confederation were academics) led to rapid concessions such as the April Laws, legitimising largely autonomous and substantively democratic rule for Hungary, as well as several draft constitutions elsewhere.

However, to the despair of Karl Marx – who visited Vienna in August 1848 as a 'revolutions tourist' – the revolution soon split into a *bürgerlich* (bourgeois) element and more radical socialists demanding direct representation. Petitions turned to demands and demands to violence. At the same time, a strong national awareness among the disparate ethnicities threatened the multi-national Habsburg state. It also divided the revolutionary priorities, even inflaming reciprocal resentments and thus weakening the impact of this first great 'European' revolt against inequity and the absence of democratic rights and freedoms.

The revolution is often seen as a failure, but it was a portent and ultimately many of its liberal and nationalist concepts were to triumph. Its principle immediate success in the Habsburg lands was the abolition, once and for all, of serfdom. It also stirred the 'Austrian' national identity in a way that had not previously been evident. The Frankfurt Assembly of Liberals set up during 1848 was attended by representatives from all over Germany, but its president was the liberal Archduke John, so that arguably the Habsburgs were still a presiding influence in most of the German territory. However, it is ominous that Austrian delegates were attacked by German radicals in the Parliament as 'only half-Germans' and attention was drawn to the danger of swamping the Protestant Teutonic world with Catholics and Slavs through the influence of the Habsburg Empire.[27]

Even more complex was the interaction of nationalism and liberalism elsewhere in the empire. That was particularly so in Hungary where a Croatian nationalist general, ostensibly acting for the Habsburgs, led a military campaign against the secessionist Hungarians. This was despite the fact that Croatia and Hungary had been united since 1102 through the union of crowns under Hungary's ur-dynasty of Árpáds.

Serbs, Slovaks and Romanians also became awakened to a sense of undervalued ethnic identity in respect of Magyar rule, Magyars, in turn, in respect of Habsburg 'German' rule, likewise the Czechs under the Habsburgs. In the Holy Roman Empire – the thousand-year Reich – ethnicity *per se* had generally played second fiddle to both dynastic claims and religion, on both of which the Empire based its legitimacy.

Now the Habsburgs were faced with a multiplicity of restive peoples who increasingly asserted their ancient rights as individual nations, even if, in some cases, these had never really existed.

CHAPTER 9
FROM AUSTRIAN EMPIRE TO DUAL MONARCHY

Inauspicious Beginnings
On the death of Emperor Francis in 1835, his slightly disabled and epileptic son Ferdinand ascended the throne. Ferdinand's physical shortcomings were the result of Habsburg inbreeding, his parents being first cousins. It was therefore considered prudent to set up a Regency Council that took the day-to-day political decisions. This was in effect controlled by Metternich and the more liberal Bohemian noble, Franz Anton von Kolowrat. Unfortunately, the two shared a mutual detestation and spent much time frustrating each other's initiatives.

In point of fact, it was doubtful if Ferdinand was mentally retarded (he mastered several languages and became an expert botanist). In any case, the people seemed to regard him with some affection and called him Ferdinand *der Gütige* (the Benign), although the satirists changed that to '*Gutinand der Fertige*' (the benign and kaputt). The historian A. J. P. Taylor characterised Ferdinand's eminently sensible observation 'I am the Emperor and I shall have noodles' as a 'noodle calling for noodles', but Ferdinand rose to the occasion when the 1848 revolution broke out. He immediately agreed to most of the demands for more responsive government to avoid bloodshed and at one point even rode around Vienna in an open carriage to be received by cheering crowds. His most significant concession was to Hungary, which obtained its *pro forma* independence with the 'April Laws'. Naturally this was too much for the Regency Council (now minus Metternich, who had fled to England). Ferdinand was forced to abdicate in favour of his nephew,

Francis Joseph I, and was sent off to retirement in Prague. The heroes of the revolution from the Austrian point of view were two able commanders: the octogenarian Field Marshal Radetzky and General Windisch-Grätz. The latter restored order in Bohemia, initially facing down a mob in Prague that had already killed his wife; the former, with magnificent generalship, recovered the Italian possessions. The famous *Radetzky March* (1848) by Johann Strauss Senior was composed in his honour and is played each year as the encore of the internationally broadcast New Year's Concert of the Wiener Philharmonic. It is a bit like 'Land of Hope and Glory' at the London Proms, but without words and therefore without the equivalent bombast.

Peace was restored in Vienna by Windisch-Grätz's intervention, though not before the Minister of the Interior, Latour, had been lynched by the mob and hanged from a lamppost. Eighteen-year-old Emperor Francis Joseph began a twin programme of pacification and constitutional reform under the guidance of his chief minister Prince Schwarzenberg. Various patents and diplomas attempted to tread a delicate line designed to suggest that constitutional reforms stemmed entirely from the emperor's paternalistic grace and not the 'power of the people' (*Macht des Volkes*) that the revolution had unleashed.

Meanwhile, retribution was to be meted out to the main protagonists of that revolution. This was particularly the case in Italy and Hungary, where a psychopath called Baron von Haynau came to be known as the Hyena of Brescia and the Hangman of Arad respectively, because he had naked women whipped as supporters of insurrectionists* and thirteen Hungarian generals hanged. On the very same day in 1849, the

---

* Admittedly this was in reprisal for massacre by the mob of Austrian invalid soldiers in a hospital.

judicial murder of Count Batthyány, the first Prime Minister of an autonomous Hungary, took place. Whatever concessions had been made (for example, through the April Laws), Prince Schwarzenberg was determined to make it clear that all revolutionary leaders were now to be treated as traitors.

Francis Joseph's reign thus began in a welter of savagery not seen since the Counter-Reformation. The centralised absolutism administered by the formidable Schwarzenberg in his name was even reinforced by a Concordat in 1855 with the Papacy. This reinvolved the Church in primary education and privileged Catholic doctrine in certain aspects of civil society such as marriage. Its provisions remained in force until 1870. In that year, however, the First Vatican Council brought its long-running attacks on liberal society to a head with Pius IX's (Pio Nono) declaration of Papal Infallibility. This was too much even for many devout Catholics to stomach and in Austria a group calling themselves Old Catholics broke away and formed their own congregations. In Vienna, they still have their own church, the lovely Renaissance Salvatorkapelle, which is part of the Altes Rathaus (former City Hall).†

> *Empress Elisabeth of Austria – 'Sisi'*
> Francis Joseph's reign reverted to the Habsburg capacity for longevity (sixty-eight years in his case) as the most reliable way of outmanoeuvring your enemies. Although he was hated at the beginning of his reign, this osmosed gradually into grudging respect and finally ironic appreciation, whereby he

---

† The Austrian Old Catholics are part of the Union of Utrecht of Old Catholic Churches which was formalised in 1889; however, the trigger for what was, in all but name, secession from the Vatican, was the multiplicity of doctrines that Pio Nono (Pope Pius IX from 1846–78) promulgated from the time of the Risorgimento onwards in an effort to regain the Church's influence in increasingly secularised societies.

became an iconic fixture in everybody's life like the tower of the Stephansdom itself. Dull though he was, he acquired one considerable (if double-edged) advantage by marrying the lively Elisabeth of Bavaria – Sisi – esteemed a beauty and capable of charming both '*das Volk*' and potential enemies.

Francis Joseph, the penultimate Austrian Emperor. His death in 1916 and magnificent funeral during World War I was widely considered as ominous. Two years later, 640 years of Habsburg rule in Central Europe came to an end.

A Bavarian duchess, Elisabeth – known as Sisi – was first cousin to her husband Francis Joseph. In learning Hungarian and mixing easily with Magyar aristocrats, she did much to cement the alliance with Hungary in 1867.

Sisi's first challenge on arriving at the stuffy Habsburg court was standing up to Francis Joseph's mother, the imperious Archduchess Sophie. Rather slushy movies about Sisi portray Sophie as the mother-in-law from hell – sour, devious and envious of her daughter-in-law's good looks and unconventionality. Sisi's modern ideas included having a personal gym built for her in the Hofburg. An anorexic, she followed an obsessive diet and exercise regime, and was much admired for her equestrianism, which was another facet of her determination to live an independent life.

Sisi provided an heir to the throne (in 1858) and three

daughters, but is remembered most for playing a vital role in the rapprochement between the Hungarians and her husband. She learned Hungarian (*magyarul*) and was close to Count Andrássy, the most influential of the Magyar noblemen. After her coronation as Queen of Hungary in June 1867, the appreciative Hungarian government gave her as a summer residence the Gödöllő estate north-east of Pest.

Eventually, she grew bored of Francis Joseph and the dreary state dinners where the emperor, having finished his meal would leave before those at the bottom of the long banqueting table had even been served the main course. Once the emperor had departed, the banquet was officially over and legend has it that Hotel Sacher, located next to the Hofburg, built its fortunes on still famished dignitaries fleeing the Hofburg dinners in search of something to eat.

Sisi took to restless wandering around Europe – from Gödöllő to her Achilleion palace on Corfu (where she could write poetry in the manner of the then fashionable Heinrich Heine) to Monte Carlo, where she played the tables, and to England and Ireland, where she hunted with Bay Middleton, regarded as the finest horseman of his day.

The cliché is that Francis Joseph was emotionally repressed and psychologically damaged, but his tender letters to his wife when she was abroad show that he was simply heartbroken. There is a good deal of pathos in his project of building for her, and at vast expense, the Hermes villa (1886) on the south-western outskirts of Vienna. Her bedroom was decorated with Hans Makart's scenes from *A Midsummer Night's Dream*, her favourite play. However, she intensely disliked the place, only reluctantly turning up for a week or two in summer. As an attempt to win back her affections, the villa had proved to be an abject failure.

The double suicide of Sisi's son Rudolf and his lover Marie Vetsera at Mayerling in 1889 threw Elisabeth into deep melancholy. Nine years later, she herself was stabbed to death

Empress Elisabeth's funeral provoked widespread mourning both in the empire and abroad in countries like England where she was well-known and liked.

beside Lake Geneva by an anarchist (killing royalty had become fashionable – between 1867 and 1913 seven kings or queens and one crown prince were assassinated).

From Neo-Absolutism to the Ringstrasse

Francis Joseph's Neo-Absolutism lasted nearly two decades, but was what progressive historians would describe as being 'on the wrong side of history'. The emperor had been baptised in memory of two significant predecessors, Francis I and Joseph II: one a proponent of autocratic stability, the other a protagonist of autocratic reform. Around 1857, the Joseph II model re-emerged, but with distinctly liberalising features. Urged by Alexander von Bach, his talented chief minister, Francis Joseph announced that the walled fortification of Vienna, of Italian design and dating mainly from the seventeenth century, would be demolished and replaced by a Ringstrasse. This, in time, gave its name to a bustling era of burgeoning commerce and real estate development.

The Ringstrasse was to be lined with major public buildings constructed in Historicist style. The first to be commissioned was the Memorial Church (Votivkirche), commemorating Francis Joseph's narrow escape from assassination by a Hungar-

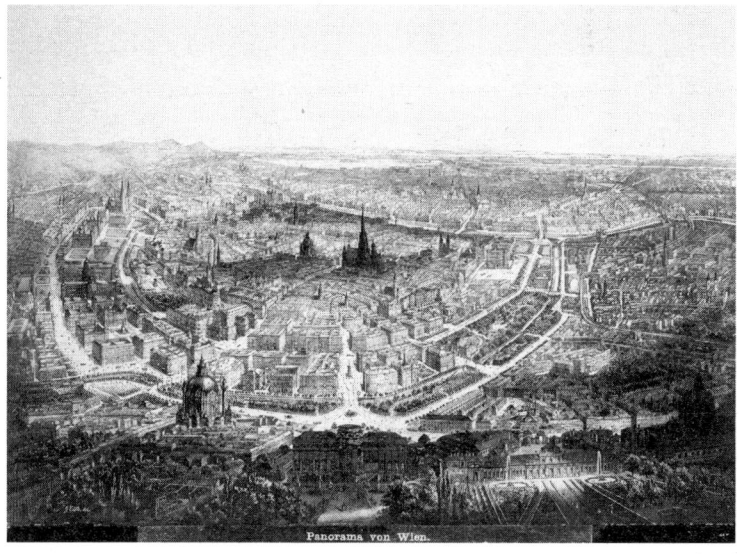

In 1857, Francis Joseph issued an historic ordinance: Vienna's defensive and redundant city walls were to be demolished and replaced with a 5-kilometre-long Ringstrasse, flanked by iconic institutions.

ian tailor as the emperor took his post-prandial stroll on the bastion. The money was raised by his unlucky brother, Maximilian, who was briefly Emperor of Mexico, but was executed in a revolution in 1867.

Later, came one of the great buildings of Viennese Modernism, the Post-Office Savings Bank (1905), built by Otto Wagner, who had also designed the city's metro stations in Art Nouveau

(Vienna Secessionist) style. Some spectacular palaces of the so-called *Geldadel* (nouveaux riches) also went up on the Ring, while a luxury hotel was made out of the former palace built for the Duke of Württemberg and his Austrian wife. As the Hotel Imperial, it is used for guests of the state and has hosted Hitler, Queen Elizabeth II and John F. Kennedy.

This explosion of creative and commercial energy was to be capped by the World Fair held in the Prater in 1873 on the pattern of London's 1851 exhibition and similar shows in Paris. Unfortunately, 1873 also saw the first meltdown of modern capitalism in Austria with a run on the banks and a stock market crash. Contemporaneously there was an outbreak of cholera.

However, Austria's belle époque barely paused for breath and the last years of the nineteenth century were a time of contrasting extravagance and poverty, of grand opera and sometimes drivelling operetta, of portentous architecture and ivory tower symbolism in the arts, of tradition and secession, of press scandals and coffee-house culture, of complacency offset by Freudian gloom. In short, it was the best of times and the worst of times.

Assailed on Two Fronts

Despite the transition to a modern state through administrative reforms carried through by Alexander von Bach and Franz von Stadion, it was evident by the 1860s that the position of the Austrian Empire was becoming precarious. The war in Italy preceding Italian unification had not gone well for Austria. Napoleon III had given the Italians military support, while poor generalship on the Austrian side culminated in the disaster of Solferino in 1859, where Franz Joseph himself held the command. Metternich may have referred to Italy as merely 'a geographical expression', but liberal nationalism and deft diplomacy by the Count of Cavour, later to be Italy's first prime minister, proved that this was no longer true. By 1866, Lombardy and Venetia had become part of the emergent Italian state and only Trieste, important as Austria's only port of significance, remained in imperial hands.

The loss of Italian territories was painful, but a far greater loss of prestige was implied by the empire's defeat at the hands of the Prussians at Königgrätz (Sadowa), in Bohemia, in 1866. In this, Francis Joseph and his advisers fell into a trap cunningly set by Otto von Bismarck, the tactically astute Chancellor of Prussia. The Austro-Prussian War had begun as a somewhat ridiculous dispute over the governance of Schleswig-Holstein at the northern tip of Germany, but Bismarck's quickly arranged treaty with Italy presaged a war in which Austria would be obliged to fight on two fronts. Further provocations to states in the German Confederation (the Catholic dominated remnants of the Holy Roman Empire) lured Austria into war.

The epoch-ending Battle of Königgrätz was, in fact, closely fought, but the Prussians had a modern breech-loading gun which fired off five times as many shots per minute as the old-fashioned Austrian muskets. The casualties tell the end result starkly: 9,000 Prussians as against 44,000 Austrians, with another 22,000 of the latter captured. The long, sometimes tormented, sometimes glorious history of Habsburg dominance in Germany was at an end and Prussia consolidated its pivotal position, or, as Bismarck had insultingly put it, 'the trim seaworthy frigate of Prussia [was no longer chained] to the ancient worm-eaten galleon of Austria.'

The gradual transformation of the Kingdom of Prussia into the Empire of Germany through the nineteenth century was a complex process of diplomacy and force. Landmarks along the way included the Peace of Prague in 1866, when Prussia annexed four of Austria's allies in northern and central Germany – Hanover, Hesse-Kassel, Nassau and Frankfurt. Twenty-one states north of the Main River became the Prussian-controlled North German Confederation. She now controlled two-thirds of Germany's population and had full access to the resource-rich Ruhr region.

After smashing the French and occupying Paris in 1871 – the culmination of the Franco-Prussian War – Prussia designated itself an empire. In the 1870s, Bismarck conducted a so-called *Kulturkampf* (Cultural Struggle) to extinguish the influence of the Catholic Church in Protestant Germany. Perhaps most decisive of all, the earlier *Zollverein* (Customs Union) of 1834 across German states advantaged an expansionist Prussia. Austria was excluded because its trade was structured to its Central European empire and it had always based its policies on protectionism. This worked after a fashion (assigning Hungary the role of breadbasket and Bohemia the role of industrial production), but was too rigid for fast-developing modern economies. The Prussian Empire, by now all of Germany except Bavaria, was becoming the geopolitical and industrial hegemonic power of Europe.

The Austro-Hungarian Empire

School history teaches us about some nine empires affecting European history from the ancient Persian to the British. The overnight appearance of another one in the second half of the nineteenth century is somewhat remarkable. We are reminded that the Hungarians, now in a new and complementary partnership with the German Austrian Habsburgs, were actually an ancient people called Magyars who had occupied the Carpathian Basin and associated lands for some 1,000 years.

Scholars have often struggled to contextualise an empire

even more difficult to define than the Holy Roman Empire, which is saying something. For a start, the Austro-Hungarian Empire was ruled both by an Emperor (of Austria) and a King (of Hungary), who happened to be the same person (hence the nomenclature *'kaiserlich und königlich'* – 'imperial and royal' – to describe it). Secondly, it consisted of two independent states with their own parliaments and constitutions, except that foreign affairs and defence for the joint entity were reserved to the emperor.

The Austro-Hungarian Empire, 1914

The Austrian Constitution (*Staatsgrundgesetz*) of 1867 incorporated most basic freedoms of a modern democracy and the first Hungarian government under the new arrangements also passed liberal measures, particularly in regard to education. There were two languages of state, German and Hungarian, although there was an ongoing dispute about the language to be used for the military, which the Austrians thought should be German and the Hungarians thought should be Hungarian.

Fourthly, Bohemia, where Czech nationalism grew

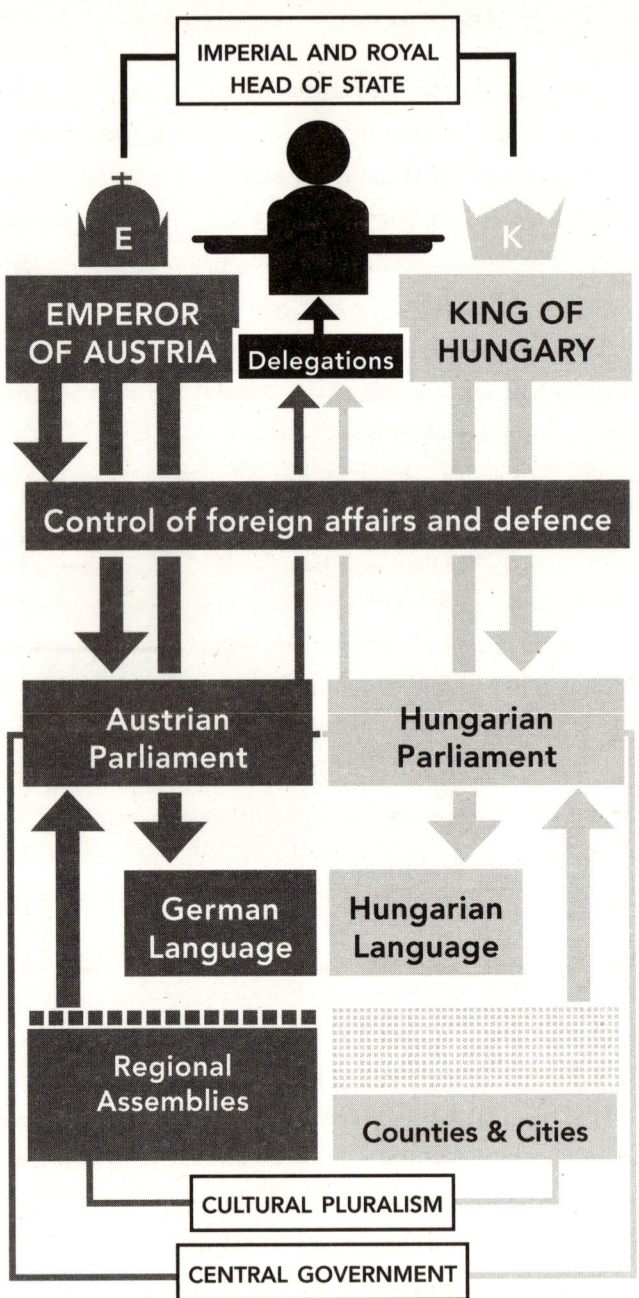

The peculiarities of the Austro-Hungarian Empire included being ruled by someone who was both Emperor of Austria and King of Hungary, while domestically each state acted independently with its own parliament.

stronger by the day, remained in the Austrian (so-called 'Cisleithanian') part of the empire. Since the tax revenue of Bohemia was more than the total for all the rest of Cisleithania, the Czechs did not view the Dual Monarchy as an equitable arrangement. And if Hungarian was to be a language of state, why not Czech?

Lastly, the empire's demography was as wide as the Roman Empire's, consisting of Czechs, Slovaks, Slovenes, Croats, Serbs, Slovaks, Ruthenians (Ukrainians), Poles, Romanians (inhabiting what the Romans called Dacia), Magyars, Germans (Austrians, Saxons, Swabians), Italians and Jews, plus the odd Aromanian, Greek etc. It was thereby a multi-ethnic state which for the first time since the Romans tried to combine central government with cultural pluralism, although in Hungary the latter was largely abandoned after the early days of liberal reform gave way to 'Magyarisation'. However, the claim by the bon-vivant revolutionary Friedrich Engels that the Dual Monarchy was a 'prison of nations' is no more than a useful falsehood which was exploited by nationalist radicals and later by Communists – who really did erect a prison of peoples with a wall around it in the Communist bloc.

The Compromise with Hungary

After the defeat at Königgrätz, Francis Joseph had little choice but to seek some accommodation with his diverse subjects to shore up his tottering empire. The Hungarians themselves were in conciliatory mood, led by a shrewd lawyer Ferenc Deák, a veteran of Hungarian Reform Era politics (1825–48). A constitutional arrangement (known as the *Ausgleich* (compromise) in German, *kiegyezés* (settlement) in Hungarian) was negotiated. It preserved Hungarian internal independence, but reserved external matters, as already stated, to the Austrian emperor. That proviso ultimately proved disastrous for Hungary, since it was obliged thereby to enter World War I on the German side, despite the strong misgivings of its Prime Minister István Tisza. As for Austria, it pursued a gradual policy of reform after 1867, yet was increasingly subject to the same pressures of ethnic assertion as Hungary, particularly in Bohemia.

More ominously, among the Austrian Germans themselves a split was widening between the *grossdeutsch* faction, wanting what they regarded as a 'return' to their German 'home' dominated by Prussia, and those loyal to the emperor. The Austrian ethno-political identity, hitherto masked by its imperial and universalist roles, was now becoming a matter for political debate.

CHAPTER 10

FIN DE SIÈCLE TO FINIS AUSTRIAE: 1873–1918

The Dash for Modernisation
A major recent reassessment by Pieter M. Judson shows that the Dual Monarchy, particularly the Austrian half, was not as 'backward', either constitutionally or economically, as is too readily assumed.[28] Nor was the aging Franz Joseph, rising at 4 a.m. each day to start his eight hours perusing state documents, entirely unresponsive to the changing political and social environment. Indeed, he presided over a cultural boom: first in respect of building out Vienna and other cities of the empire with great representative buildings (he financed the Budapest opera house out of his own pocket); secondly in respect of the arts, which developed from elegant historicism to the early modernism of the Vienna Secession. As Judson comments:

> In popular geographies and scientific publications, in folk art, and in public architecture, the imperial regime articulated a vision of empire meant to reinforce a popular sentiment for unity among its culturally diverse peoples.[29]

An outstanding example of this concept is the Austrian architectural practice of Fellner and Helmer (founded in 1873) that built forty historicist-style theatres and opera houses across the empire and beyond. Designs for theatre curtains and ceiling paintings were often made by the Klimt brothers, long before the eldest, Gustav Klimt, made his name as the most fashionable artist of his age.

The clichéd narrative of Franz Joseph is one of failed

generalship and imperial decay that depicts the aging emperor as a man stranded in a previous age, desiccated and emotionally dead, presiding over an empire of which the wheels were coming off in slow motion. This, however, is mostly written with the benefit of hindsight and strongly influenced by left-liberal republicanism. It may be more justifiable as the jaundiced view of a brilliant doctor, Viktor Adler, who saw the appalling misery of the urban poor at first hand and was moved to found the Social Democratic Workers Party in 1888–89. He memorably described late imperial governance as 'absolutism mitigated by muddle'.[30]

Austro-Marxism

The most notably 'Austrian' feature of Austro-Marxism was its willingness to compromise and for the most part to operate within the norms of a bourgeois liberal society. The exception was when it was attacked head-on, as during the brief Civil War of 1934. Indeed, the prestigious leader and founder of the Social-Democratic Party in 1888, Viktor Adler, declared in 1889 at a Paris conference that 'except for France and England, Austria has perhaps the most liberal laws in all Europe; so much so that it resembles a republic which has a monarch in place of a president at its head.'[31]

Nevertheless, the leading Socialist thinkers, such as Otto Bauer, Karl Renner and Max Adler (no relation) called themselves Austro-Marxists and had an influence on foreign activists living or studying in Vienna in the early twentieth century. Leon Trotsky lived in Vienna between 1911 and 1914 and met that threesome every Saturday at the Café Central. Antonio Gramsci, the great Italian theoretician of Marxism who coined the idea of 'the long march through the institutions', was in Vienna in 1923. He came to the same conclusion as the Austrians, namely that functioning capitalist societies could be changed by 'entryism' rather than revolution. Likewise Karl Kautsky, who studied in Vienna and became a leading theorist of orthodox Marxism in Germany, was of the view that 'history cannot be hurried' and conditions favourable to a Communist takeover had to develop first. He eventually retired to Vienna.

However, Trotsky, Stalin and Tito deplored the moderation of the Austrian Social-Democratic leadership. Between the wars, Josip Broz (Tito), who had been taken prisoner by the Russians in 1915, worked in a Wiener Neustadt factory while plotting a Communist party takeover for Yugoslavia. Stalin worked on a thesis in Vienna before the Bolshevik Revolution, but by 1913 was already accusing the Austro-Marxists of being 'fellow-travellers of the bourgeoisie' and they were excluded from the Communist International from 1918 onwards for repudiating terrorism. Stalin was being assisted in his work, a polemic against Austro-Marxists,[32] by Nikolai Bukharin, who studied economics at the Vienna University between 1912 and 1914. Later a key figure in the Soviet government, Bukharin fell out with Stalin and was executed following a show trial in 1938.

Despite the violent hostility displayed towards it by Communism on its post-war winning streak, it is Social Democracy Austrian-style that has prevailed in Western Europe where Communism has imploded under the weight of its own ideological contradictions and totalitarian violence.

Founders' Era

Marx and Engels believed that capitalism was doomed to regular boom and bust in decade-long cycles. The experience of the Austro-Hungarian economy was more like the biblical seven fat and seven lean years. After the disaster of the war with Prussia and the settlement with Hungary, the seven fat years – the *Gründerzeit* (Founders' Era) – ran from 1866 to 1873, during which time, for example, the extent of the railway network in Austria increased by 150 per cent from 6,125 to 15,579 kilometres. In 1867, Hungary had a 'miracle harvest' when much of the rest of the western world suffered a bad one. The unexpected windfall helped balance the books for several years through massive exports of wheat. Water transport on the Danube boomed, as did steel production in Styria based at Mürzzuschlag.

The first part of the splendiferous Ringstrasse replacing Vienna's old bastions and glacis (defensive slopes fronting the bastions) had already opened in 1865 and the rest was underway. Vienna over the following twenty-five years has been described as a vast building site – and indeed between 1872 and the 1890s the great museums, a new city hall, a new university, the first modern parliament and stock exchange, as well as the new imperial *Burgtheater*, all arose along the Ring. Infrastructure in the form of regulation of the Danube (1870–75) limited urban flooding, while, in 1873, Eduard Suess's aqueduct, running 95 kilometres from the Alps, enabled many households that had mostly relied on wells to enjoy running water and proper sewage disposal. Alas, the system was functional just too late that year to obviate Vienna's last cholera epidemic during the World Fair. A huge new cemetery was also opened, together with an equally impressive meat market at St Marx on the eastern periphery. New railway stations were built and the preparation for an intracity travel network got under way.

The speed of Vienna's development had, of course, a downside. The population grew rapidly with a flood of impoverished migrants from the Crown Lands arriving to seek work. In the suburbs, so-called *Mietskaserne* ('rent barracks') arose and the poorest families had shared facilities. Often beds had to be used by more than one person as they were rented out during the day for a few hours to a so-called *Bettgeher*, who had nowhere else to go.

Poor Orthodox Jews from Galicia and the Bukovina settled in the Leopoldstadt, while middle class and non-Orthodox Jews built up status and money in the free professions to which they had access. All civic inequalities on Jews were abolished by the civic reforms (*Staatsgrundgesetz*) of 1867. Fifteen years later, 60 per cent of the doctors in Vienna were Jewish. By 1887, some 394 lawyers out of 681 in total were Jewish and Vienna's most influential newspapers were 'largely owned and staffed' by Jews. It is an unwelcome irony that Moriz Benedikt, the Jewish editor of the *Neue Freie Presse*, the leading newspaper of the metropolis, was also a worshipper of Bismarck and pan-German ideology. By 1890, there were to be more than 118,000 Jews in Vienna, the majority arriving from Galicia on the new railway connection.[33]

The World Fair

The acme of the seven fat years came with the impressive World Fair of 1873. It was staged at the Prater, the huge park in the eastern suburb originally opened to the public under Joseph II. Later, the well-to-do bourgeoisie promenaded in their carriages along the 4.4 kilometres of its great chestnut-lined Hauptallee. The Fair featured some 26,000 exhibits, based on the concept of the geopolitical positioning of Austria-Hungary between West and East – a motif that was both very ancient and very modern.

An intriguing example of this in action can be seen in the enthusiasm of the Japanese to participate (shortly after the westward-looking Meiji Restoration in Japan). They constructed one of the biggest pavilions, extensively displaying aspects of Japanese society and landscape. Japonaiserie now became influential in western Europe and left its mark on the work of numerous European artists, including those of the Vienna Secession.

Although somewhat marred by an outbreak of cholera and a stock market crash, Vienna's World Fair of 1873 attracted visitors from across the world.

Between May and November 1873, the World Fair attracted in all 7.25 million visitors, and did wonders for the city's hotel industry. However, it was, ironically, at one of the new hotels built for the fair that a British visitor was the first to be recorded as a case of cholera (at least the first one admitted by the authorities in Vienna's last-ever epidemic), having unwisely taken her afternoon tea with a glass of tap water.

Indeed, the 7.25 million visitor numbers were only a third of what Austria had hoped for, principally because news of the cholera break-out evidently put many people off. Nevertheless, Francis Joseph gallantly led crocodiles of visiting dignitaries around the exhibition. One of these was the Shah of Persia, who visited while touring Europe in search of ideas to modernise his country. In his travelogue, he recorded his disobliging view that the fair resembled a glorified souk. At a Hofburg dinner, though, he was so entranced by the *décolleté* of Sisi, bathed in candlelight opposite him, that he made a not ungenerous offer to Francis Joseph to purchase her. This was politely rebuffed – the Habsburg marriage brokerage was content to dispose of Habsburg daughters, as Marie Louise had been awarded to Napoleon, but was not yet reduced to selling off imperial wives. Still, Persian rugs from the Persian pavilion became one of the show's most popular items, and were soon part of the standard accoutrement in the homes of well-to-do Viennese.

The Stock market Crash of 1873

The World Fair had been built on a wave of optimism when Liberal principles of free trade, risk-taking and individual betterment, coupled with unprecedented and rapid technological development, promised a bright future of unparalleled prosperity. Two things were overlooked: the plight of the poor in an ever more dramatically unequal society, and the fact that technology generally takes years of investment to be successfully monetarised.

What followed was strikingly similar to the dot-com bubble of the late 1990s and the great financial crash of 2008–09. The naive and greedy were easily seduced by worthless investments on offer from an ever-expanding army of sharks. The newspapers egged the price spiral onwards and profited hugely from hyperbolic promoting of swindles (some papers were actually partially owned by the banks). Of course, after the crash, some of their commentators wrote sanctimonious articles explaining how they had foreseen it all from the beginning. And at the top of the hierarchy of deceit and conscienceless avarice sat the ever-wealthier bankers. The parabola of the disaster may accurately be mapped by the founding of new 'banks' – nineteen between 1868 and 1870, twelve more in 1871, twenty-nine in 1872. The house of cards collapsed on 'Black Friday', 9 May 1872, with the police having to close the Stock Exchange at 1 p.m. The opening hours had already seen 120 'bank' insolvencies. Half of the newly founded 'companies' simply vanished.

The Music of Oblivion

Austria's equivalent of the *belle époque* was an age drenched in champagne and bad debts. Even the stock market crash and the cholera epidemic barely stemmed the flood of Heurigen diners and ballgoers (who could, if they wished, dance to a 'Crash Polka' specially written in honour of the financial calamity). The people headed for the fine ballrooms constructed in the Biedermeier era when the waltz became all the rage.

The waltz (in three-four time) had originated as an eighteenth-century folk dance in German Bohemia, Bavaria and Austria, where it was known as a *Ländler* or *Schleifer*. Its Viennese variant was the basis of the astounding success of the Strauss dynasty. The most successful of them was Johann Strauss Junior (1825–99), whose *Blue Danube Waltz* was at first a failure, having been premiered by a rather dreary male voice choir just after the Königgrätz disaster. Since then it has become the epitome of nostalgic local patriotism. As late as 1911 that local pride was still very much alive when Richard Strauss (no relation to the dynasty) collaborated with Hugo von Hofmannsthal on *Der Rosenkavalier*. The wistful waltz motif, redolent of *alt-Wien* ('old Vienna'), made the opera one of the most successful ever written. The satirist Karl

Kraus (1874–1936), however, was strongly opposed to sentimentality about 'the olden days', writing: 'I have news for the nostalgists: "Old Vienna" was once new.'

The 'waltz kings', the Strauss dynasty – Johann Senior (1804–49), Johann Junior (1825–99) and assorted siblings – dominated popular music in nineteenth century Vienna.

Johann Strauss Junior's music was taken seriously by composers of classical music. Mahler was a fan and Brahms said he would have given anything to have written the *Blue Danube Waltz*. But Johann Strauss Junior was also the first pop star, so besieged by fans who wanted a lock of his hair that he was reduced to sending them clippings from his poodle. His enduring popularity even induced the Nazis to alter the birth registration of his forebears to remove a trace of Jewish blood. His operettas (for which a huge audience had emerged) offered escapism and (critics sniffed) encouraged an attitude of irresponsible *carpe diem*. A line from his operetta *Die Fledermaus* (1874) might sum up the attitude of contemporary operetta goers: 'Happy is he who forgets what anyway cannot be changed.' Interestingly, the origin of this maxim can be traced back at least as far as Frederick III (1415–93), the greatest Habsburg survivor of them all, whose motto it was – *Rerum irrecuperabilium felix oblivio.*

Nationalist Politics to Class-Based Politicians

Until 1907, the Cisleithanian, which is to say the 'Austrian', half of the empire had a Parliament in Vienna in which all the national minorities were represented.* Austria's awkward official name 'the Kingdoms and Lands Represented in the *Reichsrat* (Imperial Parliament)'[34] is a clue to the imperially pluralistic yet arduous struggle for political compromise. However, the *Reichsrat* was elected on a restricted franchise based on property and collective representation, so that only about 6 per cent of the population was enfranchised in the mid-nineteenth century. Gradually, measures were passed to widen the franchise, but this tended to sharpen the conflict between nationalities. In particular, the influence of the *Großdeutsch* faction – Pan-Germans who wanted to merge Austria with Germany – under the ruthless leadership of Georg von Schönerer (1842–1921) was successfully disruptive.

Schönerer was fiercely anti-Catholic (though he converted to Protestantism rather late in his career) and equally fiercely anti-Semitic (though his wife was half-Jewish). He was a clever demagogue who wrapped the moral and intellectual contradictions of his ideology inside intimidatory rhetoric. One of his slogans was 'Without Judah, without Rome / Germania's cathedral will be built,' and he openly advocated that Jews should be 'put down'. Small wonder that, after Karl Lueger, he was Hit-

---

* Jews were very well represented in Parliament, being citizens with full rights since 1867, but they were not represented as a national minority, not least because they regarded themselves as Austrians. Their alternative identity was confessional, rather than ethnic and nationalist.

ler's greatest hero. In due course, Schönerer's *Großdeutsch* Liberalism was eclipsed by the Christian Social Party and many of its adherents later became Nazis. Remnants of its ideology have lingered in the Liberal and Pan-German wings of the far-right Freedom Party of today, whose former leader Jörg Haider once described the creation of the Second (post-1945) Austrian Republic as a 'miscarriage'.

In adopting racism and sectarianism, Schönerer was drilling into a politically productive oil field. At one stage, the German Austrians in Bohemia were boycotting the local Prague Assembly, while Czechs in Vienna were boycotting the *Reichsrat*. An example of the problems to be overcome may be seen in the language law passed in 1897 under a liberal prime minister, Count Badeni, which stipulated that all civil servants in Bohemia had to be bilingual (German and Czech). This met with fierce opposition from the ethnically German Bohemians. It effectively excluded many of them from desirable jobs in the bureaucracy since they maintained that they would not, or could not, learn Czech. (Czechs, on the other hand, learned German at school.) The anger this provoked spread also to Austrian cities, and the project had to be abandoned when an alarmed Francis Joseph dismissed Badeni shortly afterwards. In general, the judgement of the Austrian historian Helmut Rumpler holds good, namely that the Cisleithanian Parliament was not appropriate as a vehicle for western parliamentarianism with its majority principle, because each party in the *Reichsrat* saw itself first and foremost as representing its nationality interest (rather than the common good of the empire).

After 1907 and the introduction of universal male suffrage, the rise of mass parties based on economic interest and ideology becomes apparent. The Social Democratic Party had been founded in 1889, while its great opponent, the Christian Social

Party, appeared four years later on the basis of Catholic social conservatism formulated by Karl Freiherr von Vogelsang, a Catholic convert. Von Vogelsang presided over political debate in the evenings at a Viennese restaurant called the *Die Goldene Ente* (*The Golden Duck*, hence the *Enten-Abende*, a forerunner of the modern think tank). Karl Lueger, subsequently the famous (or infamous) Mayor of Vienna, was a regular attendee. Vogelsang's political philosophy reflected the influence of Pope Leo XIII's encyclical *Rerum novarum* (1891) which sought alternatives to the materialistic and competitive ideologies of Socialism and Liberalism. It aimed at combining Roman Catholic doctrine with much-needed social reform.

Vogelsang's seminal article 'The Material Situation of the Working Class in Austria' (note the remarkable similarity of its title to Engels' 1845 tract *The Condition of the Working Class in England*) eventually led to the social reforms of the Conservative government under Eduard Graf Taaffe. These included limits on working hours, Sunday rest, accident and health insurance, as well as a cooperative law.

Karl Lueger

From the beginning, Karl Lueger's Christian Social Party propagandised against 'Jewish capital' and its populist leader used anti-Semitic sentiment to great effect in attracting support from the newly enfranchised '*5 Gulden Männer*'. The latter constituted the large number of lower middle-class voters benefitting from the tax qualification for suffrage being lowered to only 5 Gulden per annum. Lueger (1844–1910) understood very well the anxieties of this class threatened by modernisation. Early in his political career, he had provided social and political support for 'the little people' in collaboration with a Hungarian-born Jewish doctor, Ignaz Mandl. Anti-industrial, anti-capitalist and anti-Semitic feeling was strong in this layer of society and Lueger spotted its potential for exploitation.

Having built up a personality cult with sophisticated self-promotion, 'Handsome Karl' eventually became Mayor of Vienna in 1893. This came after he'd been disqualified three times by Francis Joseph, who strongly disapproved of anti-Jewish agitation and only relented after the intervention of Pope Leo XIII. Lueger rewarded his supporters with populist measures such as the municipalisation of energy suppliers, which were foreign-owned and tended to be unscrupulous. Under his regime, tram lines and a major new fresh water supply were built, as well as social projects, such as a care home and a psychiatric hospital. Ironically, such beneficial measures for the city as a whole laid foundations on which 'Red Vienna' was to build with great success in subsequent decades.

The darker side of Lueger's regime was captured in Hugo Bettauer's bestselling and eerily prophetic satire, *The City Without Jews* (1922). In the novel, a Lueger-like mayor expels all the Jews from the city and the church bells ring on the day the last train departs. Immediately, the *Juden-frei* city becomes dull and listless, and the economy goes into sharp decline. Bettauer, a prolific journalist and novelist, paid a steep price for his unwelcome forecast. In 1925, a furiously indignant pan-German nationalist turned up at his office and shot him. Bettauer died two weeks later from his injuries.

One of Lueger's many admirers was the youthful Adolf Hitler, who between 1907 and 1913 scratched a living in Vienna by painting tourist views (and selling them through a Jewish agent). Lueger used anti-Semitism tactically and cynically, once saying 'I decide who is Jew' (*'Wer ein Jud ist, das bestimme ich'*). In his version of perennial enemies ('Jews, Socialists and German Nationalists'), there is an echo of the tripartite Habsburg delineation of their historic foes as Turks, Protestants and Jews. After 1907, when general male suffrage was introduced for national elections, Lueger stayed in power by failing to introduce it in the municipal elections, knowing that, if he did, Adler's Social Democrats would immediately win a majority. In fact, in every free election under universal suffrage held in Vienna, the Socialists have won. From pre-war Red Vienna to post-war tourist magnet, Vienna has become a showcase for enlightened Social Democratic governance, just as well-run Bologna became the post-war showcase for the Italian Communists.

Vienna Secession

'To every age its art, to art its freedom' (*Der Zeit ihre Kunst, der Kunst ihre Freiheit*), reads the inscription on the façade of the Secession building in Vienna.

In the second half of the nineteenth century, the art market in Europe underwent a major upheaval. The changes started in France with the Impressionists – whose work Baudelaire called 'the painting of modern life'. The all-powerful Academies or the official *salons* that had monopolised the exhibition scene and effectively dictated what styles and genres were acceptable, now found themselves outflanked by new artistic groupings. These were mostly eclectic and very individualistic, as with the Vienna Secession (*Wiener Sezession*). Private commissions from the nouveau riche industrialists, bankers and well-to-do practitioners from the free professions began to supplement or replace those of the state on which Historicism had largely relied.

The hugely significant Munich Secession (founded 1892) preceded and inspired its namesake in Vienna. Under the Dual Monarchy, new artist groups were founded in Poland (the *Sztuka*), Prague (the *Mánes*) and in Hungary (the *Nagybánya* art colony). Then, in 1897, seventeen artists headed by Gustav Klimt 'seceded' from the Viennese *Künstlerverein* (Artists' Association). Within a year, they had built their own Secession exhibition hall, designed by Joseph Maria Olbrich and largely financed by Karl Wittgenstein, the industrialist father of the philosopher Ludwig and the one-armed concert pianist Paul.* The building looks a little like an imagined ancient Assyrian piece of architecture. With a huge openwork gilded ball of laurel leaf at the centre of its roof, it's known to market criers in the nearby *Naschmarkt* as 'the golden cabbage'. It could hardly be further in style from the stolid Historicism of the *Künstlerhaus* or the likewise nearby Academy of Fine Arts. On the facade is the Secession's motto provided by the art critic Ludwig Hevesi – *Der Zeit ihre Kunst, der Kunst ihre Freiheit* ('To the Age its Art, to Art its Freedom'). Not only did this fire the starting gun for Secessionist architecture in Vienna, the style also spilled over into handicrafts with the formation of the *Wiener Werkstätte* (Vienna Workshop) in 1903.

---

* After being wounded in World War I, Paul Wittgenstein was taken prisoner by the Russians and his right arm had to be amputated.

Since the rediscovery of the Secession in the 1980s, Gustav Klimt has become something of a cult. His work more than any other manifests the breaking of visual taboos, such as full-frontal nudes complete with pubic hair, the turn to Symbolism and the Freudian identity crisis of the intellectuals of his day. In particular, his faculty paintings for the new university's aula caused a scandal because of their evident nihilism and bleak view of humanity: *Philosophy*, highlighting mankind's vulnerability and abandonment to a tragic fate; *Medicine*, stressing the hopelessness of what is mere postponement of death. Indeed, they flatly contradicted the faith in scientific progress based on the philosophy of positivism to which the university professors were almost all dedicated. Klimt, on the other hand, believed that only art could unveil the deepest truths about humankind. As he put it: 'Only the ever-greater penetration of the whole of life by artistic ideas will guarantee the progress of civilisation.' In the faculty pictures, however, the doom-laden aphorism from one of the coming generation, the Expressionist painter Egon Schiele (to whom Klimt was both mentor and friend), seems to be the energising motif. As Schiele put it: 'Everything is living death.'

CHAPTER 11

THE ROAD TO WAR AND DISASTER

World War I

By the late nineteenth century, the Ottoman Empire was crumbling and its ethnic parts were beginning to seek independence. Concurrently, Russia was heavily promoting pan-Slavism with considerable success in the Balkans. Even the newly and fiercely independent and non-Slav but Orthodox Greece had a Russian political faction, and Kapodistria, the first Governor of Greece (1827), was a former Russian Foreign Minister, though by no means a Russian puppet. Having secured independence from the Ottomans in the mid-nineteenth century, Serbia, on the other hand, now owed most of its political leverage, as it still does, to heavy Russian backing. The Habsburgs' last territorial expansion in their long history – the annexation of Bosnia Herzegovina in 1908 – therefore irritated almost everyone, allies and foes alike.

At the same time, the heir to the Habsburg throne, Archduke Franz Ferdinand, was developing plans for a 'trilateral' empire in which the Slav element was to have the same political rights as the Germans and Hungarians in the Dual Monarchy. Again, this irritated almost everyone – the Magyars obviously, who foresaw the loss of Croatia which had been part of historic Hungary since 1102, but also the Serbs, who saw their own ambitions for Balkan dominance diminished thereby.

Against this background of bubbling unrest, on 28 June 1914, Franz Ferdinand and his wife were assassinated by a Serbian nationalist while on a visit to Sarajevo in Bosnia. Austria issued an ultimatum to Serbia which no country could have accepted and a month later declared war. This triggered the mobilisation of Russia to protect Serbia. On 1 August 1914, Germany declared war on Russia and then on France, while Austria-Hungary declared war on Russia on 6 August and the British and French declared war on Austria-Hungary four days later. In May 1915, Italy entered the war on the Allied side after being promised Austrian South Tyrol (*Südtirol*) at war's end. Romania joined the conflict, likewise on the Allied side, in 1916 after another secret agreement approving its seizure of the long-coveted Transylvania from Hungary. The Ottomans rashly attacked Russia in October 1914 and the latter duly declared war on their moribund empire a month later. Finally, in 1917 the USA entered the war and thereby tilted the balance in favour of the Allies.

Detailed discussion of World War I is beyond the scope

of this book.* However, contrary to the once held view that Germany was entirely responsible, historian Christopher Clark argues that the war was triggered by a concatenation of existing geopolitical pressures and old-fashioned unwieldy alliances, exacerbated by missteps and misappreciations by the leading individual actors. For Austria, it meant the end of some six and a half centuries of Habsburg Empire. Factors that went beyond the immediate responsibility of Austria-Hungary included the growing strategic tension between Britain and Germany, as the latter rapidly expanded its navy to rival that of the UK; the longing of the French for revenge in respect of their humiliation by Prussia in 1871; the British guarantee of Belgian neutrality that was brought into play when the Germans overran that country, and the ever-widening power vacuum in the Balkans and Middle East as the Ottoman Empire imploded.

The Austrian Idea

There is an almost unbearable pathos in an article by the Austrian writer Hugo von Hofmannsthal entitled *The Austrian Idea*, published in the French *Revue d'Autriche* in November 1917 and the *Neue Züricher Zeitung* the following month. Hofmannsthal can see that the war is lost and seeks to console himself and his readers with a nostalgic eulogy of Austria's historic mission. That is: to defend the Christian West and bring a stabilising culture to the restive 'half-European, half-Asian peoples' of the East, a mission it had inherited from Rome.

Hofmannsthal worked with other writers in the war propaganda unit of the Austro-Hungarian Defence Ministry, the first time that leading intellectuals had been co-opted in this way.

---

* For a detailed re-evaluation of the war, see Christopher Clark: *The Sleepwalkers: How Europe went to War in 1914* (2012).

Karl Kraus was an acerbic satirist and moralistic wit who wrote pungent critiques of politics, culture and (especially) the press of his day.

In stark contrast, the satirist and pacifist Karl Kraus despised such intellectual appeasement. In one of his most biting satires, he wrote of the war – and war in general: 'First, one hopes to win; then one expects the enemy to lose; then, one is satisfied that he too is suffering; in the end, one is surprised that everyone has lost.'

End of the Habsburgs

Just after 9 p.m. on 21 November 1916, Francis Joseph died in the Palace of Schönbrunn in Vienna. He was eighty-six. The war had not gone well and the newly opened (River) Isonzo front with Italy in the Julian Alps (now in north-west Slovenia), was to go even worse, with many soldiers dying from the bitter cold, avalanches, snowstorms and epidemics.

Francis Joseph was succeeded as emperor by his grand-nephew, Karl (Charles) I, who inherited a calamitous situation of shortages, famine, disillusion and unrest. Only a month before Charles took office, Friedrich Adler, the 37-year-old son of the Social Democratic leader, protesting against the conduct of the war and the authoritarian measures imposed to fight it, assassinated the Prime Minister, Count Stürgkh, while Stürgkh was having lunch in a restaurant in Vienna's *Innenstadt*. Adler was sentenced to death, but Charles had this commuted to eighteen years in prison. During the final days of the war, Charles had him released.

One of the cruellest of fronts in World War I was in the Italian Alps. Here Austrian troops wait in an ice tunnel on Mount Ortler in the Eastern Alps.

Having failed either to end the war or prevent the emergence of declarations of independence by nations within the empire, Charles resigned from the business of government on 11 November 1918. The National Assembly of the newly formed rump Austrian state, the German-Austrian Republic, formally dethroned him in April 1919. Habsburgs were banned from the country unless they renounced all monarchical claims. After two unsuccessful attempts to regain his position as King Charles IV of Hungary, he went into exile in Madeira, where he died in 1922. He was, however, beatified in 2004 by Pope

John Paul II in honour of his sincere – if hideously bungled – attempts to bring about peace. The Socialist French writer Anatole France wrote of him:

> Emperor Charles offered peace; he is the only decent man to have appeared in this war, and he was not listened to.

The Peace Treaties

Several agreements during or at the end of World War I shaped the geopolitics that still largely obtain in Europe and the Middle East: The secret Sykes-Picot Agreement of 1916 carved up the Middle Eastern part of the declining Ottoman Empire between Great Britain and France as 'spheres of influence', from which

Austria's Karl Renner signing the Treaty of Saint-Germain-en-Laye in 1919. Renner himself leant towards loose integration with what he hoped would be a Socialist Germany, but any move in that direction was vetoed at the negotiations.

emerged a slew of troubled post-colonial states. The Treaty of Brest-Litovsk of 1918 induced a hard-pressed Bolshevik Russia to surrender control of the Baltic States, Finland, Poland, Belarus and Ukraine, which became sovereign independent states. Finally, the Treaty of Versailles (1919–20) with its various annexes reorganised Austria-Hungary as (in theory) ethnically uniform states; her Slav populations became the amalgams of northern Slavs (Czechoslovakia) and southern Slavs (Yugoslavia). For a short while the agreed Russian borders corresponded quite closely to what would emerge following the collapse of the Soviet Empire in 1991, but by 1922 the Bolsheviks had regained almost all of the Tsarist Eurasian territories.

The Treaty of Saint-Germain-en-Laye (1919) settled matters with Austria and officially dissolved the Austro-Hungarian Empire. Germans from the former imperial territories such as the Sudetenland began to stream into Austria. 'We have thousands

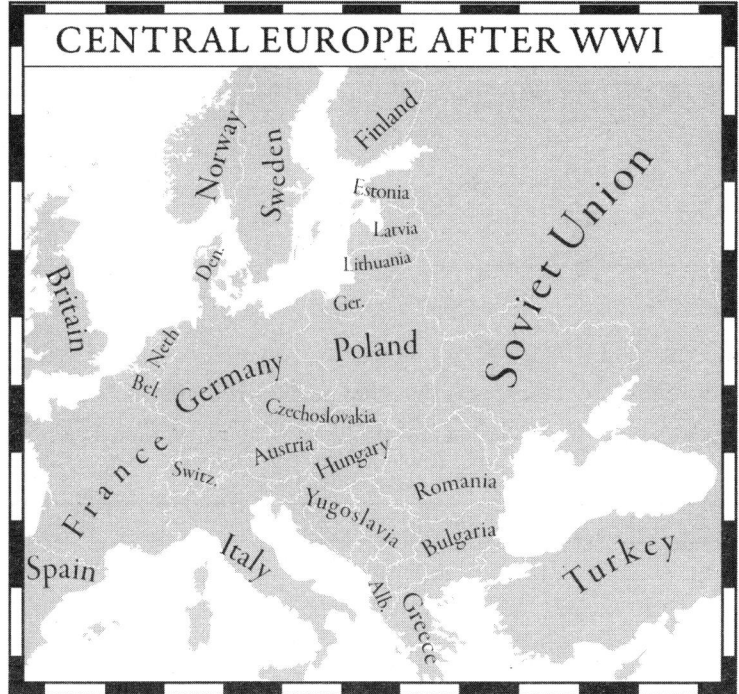

more officials than we need,' lamented a delegate to Versailles, 'and at least 200,000 workmen. It is a fearful question to know what to do with them.'[35] These unneeded bureaucrats and homecoming soldiers gave Vienna the nickname of *Wasserkopf* or hydrocephalus – the swollen head being too big for the body – but the city's population began to fall due to desperate living conditions, lack of food and insufficient housing.

Austria's delegation at Saint-Germain-en-Laye was led by Karl Renner, the head of a government that had proclaimed itself the German-Austrian Republic in 1918 and announced its intention of becoming part of a democratic Germany. This was swiftly forbidden by the victorious allies who were in the business of limiting German power, not increasing its territory. The Italians were the most aggressive of the allied negotiators, keen to ensure that the Machiavellian promise given to them under the secret wartime Treaty of London (1915) should be honoured. This involved Italy's annexation of South Tyrol, of which only about 10 per cent was Italian-speaking, along with Istria and Trieste. There was talk of reparations, but the Austrians visibly had no money.

The Treaty of Trianon (1920) settled matters with Hungary. In contrast to Austria, the Hungarian half of the Dual Monarchy was expected to pay reparations in gold and materials. It managed this until its economy collapsed in 1923, at which point the procedure was reversed and both loans and aid were instead provided *to* Hungary. Besides losing Burgenland (which Austria had occupied with the Gendarmerie), historic Hungary was slashed to pieces, being reduced to less than one third of its previous territory and losing 60 per cent of its population. This left substantial Magyar minorities in newly created and extremely hostile neighbour states. Not surprisingly, a sense of betrayal lingers in the political DNA of Hungarians. A major factor in the decision to treat Hungary so harshly was, however, its short-lived Communist revolution in 1919, which had lasted some nine months.

CHAPTER 12

THE FIRST REPUBLIC

The Pain of Rebirth

The First Austrian Republic (1918–38) was born under an unlucky star,* and had 6 million inhabitants, 2 million of whom lived in Vienna. In 1940, the historian Reinhold Lorenz dubbed it '*der Staat wider Willen*' ('the reluctant state'). Lorenz saw the *Anschluss* (literally 'Connection') of 1938 to Hitler Deutschland as a psychologically liberating 'unification' for the Austrians, something that had only been postponed by geopolitical *force majeure*. Another commentator, journalist Helmut Andics, later depicted interwar Austria as '*Der Staat, den keiner wollte*' ('the state that no one wanted'). Andics's view, written in 1962, was strongly influential, though nowadays historians examine the achievements of the First Republic, especially the pathfinding social reforms of *Rotes Wien* (Red Vienna), in a more discriminating way.

Red Vienna

By 1919, the gerrymandering of Karl Lueger was a thing of the past and in the first free vote on a universal franchise for the Vienna City Council, the Social Democratic Party won a majority of 54 per cent and a hundred councillors. The skill with which, at the national level, wily Karl Renner and Marxist Otto Bauer had distanced themselves from Communist radicalism was repeated at the metropolitan level. The Social Democrats' focus was on practical measures to

---

* Misfortunes included the Spanish flu that killed more people in Europe than World War I. Its victims in Austria included the cream of the Secession and Expressionism – Otto Wagner, Gustav Klimt and Egon Schiele.

remedy the living conditions of the working class. Most famously this was achieved by the rapid building of high quality *Gemeindebauten* (social housing that accommodated 65,000 people), which came to be admired by town planners from all over Europe. To this day, you will see large blocks of well-built flats all across the city bearing a red-lettered inscription on the front stating that it had been constructed with the proceeds of the building tax.[36] The most ambitious buildings bear the name of international heroes of Socialism (Karl Marx, Friedrich Engels, Ferdinand Lassalle). After World War II, the names of responsible councillors also appeared on facades – soft propaganda for the good works of the decision-makers of the City Council in Red Vienna. Many of these housing blocks arose along the outer Ring Road of the city (*Gürtel*), that was dubbed 'The Ringstrasse of the Proletariat'.

The most famous building of the Red Vienna era, the Karl-Marx-Hof (built 1927–33) is a vast, virtually self-contained block of tenements with a library, launderettes and offices.

Many of the social or socialist measures brought in by Lueger were there to be built on, but these were mostly infrastructure projects or otherwise aimed at his lower middle-class base of voters. The Social Democrats concentrated on their working-class voters, making provision for kindergartens, secular secondary education (against bitter Catholic resistance), childcare, maternity clinics, medical and dental provision, sport and cultural events. There was a well-planned attempt to instil a 'workers' culture' with, for example, a Workers' Symphony Orchestra, a Workers' Choral Society and numerous associations for things like nudism, bicycling and cremations. Opera and operetta continued, and the coffee houses remained packed with chattering intellectuals. To a degree, all this was an upwards bourgeoisification of the working class, rather than attempt to proletarianise society by force – as happened, for example, under the Soviet Union and its satellites.

Under the able management of Finance Councillor Hugo Breitner, all the social services and social housing were self-financed by steeply progressive taxation (rather than credit from the distrusted banks). The conservative opposition to 'Austro-Marxism' was fierce but largely impotent after 1922 when Vienna was administratively separated from Lower Austria. Thereafter, Vienna could run its affairs with an assured Social Democrat majority in the City Council until the Civil War of 1934 removed its autonomy. Since 1945, the Socialists have been in permanent overall control of City Hall, governing in coalition with Conservatives (*Volkspartei*) and smaller parties. As Vienna regularly comes out top, or near the top, of the world's most liveable cities according to the *Economist Intelligence Unit* (e.g. top in 2022 and 2023 among the 172 cities surveyed, having previously won in 2018 and 2019), it would seem that their brand of pragmatic Socialism has definitely paid off.

Ideas that Changed the World

Notwithstanding the gloomy prognosis for the First Republic, Austria between 1920 and 1938 was notable for its flowering of academic and cultural genius, producing a number of Nobel Prize winners. Until his exile to the US in 1929, Hans Kelsen (1881–1973) was one of the most distinguished legal philosophers of his age, a proponent of legal positivism and the originator of the liberal Austrian constitution still in force. Richard Coudenhove-Kalergi (1894–1972) was a well-connected idealist who planted the seed for a European Union to keep the peace among nations with his project for a Pan-Europa Union. Most of his contacts, which included Einstein, Adenauer and Churchill, thought the idea good but impracticable. In 1950, Coudenhove-Kalergi was the first recipient of the Charlemagne Prize awarded by the city of Aachen for services in respect of the unification of Europe.

Sigmund Freud's (1856–1939) pathfinding psychoanalysis was even more influential outside Austria than within.* His daughter Anna Freud was a pioneer of child psychology. The same international success could be ascribed to the philosophers Ludwig Wittgenstein (1889–1951) and Karl Popper (1902–94), the economists Friedrich von Hayek (1899–1992), Ludwig von Mises (1881–1973), who with Hayek was a founder of the 'Austrian school' of monetarist economics, and, lastly, politician and economist Joseph Schumpeter (1883–1950). Schumpeter was briefly finance minister and coined the phrase 'creative destruction' to describe the cycle of insolvency and new business creation in capitalism.

Art historian Ernst Gombrich (1909–2001) wrote the per-

---

* Freud's invention of psychoanalysis became a huge industry in the USA, but some of his ideas have been subject to increasing scepticism. Karl Kraus opined that 'psychoanalysis *is* the disease of which it purports to be the cure.'

ennial bestseller *The Story of Art* (1950) in his English exile. The Vienna circle founded by Moritz von Schlick (1882–1936), which issued its 'manifesto' on Positivism in 1929, also built on the earlier work of the physicist and philosopher Ernst Mach (1838–1916), who has bequeathed to the world the Mach number (the ratio of the speed of an object to the speed of sound). Erwin Schrödinger (1887–1961) was a pioneer of quantum mechanics. Eccentric polymath Otto von Neurath (1882–1945) invented ideograms and addressed his first English colleagues with the words 'I speak broken English fluently'. Hedy Lamarr (1914–2000) was not only a famed movie star but a talented inventor who discovered a radio device to obviate

Hedy Lamarr made her name in the 1933 erotic Czech film *Ecstasy*. After moving to the US in 1937 (she was half-Jewish), she built a Hollywood career as a *femme fatale*. Taking up science as a hobby, she co-invented a device to keep torpedoes on target.

the jamming of torpedoes by the enemy. (The US Navy turned it down and said she should exploit her glamour to sell war bonds instead, which she did!)

There are multiple less well-known but equally influential Viennese characters such as Viktor Gruen (1903–80), the inventor of shopping malls. Peter Drucker (1909–2005), the pioneer of management science, whose books sold more than 35 million copies worldwide, was also Viennese educated, though he studied in Germany and emigrated to the USA.

Communist activist, architect and interior designer Margarete Schütte-Lihotzky is best known for her 1926 invention of the highly functional fitted kitchen, the Frankfurter Küche.

One of the relatively few Austrians who bravely participated in the World War II resistance was the Communist architect Margarete Schütte-Lihotzky (1897–2000). She was the originator of the first fitted kitchen (1926), known as the Frankfurter Kitchen as it was designed at the request of the New Frankfurt housing project looking for compact, labour-saving designs. 'Viennese ideas saturate the modern world,' writes Richard Cockett in *Vienna: How the City of Ideas Created the Modern World*, and it is hard to overestimate the city's influence on modern society.

Cockett's book focuses chiefly on the twentieth century, but the phenomenon he describes begins in the late nineteenth century, particularly with the Vienna School of medicine. There were a number of pioneer feminists, too, such as the educational reformers Eugenie Schwarzwald (1872–1940) and Rosa Mayreder (1858–1938), the latter also becoming a peace activist like Bertha von Suttner (1843–1914). It was Suttner who first persuaded the armaments manufacturer Alfred Nobel to dedicate some of his profits to endowing a peace prize. Her hugely popular 1889 novel *Die Waffen nieder!* (*Lay Down Your Weapons!*)

In 1905, peace campaigner Baroness Bertha von Suttner became the first female Nobel Peace laureate.

spawned an association of the same name dedicated to pursuing peace. Suttner was involved in the attempt to establish an international court to regulate the conduct of war, although she pointed out that the aim was to ban war, not regulate it. In 1905, Suttner herself was awarded the Nobel Peace Prize.

It is worth noting that the positivist philosophy of the Vienna Circle went hand in hand with the pragmatic empiricism of Viennese medicine, both influencing intellectual developments far beyond their homebase, crowded with genius as it was. As the Circle's philosophers were at pains to argue, and its English adherent A. J. Ayer defiantly proclaimed, statements not empirically verifiable (known broadly as metaphysics) were 'meaningless'. This controversial assertion could be taken, or at least was taken, as a denial of the validity of religious belief. It cost Moritz von Schlick, the founder of the Circle, his life. In 1936, he was assassinated on the steps of the university by a former student and Catholic zealot.*

These men and later women were all products of the rigorous Austrian educational system inherited from the days of the Habsburg Empire. With a few exceptions among those who died in the 1920s, all tragically ended up in exile due to the increasingly hostile and dangerous political climate.

The contribution to literature was hardly less impressive and names like Rainer Maria Rilke (died 1926) and Franz Kafka (died 1924) – both Prague born – Stefan Zweig, Joseph Roth and Elias Canetti (a cosmopolitan relic of empire), Hermann Broch and Robert Musil are just the best known.

If there was a 'Vienna Circle' in philosophy and political economics, and a second Viennese School in medicine, there was also a 'Second Viennese School' in music led by Arnold Schoenberg and his followers Alban Berg and Anton Webern. The label is quite an honour when one thinks that the first 'Viennese School' included Haydn, Mozart and Beethoven. One could go on with a list of outstanding talent like Karl Kraus and the novelist Heimito von Doderer, appreciation of whose work, however, resists adequate translation.

One aspect of these writers worth highlighting is their attitude to the demise of the monarchy. Arthur Schnitzler (1862–

---

* The motives are not entirely clear, however. After the *Anschluss*, the assassin claimed that he had killed von Schlick because he believed he was a Jew (which he was not).

1931), whom Freud regarded as his *Doppelgänger*, chronicled the spiritual and moral malaise of a society in turmoil and (like Freud and Klimt) can be considered a sort of anti-pole to the Positivists. Perhaps his best-known work is the play *Reigen* (*La Ronde*, 1897), ten interlinked scenes of sexual liaisons that cast a jaundiced eye on the sexual mores of Viennese society. An even more provocative play, *Professor Bernhardi* (1912), explores the clash of a Jewish doctor's secular ethic with the power of the Church, which ends with Bernhardi being falsely accused and removed from his profession. A brilliant Ibsenesque work that laid bare the rifts in Austrian society, it was too much for the authorities, who promptly had it banned.

Joseph Roth was a melancholic chronicler of the tolerant ethos and atmosphere (as he saw it) of the late Franz Joseph era.

The work of Joseph Roth (1894–1939) evokes nostalgia for a governance in which Jews like himself felt secure under the relatively benign rule of Francis Joseph's regime. His most famous novel, *Radetzky March* (1932), follows the Trotta family, loyal but eventually disillusioned servants of his imperial majesty. It constitutes a requiem for a pluralist empire embracing *viribus unitis* ('With United Forces') – the motto of the ruling house and the inspiration of its bureaucrats.

If Roth laments the collapse of empire, which left him spiritually and physically homeless, others sardonically depicted the inevitability of its fate. This leitmotif was picked up by historians for many years, setting a pattern that few liked to challenge for fear of falling into sentimental Habsburg nostalgia. Hindsight illuminates, but is also subject to its own zeitgeist. For example, Robert Musil's ironic and unfinished three-decker masterpiece *The Man without Qualities* is a retrospective judgement, appearing in 1930 when Austria was already riven by ideological conflict. His imaginary state is Kakania, referring to the abbreviation 'k. und k.' for the Dual Monarchy, but the echo of the word *caka* (excrement) is impossible to overlook. Ostensibly the novel's central theme is bureaucratic preparation for a great event to celebrate the imperial jubilee of 1918, for which no one knows what is quite appropriate. In reality, it is a philosophical and sometimes nihilistic meditation on political stasis and spiritual stagnation. A line from *Yes, Minister*, the 1980s British TV satire on Whitehall manoeuvres, comes to mind: 'Something must be done. This is something. Therefore we must do it.'

Ironic and scornful of nationalism, Robert Musil's *The Man without Qualities* stands as a major achievement of Central European literature.

In fact, as a positivist, Musil saw the rise of science and mass access to hitherto esoteric learning as the beginning of a great adventure for Austrians and indeed for humankind. The late Habsburg Empire represented a transition – the exhaustion of hierarchical rule and the dissolution of its certainties and traditions.

> For Kakania was the first country in our present historical phase from which God withdrew His credit: the love of life, faith in itself, and the ability of all civilised nations to disseminate the useful illusion that they have a mission to fulfil.[37]

The Man without Qualities casts a long shadow, and there is an irresistible *Schadenfreude* in watching, with the benefit of hindsight, the deckchairs being rearranged while the *Titanic* sinks. But Musil's is ultimately an ahistorical approach. The remarkable achievements of the First Republic shouldn't be underrated. These included surviving hyperinflation, which had reached 2,877 per cent by 1922. Ignaz Seipel, a priest and leader of the Christian Social Party, managed to persuade the League of Nations to provide a bail-out and assist reconstruction. In 1925, the Austrian Krone (the currency since 1892) was replaced with the Schilling at a conversion rate of 10,000 Austrian crowns to the Schilling. Excluding the Nazi period, this remained the currency until Austria joined the Euro in 2002.

Adolf Hitler – A Case of Mistaken Identity?

> One quite commonly finds that great national leaders, or the founders of nationalist movements, do not even belong to the country they have glorified. Sometimes they are outright foreigners, or more often they come from peripheral areas where nationality is doubtful.
>
> George Orwell

Orwell describes the case of Adolf Hitler very well.

Hitler's relationship with his father, Alois Hitler, was turbulent and Adolf rebelled by failing to finish secondary school. This proved fateful: after failing the exam for entry to the Academy of Fine Arts in Vienna in 1907, his lack of a *Matura* (secondary school certificate) meant that he was also unable to apply to the School of Architecture. He was subsequently forced to scrape a living in the capital (1907–11) by painting tourist views from postcards.

In Vienna, Hitler became a passionate, rootless and resentful political dreamer. His love-hate of the city with its deeply impressive imperial Ringstrassen buildings curdled into political contempt for the tottering Austro-Hungarian Empire. At the same time, he was exposed to the Pan-Germanic anti-Semitism of Georg von Schönerer and the opportunistic Austrian anti-Semitism of Mayor Karl Lueger. His father had angrily dismissed his dreams of becoming an artist; now Vienna too spurned his aspirations.

Hitler, by then living in Bavaria in Germany,* enlisted in World War I and in 1918 was awarded the Iron Cross for bravery on the recommendation of his Jewish superior officer. Having discovered his true gifts as a genius political activist, Hitler benefitted from the anger felt by Germans at the vindictive terms – reparations, disarmament – of the Versailles Treaty. Although a first attempted putsch in Bavaria (1923) failed, the ensuing prison term afforded Hitler the chance to write his book *Mein Kampf* (*My Struggle*, 1925–26). The text mixed embroidered autobiography with the author's anti-capitalist, anti-Semitic and anti-Communist programme, and in 1933 – the year that Hitler came to power in Germany – it sold more than a million

A Jewish serpent chokes the German eagle in an anti-Semitic 1920 Christian Social election poster. 'German Christians. Save Austria,' the caption reads.

---

* Hitler acquired, and never lost, a Bavarian accent in his youth which, together with his rasping delivery, made him sound totally un-Austrian in his speeches.

copies. Subsequently, a state-sponsored free copy was handed out to the happy couple at civil marriages.

The real chance for the Nazi Party – the National Socialist German Workers' Party, co-founded by Hitler in 1920 – came with the Great Depression after the Wall Street Crash of 1929. Hitler's popularity rose steeply, stimulated by his gift for demagogic oratory and his vision of a resurgent Germany, where unemployment would be a thing of the past. Some enthusiasts compared his programme with Roosevelt's contemporaneous New Deal in the USA (1933–38). Hitler would be Europe's first modern politician: he used air travel just as US politicians made

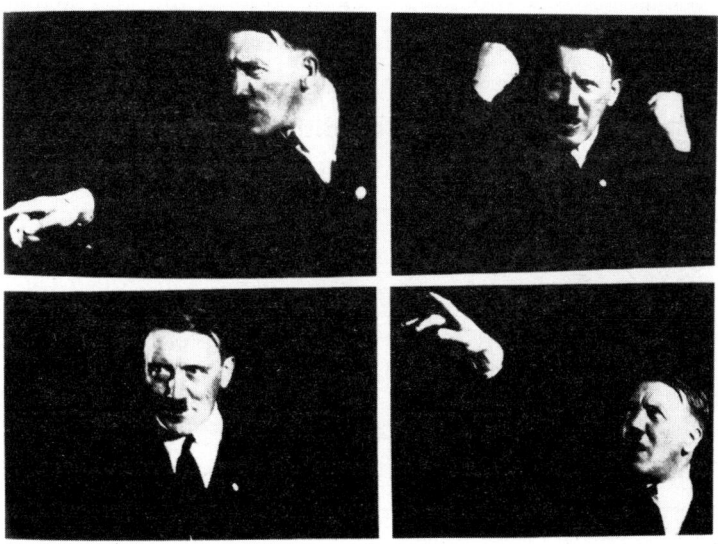

Hitler rehearsing. Although Hitler's speeches often seem ridiculous to us now, they were carefully contrived and he took instruction from professional actors in regard to gesture and eloquence.

whistle-stop tours of America, he studied the methods of self-projection of actors and employed the latest techniques of photography and propaganda.

Between 1925 (when he renounced his Austrian citizenship) and 1932 (when he acquired German citizenship), Hitler was stateless, therefore technically not allowed to run for office. In 1928, the Nazis gained only 3 per cent of the vote; by 1933 they were polling a respectable 18 per cent. Their programme was attractive, promising above all employment for the millions thrown out of work in the Depression following the Wall Street Crash, an end to crippling reparations bills, restoration of territory lost at the Versailles Treaty and (ominously) unification of a restored Germany along ethnic lines. Hitler was also favoured by the fact that, as numerous contemporary commentators show, he was not taken seriously by much of the liberal establishment, some even portraying him merely as a cartoon-like comical figure. However, his political guile was such that he technically gained power through democratic manoeuvring against a threatening background.

In 1933, the German President, von Hindenburg, was persuaded by the politically incoherent conservatives and influential industrialists to appoint Hitler – whose popularity was assuming star proportions – as chancellor. By the Enabling Act that March, Hitler was 'temporarily' granted plenary powers, having persuaded the Centre Party and Conservatives to back him, while Nazi troops circled menacingly outside the building. The mysterious Reichstag fire the previous month had also strengthened his hand as fear and uncertainty spread. Hitler adroitly blamed the fire on the Communists, spreading alarm regarding an imminent coup.

On Hindenburg's death the following year, Hitler merged the positions of president and chancellor, henceforth calling himself *Führer und Reichskanzler* (Leader and Chancellor of the Reich). The army was largely Nazi-supporting and swore its oath to the holder of this combined office. From this position, he assumed complete power through demagoguery, elimination (including murder) of opponents and sham elections.

The oft repeated observation that Hitler came to power democratically is technically correct but omits the evidence of his immense cunning and ruthlessness in the unwavering pursuit of absolute power. He offered to make Germany great again and at the height of his popularity appeared to be doing so. His ambivalence about Austria was now replaced with elaborate plans to make Linz, hardly a place where the young Adolf had passed happy years, a glittering cultural capital of the Nazi Reich, overshadowing Vienna which had snubbed him. In reality, Hitler had been forced by his father to attend the *Realschule* (secondary school) in Linz, which he'd hated and deliberately slacked in the hope of being thrown out. His father wanted Adolf to follow him into the secure job of Customs and Excise. However, fortuitously for Adolf, his detested father died in 1903 when Hitler was fourteen, and his mother removed him from the school. Four years later, financed by orphan's benefits and his mother, Hitler left for Vienna to follow his artistic dreams. Thwarted in this, he increasingly concentrated his considerable gifts on politics and the dream of restoring German (not Austrian) greatness.

From Civil War to Anschluss

> I identify with Austria, at the same time without even the merest slither of ambition that Austria identifies with me.
> Karl Kraus, 1933

The silver age of science, art, music (operetta was in its prime) and literature in interwar Austria played out against an increasingly grim political backdrop. Clive James' splendid comment on the thriving coffee-house society – 'everyone wanted to be a Johnson; nobody wanted to be a Boswell' – mirrors the educated wit that in retrospect seems to be somewhat narcissistic while Rome itself was burning. Nazi support was to rise sharply after Hitler became German Chancellor in 1933. This was against a background of deep political polarisation between Christian Socials and Social Democrats, but also a worldwide depression. The economic situation in Austria was still bedevilled by the financial fall-out from World War I. By the time of the attempted Nazi putsch in 1934, unemployment had risen from 200,000 in 1919 to 478,000, 12 per cent of the working population. About 100,000 civil servants had been dismissed as part of the League of Nations' stipulation for a post-war reconstruction loan. In 1931, Austria's largest bank, the Creditanstalt, whose balance sheet was as large as the entire government expenditure, became insolvent. It was financially networked nationwide and a run on the banks ensued. Financial insecurity coupled with political polarisation meant that there were a great many anxious and discontented people in Austria, many of whom began to look to Germany – and the Nazis – for salvation.

Things had begun to boil over in January 1927. Firstly, members of a right-wing military veterans' association (the *Frontkämpfervereinigung*) shot dead two villagers (a child and a disabled war veteran from the Croat minority) in a clash with the *Schutzbund* (Socialist) militia at Schattendorf in Burgenland. Although tragic, the incident was also somewhat farcical, as in theory both militias were there to protect Burgenland from a rumoured attempt by Hungary's Admiral Horthy to regain it. Following the acquittal of the three killers that July, enraged workers set Vienna's Palace of Justice on fire. Police fired into the crowd and eighty-nine people were killed.

Rival militias operating independently of the constitution – as they had at Schattendorf – are invariably a sign of democratic breakdown. So it was in the First Republic, which in 1933 Christian Social Chancellor Engelbert Dollfuss turned into a dictatorship. The situation came about through parliamentary deadlock, whereby the Social Democrat Karl Renner resigned as Parliamentary President (the presidents were not allowed to vote) so that he could vote as an ordinary member of parliament with his party. This caused the two vice-presidents (from other parties) to do likewise, reinforcing the stalemate. No vote could therefore be taken to end the session. Exploiting the resignations, Dollfuss declared that the Parliament had 'dissolved itself', that the constitution was dysfunctional and thereby he could establish a one-party state. Under

Engelbert Dollfuss became Chancellor of Austria in 1932. Two years later, he was assassinated in an attempted Nazi coup, but his fascistic Fatherland Front lasted until the *Anschluss* in 1938.

the Wartime Economy Authority, he assumed emergency powers and thereafter ruled by decree. Austria had become a corporate state* ruled by the Fatherland Front, as he called his party, and remained that way until the Anschluss five years later.

This state, historically known as the *Ständestaat*, or 'corporative state' as representatives were to be nominated by so-called 'corporations' or 'estates' on behalf of different societal components, was strongly anti-Marxist, anti-Nazi, to a degree anti-capitalist, but also deeply Catholic and Austrian nationalist. The model was Mussolini's Fascist Italy in its earlier form, or Portugal's Catholic *estado novo*, established by António de Oliveira Salazar at about the same time.

The *Ständestaat*'s decisive implementation in Austria took place in 1934 after a clash in Linz between government forces and the Socialist *Schutzbund*, which escalated into a four-day 'civil war'. The conflict's most dramatic moments came in the siege of the Karl-Marx-Hof, the jewel in the crown of Red Vienna, where bunkered Socialist supporters held out for a while against an artillery onslaught, images of which were printed in the press round the world.

While the *Ständestaat*, led by its Fatherland Front, was undoubtedly autocratic and undemocratic, it was not particularly violent in comparison with Mussolini's Italy, and much less so than Hitler's Germany after 1933. Although many intimidatory arrests were made of the diverse opponents of the regime, prison terms were, for the most part, short. The exceptions were a hard core of Communists, Socialists and Nazis held in two camps where, it is claimed, conditions were not particularly

---

* Corporative states are based on economic interest groups whose representatives participate formally, but not on the basis of popular votes, in policymaking. Examples are Mussolini's Italy, Salazar's Portugal and South Korea in its earlier phase of economic reconstruction. A single authoritarian leader presides over this collective at the pinnacle of a political structure with a question-begging name – such as Fatherland Front.

harsh. Nevertheless, there were nine executions after 1934 (one of a wounded Socialist who had to be brought to execution on a stretcher).

Post-war democrats like Bruno Kreisky were extraordinarily bitter about the regime that had imprisoned him. In 2024, the house where Dollfuss was born, which had been turned into a museum, became the object of controversy when it was decided to 'contextualise' the contents (i.e. make them less uncritical of Dollfuss's legacy). In the same year, the conservative government and socialist opposition ended a tradition of joint commemoration of the victims of the civil war, a sign of rising polarisation on the most conflicted issue of modern Austrian history.

Nazism in Austria

The German National Socialist Workers' Party (*Deutsche Nationalsozialistische Arbeiterpartei*; DNSAP) was formed in Vienna in 1918 and had a mixed history of factionalism and strife. They performed fairly poorly at elections where Christian Socials and Social Democrats dominated, with the Communists also featuring. Their voters were drawn from those who opposed the Versailles Treaty's forbidding of a merger with Germany – the dream of the *Grossdeutsch* faction already referred to during the nineteenth century. In 1926, the formal link to the German Nazis – the NSDAP – was established but, at the 1927 election, Hitler Nazis won only 779 votes, and only 3 per cent in the following 1930 vote. Thereafter, Germany's NSDAP doubled its membership every year because of the economic crisis. An effective slogan was: '500,000 Unemployed – 400,000 Jews – Simple way out; vote National Socialist'. When Hitler became Chancellor of Germany in 1933, Nazis were banned in Austria and fled to Bavaria. However, a hard core continued *sub rosa* to plan and execute terrorist attacks in Austria.

In July 1934, Dollfuss was assassinated by Nazis in an attempted putsch, which was foiled by Mussolini (then in alliance with the Austro-Fascists) massing troops on the Austrian border. Dollfuss's successor, Innsbruck lawyer Kurt Schuschnigg, was no match for Hitler's bullying, which included a travel blockade of Austria that deprived it of substantial tourist income. Eventually he agreed in a meeting with Hitler in February of 1938 at Berchtesgaden to appoint two Nazis to his government, one of them as minister of the interior. By now, many Austrians had become Nazi sympathisers, but Schuschnigg banked on one last throw of the dice with a referendum offering the Austrians the option to vote for a 'free, German, independent and social, Christian and united, Austria'. Opinion polls suggested 70 per cent support for Austria remaining Austria, prompting Hitler to demand, and obtain, the cancellation of the vote. Shortly thereafter, the Germans invaded.

Austria was internally demoralised and internationally isolated. The only states to protest were Mexico, Chile, China and the Spanish Republicans; the Soviet Union also did so – and then thought better of it. The League of Nations proved to be impotent – indeed when Germany later invaded Poland the matter was noted before the assembly hastily passed on to the vital question of the internationalisation of Belisha beacons for level crossings.

Austria under the Third Reich

As Hitler travelled in triumph through Upper Austria to Vienna in an open car in March 1938, he was everywhere greeted jubilantly by crowds. His version of a 'special military operation' had been inglorious, to say the least – about 30 per cent of his military vehicles either ran out of petrol or broke down, presumably because in his anxiety to forestall the Austrian referendum he had not allowed his generals time to prepare. The Aus-

Hitler addresses a rally from Vienna's Neue Hofburg on 15 March 1938, following the *Anschluss*. In his speech, Hitler celebrated the 'entrance of my homeland into the German Reich'.

trians didn't seem to mind and the press was gung-ho. At a subsequent rally in the metropolis, he appeared on the balcony of the Neue Hofburg before a hysterically cheering crowd, estimated to be 200,000 strong, to announce the full integration of Austria into the German Reich.

This wasn't originally his plan, but he changed his mind in view of the ecstatic reception he had received at Linz and elsewhere. The historian Ernst Bruckmüller describes the mood in Austria as a 'pseudo-religious experience of salvation', or at least the expectation of such. The Nazis for their part organised a confirmatory referendum from which all the undesirables – Jews, Socialists, Habsburg loyalists – were excluded, before claiming that the result was 99.6 per cent in favour of the *Anschluss*. Even before it was held, leading politicians were on their way to an internment camp. The Jewish polymath Egon Friedell had leaned out of his third-floor window, politely shouting a warning to pedestrians below, before jumping to his death.

Of course, much worse was to come, beginning with the so-called *Kristallnacht* (9–10 November 1938),* a pogrom in which Jews were murdered, assaulted, tortured and expropriated. Synagogues and business premises were attacked or burned. This mirrored what was happening in Germany and, in theory, was a response to the murder in Paris by a Polish Jew of Ernst vom Rath, a senior German diplomat. It appears that the murderer may have been a homosexual partner of Rath's and motivated by a failed blackmail attempt on the victim, but he was also a displaced German Jew who had been prohibited from returning to Poland. In reality, the *Kristallnacht* was clearly premeditated and organised, a modern version of the vicious medieval pogroms against Jews.

Austrian Nazis and local residents watch as Jews are forced to scrub the pavements of the referendum slogans for the Fatherland Front after the Nazi.

About 65,000 Austrian Jews subsequently lost their lives in the Holocaust. Of the 135,000 who managed to flee, usually after paying the surreally named 'tax on fleeing the Reich'† (some 25 per cent of their assets or confiscation of all of them if the assets were difficult to audit), 31,000 made it to Britain and

---

* So-called after the smashed glass of the windows of Jewish properties.
† '*Reichsfluchtsteuer*' – When first introduced in 1931 in pre-Nazi Germany, this tax was designed to curb capital flight from a country that was struggling under the burden of World War I reparations; however, by 1938 the Nazis had extended it to apply to all persons wishing to leave, which in almost all cases meant Jews.

30,000 to the USA, while 15,000 evaded the immigration bar imposed on Israel under the British mandate. Austria lost the greater part of its Nobel Laureates, whose world renown was both feared and hated by the Nazis. For example, Viktor Hess, who had won the prize for physics in 1936, was compelled to convert his prize money into worthless local currency before emigrating. Otto Loewi, prize-winner for neurology, was detained by the Nazis until he had deposited his prize money in a German bank. Neither ever saw the money again.

Of Roma and Sinti, some 5,500 were murdered, about half of their population; another 20,000–30,000 people with disabilities or otherwise considered 'unworthy of life' (for example, homosexuals) were also killed, mostly at Schloss Hartheim near Linz, which ran the largest 'euthanasia' programme of the Third Reich. Austria's concentration camp was at Mauthausen in Upper Austria, a granite quarry, where some 90,000 people from various nations died in forced labour, along with another 60,000 to 70,000 in the subsidiary Gusen camp nearby.[38]

Forced labour, mostly Jewish but also Romany and others considered 'undesirables' by the Nazi regime, hauling earth for the construction of the concentration camp at Mauthausen.

A young Spanish Communist, Francisco Boix, landed up here and when the SS administration discovered that he was a press photographer, he was employed to make official (propaganda) documentation of the camp. This he did, adding some illicit shots of the horrific atrocities committed by the authorities and hiding the negatives. On his release from the camp at the end of the war, he made his way to Paris and offered the film to *L'Humanité*, the leading Communist newspaper, which said it had to consult 'higher up' (i.e. the Soviets). The answer was a refusal to publish, since by definition any survivors of the camps must have been collaborators (!). The photographs were used at the Nuremberg trials to destroy the alibis of top Nazis who claimed never to have visited or not to have known about Mauthausen.[39]

> ### *Austria – Victim or Accomplice?*
> In October 1943, the Allies issued The Moscow Declaration on Austria, which stated that:
>
>> [the] Government of the United Kingdom, the Soviet Union and the United States of America are agreed that Austria, *the first free country to fall victim to Hitlerite aggression*, [italics added] shall be liberated from German domination. They regard the annexation imposed upon Austria by Germany on March 15, 1938 as null and void ... Austria is reminded, however, that she has a responsibility which she cannot evade for participation in the war on the side of Hitlerite Germany, and that in the final settlement account will inevitably be taken of her own contribution to her liberation.[40]
>
> Parallel to the Declaration on Austria was one on Italy, which significantly was phrased in more general terms and was less severe in the requirement of resistance credentials. On the other hand, it did not suggest that Italy was a 'victim' of Fascism, which was, after all, not the result of an invasion, and we should not forget the early plaudits for Mussolini

from such diverse sources as Winston Churchill, the Socialist Richard Crossman and Sigmund Freud (who incautiously labelled him 'the hero of culture').[41] It was natural therefore that Austrians should seize on the first part of the Declaration (Austria as 'victim') and rather forget about the last part.

But there was a further embarrassment: both the Cardinal Archbishop of Vienna, Theodor Innitzer (along with the Austrian Bishops' Conference) and former Socialist Chancellor Karl Renner had appealed for a 'yes' vote in the *Anschluss* referendum. Renner, as a long-standing 'Gross-Deutscher' (Pan-German), was being consistent, adding in his recommendatory newspaper article in the *Neuer Wiener Tageblatt* that he supported a 'yes' result despite 'disapproving of the means used to obtain it'. This phrasing might be deemed a shade euphemistic, but it was probably the insurance ticket for the wily Renner, who claimed that the *Anschluss* was 'a satisfaction for the humiliations of 1918 and 1919'. This was a view widely shared among Socialists. 'Shortly before his death in Parisian exile in 1938,' writes historian Lonnie Johnson, the Marxist '[Otto] Bauer described the re-establishment of Austria as a "reactionary slogan" and called for a "unified German revolution" (*gesamtdeutsche Revolution*), or, in other words, "a maintenance of the *Anschluss* after, as the German-speaking proletariats envisioned, there was victory over Nazism."'[42]

In the Church's case, the letter to Hitler expressing support was signed by Cardinal Innitzer, who gratuitously added '*Heil Hitler*' at the bottom. The Protestant Churches had long since committed themselves to the *Anschluss* and only Communists (mostly) and monarchists were against. In any case, it proved to be a huge mistake on Innitzer's part, since the Vatican immediately disowned his statement and demanded a retraction condemning the policies of the Nazis. In October, there was a huge anti-Nazi demonstration of the *Katholische Jugend* (Catholic Youth Movement) in front of the Stephansdom, the only such demo under Nazi rule in Austria. Inside the packed cathedral, Innitzer preached a sermon which ended with the words 'Christ is our leader!' – 'leader' in German being *Führer*, just as Hitler styled himself. This was rightly taken as a declaration of defiance of the regime which had set to work to destroy the influence of the Church. The next day, Nazi thugs stormed and smashed up the Bishop's Palace and defenestrated Innitzer's secretary, all undisturbed by the police.

Innitzer embodies the identity confusion of many Austrians at that time. The liberal Catholic historian Friedrich Heer has commented acidly that 'the clergy, as always, gets into bed with power,'[43] which is, in fact, far truer of the Orthodox Church than the Catholic Church, though it is also true that the Vatican was outmanoeuvred both by Mussolini and Hitler. Before the *Anschluss*, Innitzer had strongly supported the clerico-Fascist state of Dollfuss and Schuschnigg. But this in itself is something of a contradiction, since Innitzer was at heart a *Großdeutscher* (born in Neugeschrei, now in the Czech Republic). On the other hand, he had earlier shown his humanity by being one of very few prominent people to raise the alarm internationally about the genocidal Soviet induced famine in 1930s Ukraine, known as the *Holodomor*. After his initial attempt to ingratiate himself with the Nazis, he led the Church under the radar during the Nazi period and even supported its secret protection of persecuted Jews. He survived everything, remaining Cardinal Archbishop until his death in 1955, the year in which the Allied occupation of Austria ended. In a touch worthy of operetta, he even has a pastry, the *Kardinalschnitte*, named after him – still available in all good *Konditoreien*.

Austria fared no better during World War II than in World War I – in fact, considerably worse, as her 'ally' openly despised her and she was ruled like a provincial province (the 'Ostmark', later 'Donau- und Alpenreichsgauen'), which in turn was chopped up into new administrative entities (*Reichsgauen*)

Towards war's end, Vienna's Stephansdom was damaged by a fire begun by civilians looting shops, before the wind carried the burning embers onto the cathedral.

ruled by *Gauleiter*. Resentment that had arisen during World War I resurfaced against the arrogance, self-righteousness and generally aggressive *Korporalston* (slang for an overbearing manner) of the northern 'Brothers in War'.[44]

The complaints (of which faint traces remain even today) somewhat resemble the resentment of the East Germans who were subject to a takeover by West German business after German reunification in 1990. Prussians had been top dog once in Germany – and so had Austrians, until Napoleon, followed by Bismarck, dismantled their historic status. Austrians did not have their own regiments and were pressed into service on some of the worst fronts, such as Stalingrad. In view of later political controversy, it should also be noted that an exceptionally large number of Austrians were deployed in the treacherous Balkans, and war crimes occurred. Austrian military and civilian casualties in the war are reckoned at 384,700, of which 360,000 were military. There were some 20,000 casualties from British and US bombing raids. Vienna suffered most with fifty-two raids and 37,000 buildings damaged or destroyed – about 20 per cent of the city.

CHAPTER 13

THE SECOND REPUBLIC

Ten Years of Occupation

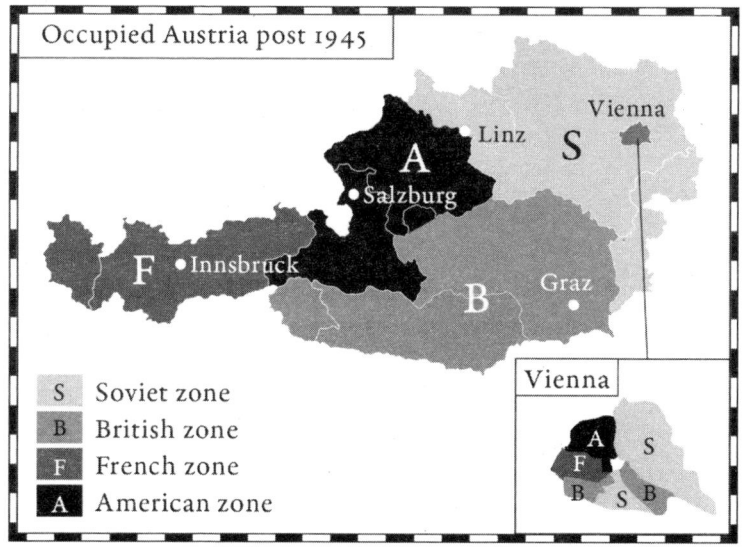

At the conclusion of World War II, Austria was divided into zones of occupation by the Allied powers: Vorarlberg and Tyrol under the French, Carinthia and Styria under the British, Upper Austria south of the Danube and Salzburg under the Americans. The Russians, who had the advantage of reaching Austria before their western Allies, got the whole of Lower Austria, Burgenland, Upper Austria north of the Danube and peripheral parts of Greater Vienna.

As elsewhere, the Russians immediately erected a self-congratulatory liberation monument in Vienna on Schwarzenbergplatz, part of which they renamed Stalinplatz. It is topped by a statue of 'the unknown Soviet soldier', the Soviets having lost some 18,000 men in securing the city in April 1945.

Erected swiftly after the war, Vienna's Soviet War Memorial was known satirically as '*der Erbse Pepi*', meaning 'Joe Peas' – in reference to Joseph Stalin and the Soviet rations of dried peas.

Today, however, this hero is familiarly known as 'the unknown plunderer' and 'the unknown rapist' due to the substantial incidence of rape of Austrian women by Russian soldiers. There were so many cases that the Catholic Church quietly relaxed the ban on abortion for the many victims. After the collapse of the Soviet Union, there was talk of dismantling the statue, but its existence is guaranteed by the *Staatsvertrag* (State Treaty) of 1955. So it remains, an Ozymandiac relic of 'liberation', though its back wall was briefly painted in Ukrainian colours after the Russian invasion of Ukraine in 2022.

Unlike the western Allies, the Russians insisted that, under their definition of reparations, they could appropriate in their sector most everything that wasn't screwed down – and indeed much that was. They were finally persuaded to moderate their claims as part of the final settlement of the *Staatsvertrag*, but the Austrians were obliged to buy back their property (officially confiscated 'German assets') at a cost of $150 million annually for six years, plus (likewise for six years) deliver 1 million tons of crude oil.* On the other hand, to protect them from Russian confiscation (and because there was no private capital available),

---

* Modest oil reserves lay in Upper and Lower Austria and the Vienna Basin.

seventy major industrial enterprises were nationalised in 1946–47, something that was later to cause headaches for a country moving towards a free market economy.

The capital itself was also divided into zones, while the old Inner City was jointly controlled. The mood of a war-exhausted and slightly sinister city is well-captured in Carol Reed's classic film *The Third Man* (1949), with Orson Welles playing an American crook (Harry Lime) who sells diluted penicillin stolen from aid agencies on the black market. It owes its remarkable authenticity to a brilliant script by the novelist Graham Greene, who had visited Vienna and seen the black-market racketeering. At the time, the official provision of rations was only about 800 calories a day.

Denazification

The National Socialism Prohibition Act of 8 May 1945 made it a criminal offence to belong to the Nazi Party and prescribed that all Nazis who had been in official positions had to be registered with the authorities. This excluded them from voting in the first democratic elections. On the other hand (and among those registered), it was thought a distinction had to be made between active functionaries and mere '*Mitläufer*' (fellow travellers) – a delicate matter, to say the least. There were in the end some 377,260 'fellow travellers', about a third of them only candidates for party membership. Some 98,260 were full-blooded 'illegals'.

After administering some denazification themselves with legal process, the Allied Powers handed the further measures to be taken back to the Austrian government, reserving only cases of war crimes committed against themselves. The Figl government removed 960 people from leading government positions and the business sector, but 36,000 of persons

> working in lower positions. This, of course, led to strategic shortages in vital professions and by 1947 the law was being applied discriminatingly, so that many considered to be less or insignificantly culpable were back at work (about 1 in 4 from the professions where being disbarred had been possible). Some eminent people in the arts (for example, the conductors Karl Böhm and Herbert von Karajan, both Nazi sympathisers) fell foul of the Prohibition Act, but their suspensions were relatively brief. Nevertheless 58 per cent of 23,477 Nazis tried in People's Courts were found guilty. There were forty-three death sentences, of which thirty were carried out.
>
> By the 1949 election, a new party calling itself the Federation of Independents (*Verband der Unabhängigen*) provided a home for ex-Nazis (except those with court convictions) and there was an unseemly scramble by both the People's Party and the Social Democrats for their votes (they won fifteen seats in Parliament). By this time, denazification was considered to be complete, although inevitably over the following years there were ongoing revelations of overlooked Nazi crimes and Nazi personnel.[45]

A provisional government was set up in 1945 under the ever-enduring Karl Renner, who had announced himself to the Russian commander in Lower Austria. The administration was regarded with suspicion by the western Allies as probably being a Soviet puppet state. However, the first nationwide free elections since 1930 were held on 25 November 1945 and produced a win for the conservative *Österreichische Volkspartei* (ÖVP – Austrian People's Party) with 49.8 per cent under Leopold Figl, followed by the *Sozialistische Partei Österreich* (SPÖ) with 44.6 per cent under Adolf Schärf. The two duly became Chancellor and Vice-Chancellor. Coalitions between the '*bürgerlichen*' (middle-class) bloc and the 'workers' bloc of voters would set the tone for a new conciliatory and consensual governance, concentrating on points of agreement and negotiating points of difference in the great task of rebuilding Austrian democracy and ridding the country of foreign occupation.

Post-War Communists
Despite a long-standing tradition of Austro-Marxism (whose intellectual founder was Otto Bauer) and the blandishments of the Russian occupying force, the Austrian Communist Party (*Kommunistische Partei Österreichs* – KPÖ) hardly made much impact after the war. In the 1945 election, they only returned four MPs (compared to the ÖVP's eighty-five and the SPÖ's seventy-six) and were given just one ministry, to the manifest surprise and irritation of the Russians. But, understandably, Karl Renner was careful to exclude the Communists from undue influence both in his Social Democratic party and his administration (although they remained a strong force in the trade unions). Also, Austrians were reasonably well informed about the Soviet purges of the 1930s, as well as the politically instigated and horrific Ukrainian famine (*Holodomor*) of 1932–33. Nor were they likely to forget the cynical pre-war Nazi-Soviet pact (in which Hitler and Stalin had agreed how to carve up Europe) which had destroyed the credibility of Soviet Communism amongst so many leftist European intellectuals.

The big moment for the Austrian Communists had come in 1918 as the First Republic was being proclaimed, when briefly Communists had taken over in German Bavaria (1918–19) to the West and were on their way to doing so in Budapest (1919) to the East. With support from both these areas, a bungled putsch had been attempted and, while being hoisted over the Parliament, the red-white-red flag of Austria was torn down and replaced with a red one. In 1950, when a fourth austerity package to tame inflation was being introduced, what looked like Soviet-inspired wildcat strikes broke out, but Austrian historians disagree as to whether they were spontaneous or not. At any rate, they failed and there followed a purge of activist Communists in the trade unions, which have remained for the most part firmly under Social Democratic control ever since.

In 2024, Communists professing democracy have returned to mainstream politics and a Communist is currently the Mayor of Graz in Styria, while in Salzburg the Communist candidate came second and became deputy mayor. However, these votes tend to depend on locally charismatic characters and in the June 2024 Euro elections they only got 2.9 per cent of the vote (and no seats), well behind the Greens and the tiny Liberal Party (NEOS).

Towards independent statehood

The decade between 1945 and 1955 proved to be difficult and frustrating. However, the country soon began to rebuild its damaged infrastructure and repair its economy with the assistance of the US Marshall Plan (about $1 billion starting in 1947), along with other international investment loans. It was striking how quickly such investment made a visible difference compared to the countries of the Soviet Empire, where Moscow blocked access to the Marshall Plan.

A more delicate matter was the rehabilitation of Austria's reputation. The official position of the Austrian government in respect of compensation and restitution (*Entschädigung und Rückgabe*) was that Austria had been *occupied* by a foreign power in 1938, which thereby had rendered the Austrian state incapable of acting. Therefore, the restored state could not be held responsible for what had occurred in between. Unfortunately, this bore a remarkable and unwelcome similarity to the position of the German Democratic Republic which simply behaved as if the Nazi regime had acted in some parallel universe and had nothing to do with the actual inhabitants. Many Nazis in East Germany became more or less zealous converts to Communist totalitarianism.

Post-war literature has lingered on Austria's love-hate with itself as it wrestles with the psychological impact of Nazism. The issue emerges strikingly in the works of Ingeborg Bachman (1926–73), whose parents had been Nazis, as well as in the brilliant and bleakly comic oratorical denunciations of Thomas Bernhard (1931–89), along with the moral confusion of Peter Handke (born 1942), who gave a tribute at the funeral of Slobodan Milošević, and the extreme quasi-pornographic psychic violence in the work of Elfriede Jelinek (born 1946). A Nobel Prize-winner like Handke, Jelinek has said that a large part of Austrian literature revolves around the 'black hole' of Hitler.

To be fair, the practical difficulties for Austria were enormous. For example, how to turn over 65,000 so-called 'Aryanised' (formerly Jewish) rental properties, or other liens, to their original occupants or owners? Especially when many of the properties no longer existed due to the bombing and their owners were abroad or no longer alive. In any case, there was also a major housing problem arising from 'displaced persons'. These included former Austrian Germans from once imperial territories fleeing the new Communist states, as well as refugees and soldiers released from the front or prison camps. All of whom needed accommodation and food. The Republic was unenthusiastic about individual compensation, too, on the grounds that it had been occupied by Nazi Germany and was not legally responsible. That said, a fund was created and a law made enabling the heirs of deceased Jews to claim their rights. It seems, however, that only about half of the applications were accepted.

Gustav Klimt's Portrait of Adele Bloch-Bauer II was one of the most significant artworks in Austria restituted (in 2006) to descendants of the original owners.

Later, the most publicised aspect of this problem was the restitution of works of art either stolen or sold under duress to the Austrian Gallery in the Belvedere, or otherwise wrongfully acquired. This rumbled on into the 1980s and 1990s and beyond. For example, after a long and contentious legal dispute, Gustav Klimt's portrait of Adele Bloch-Bauer was restituted to Bloch-Bauer's American niece in 2006 during the Schüssel government,* the first administration to try and grip this problem comprehensively.

The Staatsvertrag of 1955

As early as 1947, the Austrians began negotiating the end of their country's occupation, but Cold War events (the Korean War on the one hand, the distancing of Communist Yugoslavia from Moscow on the other) rendered progress slow. Things, however, improved rapidly after the death of Stalin in 1953. In the Moscow negotiations conducted by Chancellor Raab, Vice-Chancellor Schärf and Foreign Minister Figl, the Rus-

---

* The painting was later sold on for $135 million and now hangs in Ronald Lauder's Neue Galerie in New York.

sians tried their usual tactic of plying their guests with vodka through endless toasts, but they had met their match in three extremely seaworthy Austrians representing a country with some of the best schnapps in the world.

Foreign Minister Leopold Figl announcing the signing of the *Staatsvertrag* in 1955, which agreed the withdrawal of the four postwar occupying powers.

By 1955, all stakeholders were in agreement and on 15 May the foreign ministers of the occupying powers (Antoine Pinay for France, Harold MacMillan for the UK, John Foster Dulles for the USA and Vyacheslav Molotov for the Soviet Union), together with Leopold Figl for Austria, signed the State Treaty in the sumptuous Belvedere Palace. Figl famously declared '*Österreich ist frei!*' and they all appeared before cheering crowds on the palace balcony.

Perhaps the biggest hurdles had been the insistence of the Soviets on Austrian neutrality (to which the Americans were opposed), the retrieving of Austrian assets from the Russians and, more importantly, persuading the latter to agree to the removal of the 'guilt' clause from the Moscow Declaration of 1943. Austria had thereby finally established the principle that neither the new government in Austria, nor its people as a whole, could be held responsible for the war, a principle that influenced (not always wisely) the behaviour of successive governments and parties. Needless to say, it was in marked contrast to the stance taken by the Federal Republic of Germany (West Germany) in dealing with its own recent past.

An Austrian in late middle age when the *Staatsvertrag* was signed would have witnessed in their lifetime the collapse of the Austro-Hungarian Empire, the demise of the First Republic, an attempted putsch and a short civil war in 1934, followed by the demise of the so-called 'clerico-fascist' *Ständestaat*, the *Anschluss* to Hitler Deutschland, seven years of war and Nazi hegemony, and finally a decade of four-power occupation. After that, they might reasonably be expected to be somewhat risk averse. Yet, despite Austria's narrow escape from totalitarian Soviet rule, just a year after regaining their own freedom and facing Soviet sabre-rattling, Austrians took considerable risks in supporting (though not with weapons) the Hungarian uprising in 1956 against the Soviet occupiers. Politically this proved fortuitous, since the Communist Party in Austria lost all credibility after supporting the Soviet oppressors of its neighbour. Austria had begun its new life as a liberated liberal democracy and – above all – a neutral state.

> ### The Question of Neutrality
>
> On 25 October 1955, the Austrian Parliament unanimously passed a Declaration of Perpetual Neutrality (*immerwährende Neutralitätserklärung*), which thereby became part of the Constitution. Without such a declaration, Russia would not have agreed to end the occupation. Only recently has this become a difficulty. Even the European Union accepted Austria as a 'neutral' state when it joined in 1995. The only other neutral states in the EU are now Ireland and

Malta. The writer Robert Menasse claims that Austria's neutrality has no status in international law. He observes that it is not in the Second Republic's grounding document of the *Staatsvertrag* and theoretically is not recognised by anyone. To him it is a convenient fiction or myth sustaining the '*Land ohne Eigenschaften*' – a wordplay on the title of Robert Musil's novel *The Man without Qualities*. In an article for *News* magazine in 2023, he asked satirically of Austria's neutrality: 'What does a calming pill protect us from?'

The Austrian public do not agree. Even with the Ukraine war raging a few hundred kilometres away in 2022, 71 per cent were determined to keep the country's neutral status intact, and this despite the entry into NATO of formerly neutral Finland and Sweden. A Socialist parliamentarian has described neutrality as something that builds an Austrian identity. But the Ukraine war has upended long-held assumptions.

Critics point out that Austria is effectively freeloading under the umbrella of NATO. With the exception of Switzerland and Liechtenstein, the countries that border Austria are all in NATO. To the claim that Austria is like Switzerland, it is pointed out that Switzerland has national service and an instant militia with citizens between eighteen and thirty-four years of age retaining their service weapons at home. Austria, in fact, claims that it is upping its expenditure on the military to 1.5 per cent of GDP – which is more than Germany (under)spent on defence for years, until Chancellor Scholz announced the beginning of a new era (*Zeitenwende*) in 2022. Austria offers its small army as UN observers and humanitarian assistance in conflict areas. But to build its forces up to the effectiveness of the Swiss would, it is estimated, take two decades.

> Hitherto *de facto* pacifist states like post-war West Germany are facing a reality they assumed would never (re)occur – a return to the menace of conflict between the great powers which, if it happened, would inevitably suck in the peripheral powers. As Menasse comments with characteristic bluntness:
>
>> The claim that wars can only be ended through negotiation is idiotic, particularly in the mouths of Germans. So far as I know, Hitler was not deterred by negotiations.
>
> In this, however, he is contradicting the realpolitik of the Henry Kissinger school of political science. Kissinger himself hinted before his death in 2023 his belief that the Ukraine war would be settled with a negotiated peace rather than 'victory' or 'defeat'.

Consensus and Lessons from the Past

The first coalition government set a pattern that lasted until the mid-1960s when the People's Party acquired an absolute majority, and in the 1970s Bruno Kreisky pulled off the same feat for the Socialists. With the uncomfortable memory of the civil war in 1934 and the consequent *Ständestaat*, the Austrian coalitions were built around not only a political consensus, but also what was called *Proporz*, or an equal distribution of power and positions, from which periodically emerge allegations of corruption or cronyism.

Proporz reached well beyond government itself into parastatal and cultural positions, such as the Austrian Federal Railway (ÖBB) and museum curators. This political culture (also known as *Parteibuchpolitik* – Politics of Party Membership) has lasted, albeit in somewhat attenuated form, up to the present. It was from the mid-1980s, however, complicated by the rise to regional power and eventually government of the right-wing Freedom Party (*Freiheitliche Partei,* FPÖ). Part of this rise may be attributed to a change in the electoral system under Kreisky which, intentionally or not, favoured the FPÖ. In 1970, Kreisky had been two short of an absolute majority and this reform, which increased the element of proportionality in votes and seats, was the price for his support in Parliament by the FPÖ.

Economic Recovery and the Social Partnership
Originally the brainchild of Julius Raab (1891–1964) – the greatest of the postwar Conservative chancellors – but with the co-operation of the Socialists, the 'Social Partnership' (*Sozialpartnerschaft*) has allowed Austria to develop an extraordinarily successful way of avoiding industrial unrest while promoting economic growth. (The German *Sozialstaat* and Swiss *Arbeitsfrieden* have some similar features.) The various interests of workers, employers, entrepreneurs and industrialists are represented by a number of chambers: one for workers (AK, *Arbeiterkammer*), one for commerce (WKO, *Wirtschaftskammer*), another for agriculture (LK, *Landwirtschaftskammer*). Further, there are associations such as the Trades Unions Federation (ÖGB, *Österreichischer Gewerkschaftsbund*), which is itself divided into 'fractions' representing political party allegiance, though dominated by the Socialists. Finally, there is an association representing industry (IV, *Vereinigung österreichischer Industrieller*).

Membership of these bodies for those operating in each sphere is obligatory (except for the IV, representing industry); moreover, there is a mirror effect in government with the head of the Trades Unions Federation always having a high position in the Socialist Party and likewise the WKO for commerce and LK for agriculture being perennially led by People's Party functionaries. This web of formidable acronyms covers pretty much anyone economically active in Austria except for the free professions (although it is no surprise that the doctors have their own chamber, which is fiercely protective of its members' interests).

For many years, the deals on wages (and indirectly on prices), once they have been struck collectively by these various bodies, have been passed to government and all but nodded through. At the same time, there were long periods of coalition government that oiled the wheels of co-operative government, although it opened the door to 'Buggins's turn' style of dishing out well-remunerated positions on a party basis.

> The system was intended to co-ordinate and centralise wage bargaining and price regulation, and, in the long term, to prevent the reappearance of the culture of economic and class conflict which, between the wars, had destroyed the First Republic.[46]
>
> Jill Lewis

Originally dubbed by some critics as 'Austrocorporatism' and objected to because that smacked of the Fascists' 'corporate state', and also because the most important decisions for domestic government were taken behind closed doors, the 'Social Partnership' (*Sozialpartnerschaft*) has now become more transparent and is referred to more politely as Austrokeynesianism, or simply the 'Social Partners' (*die Sozialpartner*). The latter's highly influential activity over forty years received full constitutional recognition only in 2008 (*Österreich-Konvent*). No matter: in its heyday from the 1960s to the millennium, the *Sozialpartnerschaft* ensured that Austria remained virtually strike-free and enjoyed almost continuous GDP growth. This may favourably be compared with the adversarial system of the Anglo-Saxon economies, which brought the UK to its knees in the 1970s and threatens to do so again. While in 1960, Austria's per capita income was 20 per cent less than that of the UK, by 1972 it was ahead of the latter by 8 per cent. Journalist Paul Lendvai, the *Financial Times* correspondent in Austria, had to repeat this three times over the phone to the paper's stenographer, since it was assumed that the figure was a mistake.[47]

The Freedom Party – scandal-ridden but successful

The origins of the Freedom Party (*Freiheitliche Partei* – FPÖ) are two-fold. Its liberal wing was a relic of the Greater German constituency of the nineteenth century, which was liberal in economic and (to some extent) social policy, but a believer in a pan-German state.

However, the party's second and main component originally comprised the former Nazis who had been re-admitted to the franchise in 1949. They called themselves the *Verband der Unabhängigen* (The Federation of Independents – VdU). Their political existence owed itself to a decision by the new democratic state of Austria, and supported by the (still) occupying powers, to bring ex-Nazis (other than those guilty of crimes) back into the political mainstream. This was partly because there were an awful lot of ex-Nazis (more than 500,000 registered with the authorities) and it would do little for the cause of denazification to keep them marginalised and disenfranchised. It was also partly because both the mainstream parties, conservative and socialist, were keen to get their hands on a large pool of voters. With the

Staatsvertrag of 1955, it was decided to rechristen the VdU with a less evasive name and broaden its potential. Hence, the Freedom Party. Who could disagree with the defence of freedom as a political mission?

> Why did we become National Socialists back then? Above all because we rejected the treason of the Dollfuß system.... Anyone who has forgotten that we were national and socialist is now joining the ÖVP [Austrian People's Party].... This only proves that he never took his socialism seriously. But anyone who sees in socialism the idea of a commitment to the national community and to social justice towards every member of the people knows that their natural path is to the socialists, to the SPÖ![48]
> (From a post-war Socialist campaign leaflet aimed at attracting potential Freedom Party voters)

The Socialist Chancellor Bruno Kreisky was the first to bring the Freedom Party (FPÖ) into government when the Social Democrats (SPÖ) lost its overall majority in 1983. The FPÖ's leader at that time was a moderate liberal, Norbert Steger, who became Austria's Vice-Chancellor (1983–87). However, after an internal party putsch in 1986, Jörg Haider, the firebrand from Carinthia, took over the FPÖ leadership and moved the party sharply to the right. This resulted in increasing electoral success, culminating in 2000 in a coalition with the ÖVP conservatives under Wolfgang Schüssel. Although the coalition's programme was democratic and constitutional, the losing Socialists stirred up their sympathisers across Europe, resulting in an illegal 'boycott' of Austria at the EU. This adventure in gesture politics did neither the Socialists nor the EU any good, but on the other hand, the coalition soon began to implode due to the fractious nature of the FPÖ and the erratic behaviour of its leader (who had remained Governor of Carinthia). He himself died drink-driving in 2008.

The Start of the Kreisky Era

The era of grand coalitions came to an end in the 1960s when Josef Klaus became the conservative ÖVP chancellor, holding an absolute majority from 1966–70. Klaus was an austere, conscientious politician, who finally settled the matter of the burdensome enforced oil deliveries to the Soviet Union, a hangover from the haggling with the Russians before the *Staatsvertrag*.

To his credit, Klaus made Austrian Broadcasting (ORF) independent, discarding the system of *Proporz*, whereby its direction had been shared between ÖVP and Socialist appointees. In so doing, he more or less signed his own political death warrant, paving the way for his wittier, more telegenic rival, the Socialist leader Bruno Kreisky, to become a broadcasting regular – an important factor in Kreisky's future electoral success.*

South Tyrol Resurfaces

On 5 September 1946, Austria had signed a treaty with Italy, known as the Gruber-De Gasperi Agreement after the Austrian Foreign Minister and Italian Prime Minister who negotiated it. The treaty was intended to restore equal rights under the law and a measure of autonomy to Austrian Germans in the Province of Bolzano/Bozen Province (90 per cent German speaking). After World War I, Bozen had deliberately been united

---

* Once he was in power, Kreisky fought hard to bring the ORF back under political control.

with the larger Italian speaking Trentino province to smother local German autonomy.

The Gruber-De Gasperi measures included reinstating German as one of the two official languages and reversing other oppressive measures that were the result of an agreement in 1939 between Hitler and Mussolini. The Fascists and Nazis had envisioned a choice between complete assimilation (even the obligation to take Italian names) or emigration 'to the German Reich'. Those Austrian Germans who took the so-called option to emigrate were, in fact, sent as settlers to western Poland, which had been annexed by Germany, where they were either killed or, at war's end, expelled. Sympathy for the Nazis had been strong in South Tyrol and after VE Day the area was notorious as a 'rat run' for senior Nazis escaping European justice en route to the Middle East or South America.

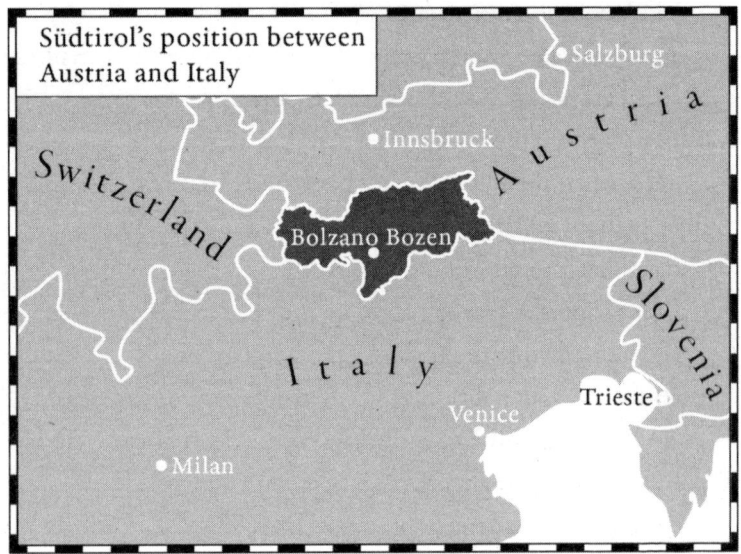

However, despite the post-war agreement (hailed at the time), South Tyrol was flooded with Italians, making German self-government virtually impossible. This, in turn, led in the

1960s to terrorist acts by irredentists against Italian installations. It was Bruno Kreisky who, as foreign minister (1959–66) took the issue to the United Nations. Italy was put under pressure to modify the agreement so that the German-speaking inhabitants were no longer under hegemonic control of the Trentino and genuinely granted wide-ranging autonomy. This was signed between the Italian Prime Minister Aldo Moro and Austria's Foreign Minister Kurt Waldheim in 1972. Due to Italian foot-dragging, however, it took another twenty years to achieve full implementation of local autonomy for a majority German-speaking region. Kreisky's astute (and not entirely risk-free) move had, though, raised his profile (and that of Austria) both at home and abroad.

Bruno Kreisky

Austria's most eminent post-war chancellor, Bruno Kreisky (1911–90) came from a prosperous Jewish family that had been settled in old Austria since the time of Maria Theresa. He had joined the Social Democrats during the *Ständestaat*, under which he was imprisoned for fifteen months in 1935 for political activism and again arrested in 1936. In 1938, he was obliged to go into exile in Sweden to avoid imprisonment or murder by the Nazis. Twenty-five members of his family perished in the Holocaust. On his return in 1950, his diplomatic and political talent was eventually recognised and he was already to be seen among the dignitaries on the Belvedere balcony after the *Staatsvertrag* was signed.

Kreisky was extremely proud as a Jew that the Austrian electorate chose him three times to be their chancellor (1970–1983), but at the same time was somewhat ambivalent about his Jewishness. This was not surprising – after his first return to Vienna from Sweden, his rise in the Social

Democratic Party was blocked on the grounds that the elders of the party did not want the party to be seen as the '*Judenpartei*' – 'the Jews' party'.

Ironically, when Kreisky first needed the parliamentary support of the ex-Nazi *Verband der Unabhängigen* (The Federation of Independents – VdU) to keep his party in power in 1970, he had in mind their leader for the position of vice-chancellor, but the man turned out to have been a member of an SS death squad. The Nazi-hunter Simon Wiesenthal exposed this, provoking an outraged Kreisky to hint unwisely that Wiesenthal had himself collaborated with the Gestapo. Wiesenthal sued him and won, but Kreisky stuck to his guns and made a number of further abusive remarks against Jews.

As with the combative Jewish writer Karl Kraus between the wars, Kreisky's attacks on those he considered to be miserable Jews took on a decidedly anti-Semitic tone. At the same time, the chancellor's apparently generous approach to ex-Nazis is said in part to have been driven by his hatred of the authoritarian Fatherland Front regime of the 1930s that had first imprisoned him. That regime was, of course, non-democratic but, in important aspects, was the ideological forebear of the Austrian People's Party (ÖVP), Kreisky's main rival.

Another ambivalence lay in Kreisky's attitude to Israel. As part of his leverage of Austrian neutrality, in 1978 he allowed the Palestinian Liberation Organisation to open an office in Vienna. As foreign minister, he had also lured OPEC, a cartel which consisted of mostly Arab oil states, to make its headquarters in Vienna. These olive branches to the Arab world did not, however, prevent the occupation of the OPEC building, as well as hostage-taking by terrorists led by Carlos the Jackal in December 1975 and a terrorist attack on the El Al check-in desk at Vienna Airport ten years later.

While Kreisky raised Austria's profile on the world stage, his able team of ministers was vigorous in implementing domestic reform in regard to labour holidays, social and health insurance, education and, greatly to the disapproval of the powerful Cardinal-Archbishop König, family law, divorce and abortion. By 1978, Kreisky himself was boasting that the welfare state was 'complete'. Critics said (and still maintain) that much of the government's measures were achieved through 'deficit financing' with dire future consequences. But by comparison with the sort of debt carried by European nations after the ravages of Covid, money-printing and inflation, the national debt of nearly 40 per cent of GDP when Kreisky left office in July 1983 seems rather modest.* Kreisky himself remained unrepentant, observing: 'As far as I'm concerned, a few billion more in debt gives me fewer sleepless nights than a few hundred thousand more unemployed.'

The Years of Scandals

They say a fish rots from the head downwards and this was most certainly the case with the Socialist Party in the later 1980s and 1990s. Partly this was because the entrenched cohesion-building Social Partners (*Sozialpartnerschaft*), for all its merits, had also become a rainbow's end for functionaries. Some of them held three different positions offering as many salaries, each with a generous pension attached. Partly also it was due to the unreformed nature of the country's largest industries that had remained nationalised since 1946.

---

* In 2024, the national debt was about 76 per cent of GDP.

Austria was now paying a high price for social peace, which might have been a good trade-off if the industries had become profitable and accountable. The hitherto successful policy of hard currency, high taxes and a generous welfare state had been thrown into question by global changes, particularly the abandonment of the gold standard by the USA in 1971. The lid then flew off the pot with the mega-scandal of the giant concern Voest-Alpine which, among other things, made high-grade weapons. Its Noricum subsidiary was found to have exported arms to both sides in the Iran-Iraq conflict of the 1980s – in defiance of both Austrian neutrality and international sanctions. Besides which, it was going bankrupt.

Internally, the Socialist party was not free from scandal, most notoriously the sudden enrichment of Kreisky's brilliant but unfortunately corrupt reforming vice-chancellor, Hannes Androsch (died 2024). Apart from being convicted of tax evasion in a trial which, as often happens in Austria, dragged on for sixteen years before a verdict could be reached, Androsch was caught in the slipstream of the biggest construction scandal of the Second Republic, namely the building of a new general hospital. The hospital's ever-exploding cost was substantially due to a huge web of corruption and bribery, principally that of the technical director, who was convicted of taking 30 million Schillings in kickbacks. The trial in 1981 was the biggest in the post-war period, involving 30,000 pages of documents and sixty-seven document files.

The investigative journalist who uncovered the scandal rejoiced in the name of Alfred Worm (the cast list of Austrian scandals often has an operetta-like feel to it). Other investigative journalists, Gerald Freihofner (*Wochenpresse*) and Hans Pretterebner, uncovered the extraordinary affair of Udo Proksch and the deliberate sinking of a cargo ship in 1977 to claim the insurance. Six people died in the sinking. At considerable personal risk and after ten years of diligent research, Pretterebner self-published, in hair-raising detail, the complex fraud in his book *The Lucona Case* (1987). He sent copies to people in shipping circles and the revelations that no mainstream publisher had wanted to touch became a best-selling real-life *Krimi*.

Udo Proksch certainly seems like a character from fiction. His parents were keen Nazis and remained so after the war. Proksch himself claimed to be apolitical, but found his milieu in the Socialist elite. He had even insured his *Lucona* cargo with a company close to the Conservatives (politicised parastatal firms are a feature of the Austrian scene) so that they would be the ones to pay out when it sank.

Among Proksch's other exploits were designing spectacle frames (from which he made a fortune) as well as, somewhat bizarrely, the establishment of an 'Association of Vertically Buried People'. The aim was to seal the dead in plastic tubes and place them vertically in the ground. This, it was hoped, would boost the plastics industry and solve the lack of space in cemeteries. By no means a handsome man, Udo seems to have possessed an irresistible charisma and charm. He had several celebrity affairs or marriages, including to the then most famous *Burgtheater* actress (Erika Pluhar) and Richard Wagner's great-granddaughter, Daphne Wagner.

Proksch owned the venerable café-patisserie of Demel on the Kohlmarkt, much beloved of tourists to Vienna. Little did they know that a 'Club 45' on the upper floors was where the fraudster 'entertained' senior civil servants and members of the Socialist nomenclature, including at least two Cabinet Ministers as regulars.

Fifteen years elapsed between the disappearance of the *Lucona* and Proksch's convictions for murder and attempted murder in 1992. A total of sixteen politicians (including the Minister of the Interior and the Parliamentary President), besides lawyers and top officials, had to resign or were sacked, in many cases also being charged or convicted of serious crimes.

Meanwhile Alfred Worm was again active in revelations concerning the Waldheim affair, revealing the Socialists' plot to exploit the would-be president's 'brown' – code for Nazi – past in the election campaign. Worm was sued for his pains but won. Later, he was sued again for calling a Freedom Party functionary a '*Trottel*', a robust Austrian word for a (usually senile) idiot. He lost this time but paid the 30,000 Schilling fine happily, saying: 'It is easily worth 30,000 Schilling to me to call this man a *Trottel*.'

> ### The Waldheim Affair
> Many see the election to the Austrian Presidency in 1986 of Kurt Waldheim as the moment of reckoning for the Austria's 1938–45 'victim' narrative. As a prelude to his electioneering, Waldheim published a 'campaign autobiography' which simply omitted his wartime service as an intelligence officer for the *Wehrmacht*. When this was pointed out, he said lamely that he didn't think people would be interested in that part of his career and denied having had any knowledge of wrongdoing by *Wehrmacht* personnel. When inconsistencies and omissions in his statements were challenged, he became angry and said that he had 'simply done his duty' as a soldier.
>
> Waldheim supporters were furious at the domestic and international attacks on him, and he was elected anyway, but as president he was a lame duck since rather few countries, other than Arab ones, were keen for him to visit. Although he had been Secretary-General of the United Nations from 1972–1981, the USA now put Waldheim on the 'watch list' for individuals with questionable World War II backgrounds,

thus denying him entry to the country. Considering the roll call of kleptocrats, murderers and psychopaths who have swanned into New York to address a respectfully attentive UNO General Assembly, this seems slightly bizarre.

In 1988, an international commission of historians set up by the government at the President's request determined that Waldheim had not committed any crimes. It did, however, say that he had detailed knowledge of atrocities committed. If his denials were true, remarked one journalist, he was the most unintelligent intelligence officer in history. Moreover, his 'enemy situation reports' would (it was argued) have facilitated deportations (for example, of the Jews from Salonica). Waldheim was a poor witness in his own defence, but neither a Nazi nor a war criminal.

The Waldheim affair finally brought the 'accomplice–victim' issue into the open and split the country. On the one hand, it facilitated the rise of the right-wing Freedom Party whose charismatic leader, Jörg Haider, was fond of making statements that sounded like Nazi apologia or anti-Semitism. There was indeed a substantial support for the view that collective Austrian guilt was unjust, and, in any case, it was wrong to hang the atrocities of Nazism round the necks of later generations, or use them as political weapons against politicians on the right who stood outside the centrist consensus. On the other hand, the affair spurred successive governments to consider long-stalled compensation for persecuted Jews or the descendants of murdered Jews, as well as restitution of property and artworks.

The Rise of Jörg Haider

Bismarck had called the Austrian Empire a 'worm-eaten battleship'. The political establishment in Austria of the late twentieth century was beginning to look vulnerable to the same accusation. Jörg Haider – youthful, demagogic, unscrupulous and agile – was pushing at an open door as he exposed what he called 'the self-service shop' of the distribution of political and parastatal office embodied by the *Parteibuch –Proporz – Sozialpartnerschaft*. Of course, the main aim of the Freedom Party under his leadership was not actually to abolish the set-up that he denounced, but to get a bigger share of the spoils. The establishment appeared helpless. The journalist Paul Lendvai relates how Chancellor Franz Vranitzky 'froze like a rabbit in the headlights' in a TV debate in 1990 when Haider laid out cards before the cameras illustrating the multiple posts and eye-watering income of a single Socialist trade union functionary in Styria.[49]

After he became the Freedom Party's leader in 1986, Haider rapidly built up national support from his base in Carinthia. The establishment basically responded with more of the same: a series of coalitions between the two mainstream parties, Socialists being the senior partner with the People's Party. Vienna tended to go its own way under its rumbustious Socialist mayor, Helmut Zilk – a national icon until it was revealed after his death that in the 1960s he'd been an informant for Communist Czechoslovakia. The personal animosity between the rival coalitionists worsened because, as a cynical Hungarian historian observed, there was so little ideological difference between them.

The most conciliatory, able and long-lasting of the coalition chancellors was Franz Vranitzky (chancellor 1986–97), the son of a Communist foundry worker and a banker turned politician. At one point, he remarked wistfully that the Austrian voters were 'in need of harmony' – and indeed the collapse of the Iron Curtain in 1989 and the subsequent entry of Austria into the EU (66.5 per cent in favour at the referendum of 1994) did provide focus points which transcended local political infighting. Most importantly, Vranitzky's visit to Israel in 1993 and his speech apologising for the 'bad things' of Austria's past, as well as defending the 'good things', helped to strike a just balance in Austria's 'coming to terms with the past'.

Go west – An East German man, brandishing his West German passport, crossing the newly opened Hungarian-Austrian border in September 1989. Within two months the Berlin Wall had fallen and in October 1990 East Germany (German Democratic Republic) and West Germany (Federal Republic of Germany) were officially reunified.

Unfortunately, these favourable developments only temporarily masked the split that had opened up in society between the establishment centre and a discontented constituency on the right, which is again in the ascendant in Austria, where the FPÖ is the party that got the most votes in the election of September 2024; and in Germany, where the AfD came second in the election of 2025. It reached 20.8 per cent of the vote on the highest turnout since the reunion of the country in 1990 following the collapse of the Soviet Union, and was ahead in the whole of former East Germany. In some respects that constituency resembles the nineteenth-century supporters of Karl Lueger, consisting now however not only of small businessmen, but of many former Socialist voters disadvantaged, they feel, by globalisation and excessive immigration. In the elections of the year 2000, the Freedom Party unexpectedly came second behind the Socialists and just ahead of the People's Party (ÖVP). Wolfgang Schüssel, the gifted leader of the ÖVP, initially tried to continue the Socialist–People's Party coalition but agreement could not be reached and he then went into government with the Freedom Party. This decision brought on Austria's biggest diplomatic crisis since the Waldheim affair.

CHAPTER 14

POST-MILLENNIUM AUSTRIA IN THE EUROPEAN UNION

Ostracising Austria

The Schüssel government of the year 2000 was electorally unusual, but entirely legitimate under Austria's constitution and proportional electoral system. The parties that came second and third in the election – the Freedom Party (FPÖ) and the People's Party (ÖVP) – had formed a majority administration, with the chancellor drawn from the third party. Owing to doubts about some of Jörg Haider's remarks, the swearing-in was preceded by a statement affirming the government's commitment to 'the intellectual and moral values that are the common heritage of the peoples of Europe' and its intention to work for an Austria in which 'xenophobia, anti-Semitism and racism have no place'. Haider himself was not included in the government line-up, though obviously he called the shots for his party from Carinthia, where he remained governor.

Of the then fourteen states of the European Union (which Austria had joined in 1995 along with Sweden and Finland), eleven were Social Democratic-led in 2000. But even conservative-led France joined in the legally improper and politically motivated EU 'sanctions' against Austria's democratically elected government. Officially these were defined as follows:

> The governments of the fourteen Member States will not promote or accept any official bilateral contacts at political level with an Austrian government integrating the FPÖ; there will be no support for Austrian candidates

> seeking positions in international organizations; Austrian Ambassadors in EU capitals will only be received at a technical level.

Europe's mainstream press piled in with pharisaical denunciation and pictured Austria, where the constitution and electoral systems are, in fact, considerably more democratic than those of some of its critics, as little more than a nest of Nazis. It is worth noting in passing that among those supporting the sanctions were the French President Jacques Chirac, who would be convicted in 2011 of abuse of office; also Gerhard Schröder, the Socialist German Chancellor, who subsequently reinvented himself as the main cheerleader in the West for Vladimir Putin, becoming, among other things, a well-remunerated Chairman of Russian energy company Rosneft.

Few in Europe were willing to admit that the attempted ostracisation was performative hypocrisy, but there were honourable exceptions. In Germany, the CDU-CSU's Karl Lamers said bluntly: 'Such a step would never have been taken against Italy' – where the extreme right's participation in government provoked barely a murmur. Within a few months, 'three wise men' were appointed to assess the state of democracy in Austria and duly recommended ending the sanctions so that the EU could back down without losing too much face.

Disturbing the Peace

It is a considerable irony that the so-called *'schwarz-blau'* government (black being the colour of the People's Party, blue being that of the Freedom Party) effectively destroyed the Freedom Party as a political force at government level for more than a decade. Under the stewardship of the conservative Wolfgang Schüssel (chancellor 2000–07), neo-liberal reforms were for the first time introduced which were ill-received by vested interests but reflected the changed global economic conditions. The bureaucracy was reduced in size and some of its privileges reduced. The bloated pensions system was somewhat reformed, the budget deficit reduced, inefficient state industries privatised, corporation tax cut from 34 per cent to 25 per cent, and the lowest band of income tax abolished.

Meanwhile in 2005, the Freedom Party split into a Haider faction, the so-called 'Alliance for the Future of Austria', and the rest, the party divisions having been manifest as early as 2002. A rising tide of scandals, such as that involving the dubious dealings of Telekom Austria (including the manipulation of stock prices and kickbacks to politicians of all parties) and a more or less perennial scandal involving corruption in respect of defence acquisition, discredited mostly Freedom Party ministers, functionaries and groupies. The party discovered the hard way that government involved taking responsibility for decisions, which proved tougher than shouting abuse from the sidelines. Vigorous attempts in the media to smear Schüssel himself were unsuccessful. The only thing that can subsequently be held against him is that after his retirement from front-line politics in 2007, he took a job with a Putin-friendly Russian firm (Lukoil), and was obliged to relinquish this post after the invasion of Ukraine. (At the same time, a post-Schüssel Socialist chancellor, Christian Kern, was likewise called out for his post on the board of the Russian railway.)

The Rise of the Greens

Austria's Greens had been around since the 1970s and featured as increasingly effective activists (much like the German Greens) under their formidable political Valkyrie

Freda Meissner-Blau. Also like their German colleagues, they were fiercely opposed not only to nuclear weapons but to nuclear energy as such. They argued that the problem of the storage of nuclear waste had not been, and perhaps could not be, satisfactorily solved.

The Greens staged their first coup with the successful mobilisation of public opinion against a completed but not yet operational atomic power station at Zwentendorf on the south bank of the Danube in Lower Austria. In 1978, a referendum was held and, to the fury of Chancellor Kreisky, narrowly decided (50.5 per cent) to prevent it being put into commission. This was the first time that '*das Volk*' had overturned an economic decision made behind closed doors and one that was strongly supported by the Social Partners, especially the Unions. Consequently, all further plans for atomic energy in Austria were put on ice. The appetite for nuclear energy waned still more after the 1986 Chernobyl disaster, and in 1997 a ban was anchored in the Constitution. This is no more beneficial to Austria (especially now, as she desperately attempts to reduce dependence on Russian oil) than Angela Merkel's panicky decision to end nuclear power was to Germany.

Kreisky's successor, Fred Sinowatz, faced an even more fierce opposition in 1984 when work began at Hainburg in Lower Austria on a hydroelectric project located in a rare biotope on the Danube floodplains. The protests inspired by the Greens escalated into violence and led to Sinowatz's resignation. Thereafter, the Greens became organised as a conventional political force but met with fluctuating fortunes at the polls. However, their former leader, Alexander Van der Bellen, was elected Federal President of Austria in 2017. Two years later, the party achieved its best ever election result (but still at only 13.9 per cent of the vote) and finally entered into government in coalition with the People's Party under Sebastian Kurz.

A Few Scandals More

Austria is placed twentieth (out of 180) on Transparency International's (Public Sector) 'Corruption Perceptions Index' for 2023, a ranking it shares with the United Kingdom and the Seychelles. This makes it one of the less corrupt countries in the world, though an avid reader of the Austrian press might be pleasantly surprised to hear this. The latest *'panama'* concerns the unravelling of Tyrolean René Benko's gigantic national and international Signa real estate empire, the largest insolvency of the Second Republic. In the media, inscrutable payments to a former chancellor are lovingly dwelt upon.

A long-standing problem revolved around the 'political' nature of the Austrian banks. Until the economic crash of 2008 brought some into foreign ownership, banks in Austria had been closely politically aligned – Bank Austria and BAWAG with the Socialists; Raiffeisen and Die Erste Bank with the People's Party. As of 2024, Raiffeisen is still heavily invested in Russia, recently making 52 per cent of its profits there and paying substantial taxes to the Putin regime. It therefore stands accused of helping to finance the Russian war machine.

The two most spectacular *'panamas'* either during or following the *schwarz-blau* era of the People's Party and Freedom Party (2000–07) were the near-insolvency of the BAWAG (Bank für Arbeit und Wirtschaft) and the disaster of the Hypo Alpe Adria in Carinthia. The latter was financed by guarantees provided by the Province of Carinthia under Jörg Haider. Fortuitously for him, the bank collapsed sometime after his death. This scandal involved dubious deals with

Bavaria, whose state-owned bank BayernLB was a 50 per cent shareholder, as well as a regulatory dispute with the EU authorities and sundry gentlemen crossing borders with suitcases full of money. The details were hard to follow, but the cost to the Austrian taxpayers who had to rescue the bank was all too clear: namely €9 billion.

The BAWAG near-insolvency was seemingly a case of incompetence, malfeasance and extraordinary greed, reminiscent of the behaviour that caused the global 2008 banking crisis. Again, it was the taxpayers who had to rescue the bank, their only satisfaction being the tracking down of the BAWAG general director Herbert Elsner, who had fled to his holiday home in France. From there, he maintained that he was too ill to return to Austria. He was, though, eventually winkled out and stood trial for his complicity in the misuse of bank assets. After several years in prison, he was partially exonerated. Arguably, it was his €6 million pension that caused more anger than his disputed participation in illegal dealings.

The Flight of Icarus
Following the resignation of Wolfgang Schüssel in 2007, the Socialists returned to the chancellorship firstly with Alfred Gusenbauer, who was deposed by his own party after only a year, and then with Werner Faymann (chancellor 2008–16). When economic conditions compelled him to break his 'no new taxes' election promise, Faymann returned the party to class warfare. He began to push for the reimposition of a wealth tax and an inheritance tax, and various duties were increased or introduced. The new €1 duty per litre of *Sekt* (Austrian champagne) is only worth mentioning because, in a delightfully Austrian way, the previous *Sekt* duty had never been abolished, only reduced to 0 per cent.

In the latter part of Faymann's chancellorship, the migrant crisis of 2015 became a portent and a strong influence on Austria's domestic politics. Thousands of migrants poured across the southern border of Hungary, which was technically (under the EU's Dublin Accords) supposed to register them and assess them for asylum rights. However, the Hungarian authorities were overwhelmed and, anyway, strongly opposed to illegal migration. Following outrage in the western press over the

Migrants reach Austria at the height of the first migration crisis in autumn 2015. The majority were hoping to go on to Germany, but many settled in Austria.

detention of migrants in deteriorating conditions, Hungary's Prime Minister Viktor Orbán agreed with Faymann, who in turn agreed with Germany's Angela Merkel, that the migrants should proceed to Austria, and thence to Germany, which in the end took in more than a million, the majority of them Syrians or people claiming to be Syrians.

Although migrants arriving at Vienna's Westbahnhof were 'clapped in' by well-wishers, there were many in Austria who were uneasy about mass migration, and this was reflected in the rise of support for the Freedom Party over the next few years. It was also an issue that brought a young shooting star of the People's Party to prominence, Sebastian Kurz, who was at the time foreign minister and minister for integration.

Kurz soon emerged as someone from the mainstream who was prepared to be frank about the challenge posed by an open-door migration policy. In October 2015, he said:

> I would like to see an honest policy all over Europe... above all in Germany. We have to finally call a spade a spade and say in no uncertain terms: the open-doors policy has to end. We are overwhelmed. Too many people are coming.[50]

This went to the heart of the anxiety those tired of being characterised as 'racists' if they opposed the abuse of asylum rules (while not opposing genuine refugees). The Kurz family had itself hosted Yugoslavian refugees in the 1990s. Many on the Left in Austria, as elsewhere, simply refused distinctions between 'economic' migrants and refugees. The distinction is indeed hard to make, since many of those fleeing poverty are impoverished because of war, famine and state implosion. Nevertheless, it was becoming obvious that democratic welfare states could not withstand the domestic pressures of unlimited migration, and subsequent elections have reflected that concern.

Kurz's rise was indeed meteoric (he was only twenty-seven when he became foreign minister) and had a cathartic effect on the People's Party, which had too long been led by dull mediocrities. In 2017, he staged a Trump-like coup on the party and became chancellor in coalition with a revived Freedom Party under Heinz-Christian Strache. At thirty-one, he was the youngest head of government in the world. He was soon to be confronted with the challenge of the Covid pandemic, which he managed with some success.

Unfortunately, Kurz had not reckoned with the revenge of the Austrian establishment, which does not take kindly to political shooting stars. Worse, a year after being elected, Kurz was being feted as the *Wunderkind* of European politics in (of all places!) the German press. In Vienna, the knives were already sharpening. The first blow, however, came from his coalition allies, the Freedom Party, when 'Ibizagate' broke. This was a secretly filmed and heavily edited viral video which showed the Freedom Party's well-refreshed leader, Heinz-Christian Strache, at his holiday home apparently being wooed into speculating about corrupt practices by a (fake) representative of a Russian oligarch. Strache had to resign immediately and since the Freedom Party supplied the minister of the interior, Kurz demanded that the latter also resign (instead of being responsible for an investigation into his own party), which he refused to do. In the end, the government itself resigned after a parliamentary motion of no confidence and Kurz prepared for new elections.

Kurz won the subsequent election in 2019 with a large margin and negotiated a coalition with the Greens. Something appeared to have gone wrong with establishment calculations, as he was more popular than ever. At this point, what can only be described as 'lawfare' was set in train and (often anonymous) allegations or lawsuits rained down on Kurz and the People's Party. Ultimately, his position became untenable and in 2021 he resigned. He is accused of buying influence with public funds, fraudulent manipulation of opinion polls and perjury before a parliamentary committee. In February 2024, he was convicted on the perjury charge and acquitted on two other counts. The verdict goes to appeal.

Envoi

In the second decade of the twenty-first century, Austria (population of just under 9 million) has achieved an enviable economic position as the fourteenth richest country in the world per capita. Its GDP per capita is $56,802 (nominal, 2023), and $69,502 (PPP – Purchasing Power Parity, 2023). Although the numbers have been generally good in the past, the problems Austria has faced since the beginning of the Ukraine War, the Covid pandemic and mass migration are common to her European partners. Particularly in regard to migration, she is effectively a front-line state since migrants believe they have better chances in Austria than in the countries en route. In 2022, she had 106,000 asylum applications (in a country a tenth the size of Germany, which had 218,000).[51]

Many of these were from Ukraine, but numbers continue to arrive through the Balkans. The officially 'closed' West Balkan route up through southern Hungary from Serbia, and others through Bulgaria or Romania, still yields a stubborn quota of illegal migrants. Partly because of this, Austria had long opposed the EU plan to open up Bulgaria and Romania to the Schengen (open borders) Agreement, but in 2023 it somewhat reluctantly dropped its objections and, as of 1 January 2025, Bulgaria and Romania are full members. Hungary apprehends a substantial number of people traffickers, who are generally tried and imprisoned, only to be freed after relatively short sentences due to overcrowded prisons, so that they are soon back in business.

Austria has experienced a number of Palestinian or Islamist terrorist attacks. In 2020, a Jihadist slaughtered four people and wounded twenty-three others in an attack around the synagogue in Vienna's Inner City. In February 2025, another lone wolf Islamist attacker stabbed people in a Villach street, killing one. Several other planned attacks have been thwarted. In the capital, Salafist influence among Sunni Muslims has become a problem in some schools. Some 60 per cent of children born in Vienna are to migrant families; 17 per cent of the Austrian population are foreign nationals (Germans being in the majority) and more than 34 per cent of the population of Vienna have a 'migration background' with Germans, Serbs, Turks and, most recently, Ukrainians the largest groups. The definition of 'migration background' applies to those not born in Austria and where at least one of their parents is not born in the country.

Vladimir Putin and Karin Kneissl at Kneissl's wedding in 2018. Kneissl was successfully suggested by the FPÖ as a 'non-party' candidate as foreign minister during the 2017–19 coalition.

Austria continues its balancing act between East and West, resulting in some embarrassment when two ex-Chancellors (one Volkspartei, one Socialist) were revealed to be on the boards of Putin-friendly Russian companies; plus the eccentric former Foreign Minister Karin Kneissl (FPÖ) invited Vladimir Putin to her wedding and was filmed dancing with the despot. She later migrated to Russia.

As of spring 2024, Austria was still receiving almost 95 per cent of its gas from Russia, due to a long-term contract negotiated by the oil firm ÖMV before the Ukraine war. However, in December 2024 it was announced that ÖMV was rescinding its contract with Russia for gas deliveries owing to Russia having repeatedly infringed the terms. Concurrently, it was announced that Austria had filled up its gas reserves over the summer and would have no difficulty meeting winter demand. Also, along with Hungary (although the latter is a NATO member), Austria does not send weapons to Ukraine, citing its neutrality law.

The intertwining of Austrian commercial interests with Russia and the fact that Austria is indirectly helping to finance Putin's war effort is, to put it mildly, a continuing source of embarrassment. Austria's second largest bank, Raiffeisen, still has a huge Russian subsidiary that has typically delivered 60 per cent of the bank's profits in previous years, but is now apparently trying to wind down its holdings (though still advertising jobs locally). It has tried to keep below the radar.

The New Government in 2025

Following the election in September 2024, it took more than five months for a government to be formed, with the formerly dominant centrist parties polling record lows. The conservative People's Party (ÖVP) received 26.7 per cent of the votes, while the Social Democrats (SPÖ) fared worse with 21.14 per cent. The 'winner' was therefore the far right Freedom Party (FPÖ) at 28.85 per cent. However, neither of the centrist parties, still less the liberals (NEOS – 9.14 per cent) or the Greens (die Grünen – 8.24 per cent), wished to form a government with the FPÖ.

Because of this taboo on collaboration with the far right (which in Germany is known as the *Brandmauer*, or firewall), the ÖVP tried to negotiate a coalition with the SPÖ and NEOS to reach the necessary majority. When this at first failed, the ÖVP reversed itself and negotiated with FPÖ, whose radical demands (particularly its Euro-scepticism and association with other far right European parties and policies) proved unacceptable. The ÖVP was driven back to the formerly envisioned coalition with SPÖ and NEOS, which ultimately was sworn in by the President on 3 March 2025.

The new government needs to make unpopular decisions (in particular, it faces EU sanctions if the budget deficit is not dealt with), but with the Socialists in charge of the Finance Ministry, it is not clear that the necessary amount of belt-tightening on the welfare state can be made. With the Conservatives leading the Ministry of the Interior, tighter control of migration and more efficient deportation of illegal migrants are indicated, these being major preoccupations of FPÖ voters.

At the same time, the delicate issue of neutrality will have to be resolved, and in any case more money has to be spent on defence. With Conservatives at the Defence Ministry, it is likely that Austria will join the European Sky Shield Initiative (ESSI), a project to build a ground-based integrated European air defence system which includes anti-ballistic missile capability. This would likely be a way of bypassing the constitutional problem of neutrality. The example of neutral Ireland unexpectedly offering to contribute to a potential security force in Ukraine shows the way the wind is blowing.

Austria's generally pragmatic centrists are therefore faced with similar dilemmas as those afflicting most other EU countries. Everywhere the so-called peace dividend from the collapse of the Soviet empire has been overspent, mass immigration – cheered on by the humanitarian Left and businesses in search of cheap labour – has become an electoral liability, and defence expenditure has languished due to serious miscalculation of Russian intentions. Complacent politicians had forgotten the old Roman adage: 'If you want peace, prepare for war'.[52]

Small is Beautiful

Nearly three generations after World War II, the Austrians' anxious contemplation of a turbulent twentieth-century past, ranging from remorse to denial, has given way to a generally dynamic and forward-looking people who carry less historical baggage than their parents and grandparents. Perhaps partly because of a certain fluidity of identity in contemporary Europe, the question 'Is there an Austrian nation?', posed in 1981 in a book by Friedrich Heer, now seems less pressing to them.[53] Jörg Mauthe's quixotic book of reflections for Austrians, 'specifically for Austrophiles, Austromasochists, Austrophobes and other Austriacs', is now no more than an entertaining museum piece. However, perhaps Austria is not quite the 'Isle of the Blessed' flatteringly proclaimed by Pope Paul VI in 1971. Apart from anything else, the country has been rocked by some spectacular sex scandals in the Church since then, as well as lurid *'panamas'* and some unsavoury political infighting.

Tourism has expanded enormously. It isn't only skiing and the Alps: vast numbers of visitors flock each year to the Salzburger Festspiele, the rich musical offerings of Vienna and its fabulous museums, to name but a few attractions. Overtourism is becoming a problem, at least in Salzburg, bringing in its wake a plague of kitsch – *Kaiserkitsch, Sisikitsch, Mozartkitsch, Klimtkitsch,* Tyrolean kitsch. *The Sound of Music* has a lot to answer for.

A plague of Mozart rubber ducks

On the other hand, the quality of life in Austria is regularly judged to be at, or near, the top of the international listings. This is a reflection of the artful means by which the Austrians combine an embedded conservatism with a taste for modernity. A Socialist chancellor put it this way: 'Everyone is in favour of change in Austria; as long as everything stays the same.' To borrow a thought from Karl Kraus: 'the sound principle of a topsy-turvy lifestyle in the framework of an upside-down world order has stood every test.'

Further Reading

On Austria:
Gordon Brook-Shepherd: *The Austrians: A Thousand-Year Odyssey* (Harper Collins, 1996)
Stephen Beller: *A Concise History of Austria* (Cambridge University Press, 2006)
Martin Rady: *The Habsburgs: The Rise and Fall of a World Power* (Penguin, 2020)
John Stoye: *The Siege of Vienna: The Last Great Trial Between Cross and Crescent* (OUP 1965 /New Edition Birlinn 2008)
Pieter M. Judson: *The Habsburg Empire: A New History* (Belknap Press of the Harvard University Press, 2016)
Paul Lendvai: *Inside Austria: Old Challenges, New Demons* (C. Hurst & Co, 2010)
Paula Sutter Fichtner: *The A to Z of Austria* (Second Edition, The Scarecrow Press, 2010)

On Vienna:
Ilsa Barea: *Vienna: Legend and Reality* (1966, New Edition Random House, 1993)
Richard Cockett: *Vienna: How the City of Ideas Created the Modern World* (Yale University Press, 2023)
Nicholas T. Parsons: *Vienna: A Cultural and Literary History* (Signal Books / OUP, 2008)

For understanding Central European history as a whole:
Lonnie Johnson: *Central Europe: Enemies, Neighbours, Friends* (Oxford University Press, Third Edition 2010)

Endnotes

1 *'O heiliger Sankt Florian, verschon' mein Haus, zünd' and're an.'*
2 Werner Freudenberger: *Kultweg Bernsteinstrasse. Auf dem Weg von Carnuntum nach Aquilea*
3 *'migration gentium'* appears in Lazius's *De gentium aliquot migrationibus* (1557)
4 Friedrich Heer: *The Holy Roman Empire* (Phoenix, 1995) P.59.
5 Stephan Vajda: *Felix Austria: Eine Geschichte Österreichs* (Ueberreuter, Vienna, 1980) P.78.
6 *König Ottokars Glück und Ende* by Franz Grillparzer, premiered 1825.
7 Benjamin Curtis: *The Habsburgs* (Bloomsbury, 2013). P.17.
8 For details see: John E. Morby: *Oxford Dynasties of the World* (Oxford, 2002). P. 124.
9 Brigitte Hamann: *Die Habsburger. Ein biographisches Lexikon* (3., korrigierte Auflage, Wien, Ueberreuter 1988.)
10 Curtis op cit. P.53.
11 Peter H. Wilson: *Europe's Tragedy: A History of the Thirty Years War* (Allen Lane, 2009) Pp. 23-24.
12 Martin Rady: *The Habsburgs* op cit. P.147.
13 David Eggenberger: *Dictionary of Battles from 1479 to the Present* (Allen & Unwin, 1967).
14 Alan Ryan: *On Politics: A History of Political Thought from Herodotus to the Present* (Penguin, 2012) Pp. 321-2. Italics in the original.
15 Quoted in Günther Hödl: *Habsburg und Österreich 1273-1493* (Böhlau, Wien, 1988).
16 Martin Rady op cit. P.122, quoting Hammer-Purgstall: *Leben des Kardinals Khlesl.*
17 Mentioned in John Stoye: *The Siege of Vienna: The Last Great Trial between Cross and Crescent.* (2nd Edition 2011, Pegasus Books) P.175.
18 Max Weber: *Die protestantische Ethik und der Geist des Kapitalismus*, 1904-1905 (translated by Talcott Parsons as *The Protestant Ethic and the Spirit of Capitalism*, 1930).
19 Curtis op cit. P.189. The Polish–Lithuanian Commonwealth was carved up ('partitioned') in 1772, 1792 and 1795.
20 Vajda op cit. P.398.
21 David Gilmour: *The Pursuit of Italy* (Penguin, 2012) P.120.
22 Quoted in David Gilmour op cit. Pp.126-7
23 Alan Sked: *Metternich and Austria: An Evaluation* (Palgrave Macmillan, 2008); Wolfram Siemann: *Metternich: Strategist and Visionary* (Harvard Belknap Press, 2019); Henry Kissinger: *World Order* (Penguin Edition, 2015) Pp. 73-76.
24 Alan Sked op cit. P.2
25 *Freiheit in Krähwinkel* (*Freedom in the Back of Beyond*) Act 1, Scene 14.
26 See Catalogue to the exhibition *Bürgersinn und Aufbegehren – Biedermeier und Vormärz in Wien, 1815–1848* (Künstlerhaus, Wien, 1988)
27 See Gordon Brook-Shepherd: *The Austrians: A Thousand Year Odyssey* (Carroll & Graf, N.Y., 1997)
28 Pieter M. Judson: *The Habsburg Empire: A New History* (The Belknap Press of Harvard University Press, 2016).

ENDNOTES 235

29 Judson op cit. P.317.
30 '*In Österreich herrscht der Absolutismus – gemildert durch Schlamperei*'
31 Quoted in Heinrich Benedikt: *Die Monarchie des Hauses Österreich* (Munich, 1968) P.181. A detailed look at the ideological deviations of Austrian Social Democracy from hard-line Marxism and Bolshevism is offered in Chapter 6 ('Austro-Marxists') of William M. Johnston: *The Austrian Mind: An Intellectual and Social History 1848–1938* (University of California Press, 1972).
32 *Nationalitätenfrage und Sozialdemokratie*, published in Berlin in 1913.
33 Gordon Brook-Shepherd: *The Austrians: A Thousand Year Odyssey* (Carroll & Graf N.Y., 1997) Pp. 98-99.
34 '*Die im Reichsrat vertretenen Königreiche und Länder*'
35 Quoted in Margaret MacMillan: *Peacemakers: Six Months that Changed the World* (John Murray, 2003) P.256.
36 '*Erbaut von der Gemeinde Wien aus den Mitteln der Wohnbausteuer in den Jahren 1926 und 1927*'
37 Robert Musil: *The Man without Qualities*, trans. Eithne Wilkins and Ernst Kaiser (Martin Secker and Warburg Lt. London, 1954. Vol 1, chapter 109), pp.575-7. Quoted in David S. Luft: *The Austrian Dimension in German Intellectual History* (Bloomsbury Academic, 2022), P.107
38 All statistics from Ernst Bruckmüller: *Geschichte kompakt: Österreich* (Böhlau Verlag Wien, 2021) Pp. 200 ff.
39 The full story is told in an ORF (Austrian Broadcasting) Universum History, ORF2, 26/01/2024.
40 Robert H. Keyserlingk, *Austria in World War II* (Kingston, Montreal 1988) S. 207 f
41 See Roberto Zapperi: *Freud and Mussolini. Psychoanalysis in Italy during the fascist regime*. (Franco Angeli, 2013.)
42 See Lonnie Johnson: 'Interpreting the Anschluss in Austria, 1938-1988' in *Anschluss and 50 Years 1938–1988*. Ed. William E. Wright. (Ariadne Press, 1995).
43 '*Der Klerus ging noch in jeder Geschichtsstunde mit jedem Machtherren ins Bett*.'
44 Dieter A. Binder und Ernst Bruckmüller: *Essay über Österreich. Grundfragen von Identität und Geschichte 1918-2000* (Verlag für Geschichte und Politik Wien /R. Oldenbourg Verlag München, 2005) P.101.
45 For a detailed analysis of denazification, see Hubert Feichtlbauer: *The Austrian Dilemma* (Vienna, 2001). Pp. 109 ff. from which these statistics have been taken.
46 Jill Lewis, *European History Quarterly*, 2000, SAGE Publications, London, Thousand Oaks, CA and New Delhi, Vol. 30(4), pp.533–552.
47 Paul Lendvai: *Inside Austria* (C. Hurst & Co, 2010). P.48.
48 Quoted in 'Out of honest conviction' in *Die Presse*, 23 January 2009. (Author's translation.)
49 Paul Lendvai op cit. P.145.
50 Sebastian Kurz: *Ein Jahr Flüchtlingskrise in Zitaten* - Österreich - VIENNA.AT
51 EU-Asylwerber in den EU Ländern/Statista
52 Translated from the 4th-century AD Roman military writer Flavius Vegetius, *Epitoma Rei Militaris* iii. (Introd.): qui desiderat pacem, praeparet bellum
53 Friedrich Heer: *Der Kampf um die österreichische Identität* (Böhlau Verlag, 1981)

Image Credits

All maps and in-house infographics © 2024 James Nunn

p.xiv: Stalinplatz renamed Schwarzenbergplatz, Vienna, 1956. akg-images / brandstaetter images/Votava
p.5: Venus of Willendorf.: Creative Commons / Bjørn Christian Tørrissen
p.6: Ötzi the iceman. Media World Images / Alamy
p.15: 1920s Poster promoting the Austrian Alps. Shawshots / Alamy
p.17: Ostarrîchi manuscript. Public Domain
p.19: Klosterneuburg, Lower Austria. Creative Commons / C.Stadler/Bwag
p.20: Statue of Blondel and the Richard the Lionheart. Creative Commons. Jerrye & Roy Klotz, MD
p.22: Ulrich von Liechtenstein. Public Domain
p.33: Frederich III. Public Domain
p.34: AEIOU symbol. Public Domain
p.35: Maximilian I by Albrecht Dürer. Public Domain
p.37: Schwarze Mander. Public Domain
p.38: Jakob Fugger by Albrecht Dürer. Public Domain
p.40: Charles V. Public Domain
p.46: Hans Makart's The Entrance of Charles V into Antwerp. Public domain
p.49: Martin Luther. Public Domain
p.55: The Council of Trent. Public Domain.
p.60: Arcimboldo's 1591 portrait of Rudolf as Vertumnus. Public Domain
p.62: The Defenestration of Prague. Public Domain
p.73: Expulsion of the Jews from Vienna, 1670. Public Domain
p.75: Woodcut of the plague of Vienna. akg-images
p.76: *Der liebe Augustin* postage stamp. Public Domain
p.78: The Battle of Vienna by Martino Altomonte. Public Domain
p.82: *Il Pomo d'Oro* stage set. Public domain
p.84: Karlskirche, Vienna. Creative Commons / Thomas Ledl
p.89: Statue of Charles VI, Hofbibliothek, Vienna. Creative Commons / Jebulon
p.91: Maria Theresa and her family by Heinrich Füger. Public Domain
p.99: Vienna General Hospital. Public Domain
p.101: Joseph II ploughing. Public Domain
p.106: Franz II in his study at Biedermeier desk. Heritage Image Partnership Ltd / Alamy
p.108: Mozart and family by Carmontelle. Public Domain
p.114: Klemens von Metternich by Thomas Lawrence. Public Domain
p.122: Johann Peter Hasenclever's Labourers before the City Council. Public Domain
p.128: Franz Joseph by Eduard von Engerth. Public Domain
p.128: Empress Elisabeth - 'Sisi'. Photograph by Emil Rabending. Public Domain
p.130: Sisi's Funeral photograph by Löwy Mór. Public Domain
p.131: Vienna panorama engraving. Granger - Historical Picture Archive / Alamy
p.144: Vienna World's Fair, 1873. Public Domain
p.147: Strauss Waltz sheet music. akg-images
p.152: Vienna Secession Building. ilolab / Shutterstock

Image Credits

p.158: Karl Kraus. Public domain

p.159: Austro-Hungarian soldiers on Italian front in ice tunnels, WW1. Public Domain

p.160: Karl Renner signing the 1919 peace treaty. The Print Collector / Alamy

p.164: Karl-Marx-Hof, Vienna. C.Stadler/Bwag / Creative Commons.

p.167: Hedy Lamarr, 1934.: Public Domain

p.168: Margarete Schütte-Lihotzky's Frankfurt Kitchen. akg-images / ullstein bild

p.169: Cartoon of Bertha von Suttner by Marguerite Martyn. Public Domain

p.171: Joseph Roth. Public Domain

p.171: Robert Musil. Public Domain

p.174: Anti-semitic propaganda poster. Public Domain

p.175: Hitler rehearsing. Chronicle / Alamy

p.179: Engelbert Dolfuss. APA-PictureDesk / Alamy

p.182: The Anschluss – Hitler in the Heldenplatz. Public Domain

p.184: Jews during the Anschluss cleaning the streets. Public domain

p.185: Mauthausen concentration camp. Public Domain

p.187: Stephansdom, Vienna, 1945. Universal Images Group North America LLC / Alamy

p.191: Statue of the Unknown Soldier, Vienna. Creative Commons / Serge Bystro

p.198: Gustav Klimt's portait of Adele Bloch Bauer I. Public Domain

p.199: Leopold Figl announcing the signing of the 1955 Staatsvertrag. Sueddeutsche Zeitung Photo / Alamy

p.217: East Germans crossing the Hungarian-Austrian border, 1989. APA-PictureDesk / Alamy

p.225: Migrants in Vienna in 2015. Mojmir Fotografie / Shutterstock

p.229: Vladimir Putin at Karin Kneissl's wedding. Public Domain

p.231: Mozartkitsch. EQRoy / Shutterstock

p.232: Vienna Hofburg statue of cherub. Public Domain

Acknowledgements

I owe what knowledge I have acquired of Austrian history and Austria's many-faceted culture to enjoyable encounters with Austrians over some thirty years. A few leading historians, who are personal friends, deserve special mention: Emil Brix, Ernst Bruckmüller, Waltraud Heindl, Walter Krause, Hannes Stekl and Peter Urbanitsch. I am further greatly indebted to my professional readers who collectively saved me from a number of errors: Wolfgang Bahr, historian and journalist, Lonnie Johnson, former head of the Fulbright Commission in Vienna and himself a historian of Central Europe. As someone still struggling somewhat with the digital world, I would like to offer a special word of appreciation to my computer guru Marcel Kneuer. Over many years, despite being an extremely busy IT expert and Green politician, he has promptly rescued me from user-induced computer sulks.

Last but not least, my wife, the art historian Ilona Sármány-Parsons, greatly improved the structure of the book. It is to her that this work is dedicated, and in addition to friends and neighbours who help to make living in Austria decidedly *gemütlich*. Special thanks to Kieron Connolly at Old Street Publishing, whose editorial professionalism knocked a deficient first draft into better shape and Ben Yarde-Buller for his solid support of the project throughout.

READ IN A DAY.
REMEMBER FOR A LIFETIME.